The new INGLENOOK® COOKBOOK

The new INGLENOOK® COOKBOOK

Inglenook Cookbooks · Since 1901

Live simply. Eat well.

Brethren Press®

Library of Congress Cataloging-in-Publication Data

The new Inglenook cookbook.
    pages cm
  Updates: Granddaughter's Inglenook cookbook. Elgin, Illinois : Brethren Publishing
        House, 1942.
  Includes index.
  ISBN 978-0-87178-192-5 (hardcover)
  1. Cooking, American. I. Brethren Press. II. Granddaughter's Inglenook cookbook.

  TX715.N5235 2013
  641.5973—dc23

                                    2013010652

17 16 15 14 13   1 2 3 4 5

Printed in the United States of America

CONTENTS

PREFACE

I remember pushing a chair across the linoleum floor of the farmhouse kitchen, determined to be a part of what was going on at the counter. Mom was cooking or baking something special. She always welcomed me, and let me help stir up all kinds of goodies even though I was only four years old.

She often used a plaid-covered book that told us what we were preparing. The pages with the best recipes were smudged, oil-stained, and worn on the edges. When I got married, my mother gave me my own copy of *Granddaughter's Inglenook Cookbook* (even better than hers, because it had a spiral binding). I began using it right away as I prepared meals for my husband, friends, church, and later my children. Often I referred to the book for ideas and quantities when helping prepare large dinners at church or other events. Soon my favorite pages became smudged, oil-stained, and worn on the edges.

As time passed, my cooking changed. Foods were more abundant and global. Fresh items could be purchased regardless of the season. New appliances entered the market, and recipes were readily available on the Internet. Sadly, my *Granddaughter's Inglenook Cookbook* began to collect a little dust.

Today we are surrounded with conveniences in food products, appliances, shopping opportunities, fast foods, and technologies our ancestors could not even imagine. Yet there is a tug at our hearts and souls: We long for our tables to hold food that is simple, nutritious, and delicious. We like sharing new recipes. We savor mealtimes at home, at potluck dinners, and at other gatherings. So after more than seventy years, it is exciting for our generation to create a cookbook suited for our times.

Every recipe sent in was pure enjoyment for me, and it was a great experience to coordinate the testing process for the project. Those involved in testing and tasting were male and female, young and young at heart, busy working and busy retired. It was a vast assortment of individuals brought together for the purpose of creating another enduring cookbook for the Church of the Brethren.

As I sent sets of recipes to these volunteer testers, many new friendships developed. I liked opening friendly e-mails to sort out problems, discuss ideas, or share stories. This work was like play. As we worked together, the testers and I shared the stories of our hearts and supported each other during illnesses, deaths, births, graduations, family reunions, recovered health. We were God's family brought together in this unique undertaking.

Best of all, I had a bank of wonderful new recipes to try myself. Anytime I cooked a meal or brought a dish to an event, everyone asked, "Is that in the cookbook?" Most often I would tell them, "Maybe, but I need your input first. Taste it and let me know what you think." Helped by everyone's contributions, tabulations, and comments, those of us preparing the cookbook have carefully chosen the recipes to be included. The biggest dilemma was limiting ourselves, because we wished we could include everyone's recipe.

The New Inglenook Cookbook is a unique addition to the Church of the Brethren's tradition of culinary excellence. Not only does this cookbook contain top-quality recipes, but it offers something more—personal stories, tributes, wise tidbits, and a peek at the essence of Brethren kitchens. On the practical side, the pages include serving ideas, recipe variations, and symbols that quickly tell the reader if the recipe fits the occasion. And the paper itself is of a higher quality than the previous editions—it may take a bit more use before your pages became smudged, oil-stained, and worn on the edges.

This is a cookbook that reflects our lives today while bringing along treasured parts of our heritage. Old and new recipes have been melded in a beautiful banquet for this time. You are invited to this special feast for the heart, the soul, and the body.

—Karen Crim Dillon
Coordinator of Recipe Testing

INTRODUCTION

INGLENOOK TRADITION

Inglenook cookbooks have a long and storied history. Many individuals have received a copy as a birthday or wedding gift. Well-worn copies are blessed with food stains, hand-written notes, and dog-eared pages. Years of loving use have preserved the memories that are inextricably bound to the pages of these beloved cookbooks. And the names placed next to recipes are our culinary progenitors, a great cloud of witnesses.

The Inglenook cookbook series is a cherished tradition within the Church of the Brethren, and beyond. Somehow through our cooking we have conveyed our core values of humility, hospitality, peacemaking and service, and the sharing of common, simple meals. Whether you are a cradle Inglenook cook or a newcomer, there's a place for you at the table.

The Inglenook Magazine

It all started with *The Inglenook* magazine, a weekly literary magazine published by the Brethren Publishing House (now Brethren Press) from 1900 until 1913. Its content was for young and old alike: "Its pages are clean, its articles instructive, and it is a fitting companion for the spare moments of the schoolboy and the graybeard" (Sept. 1, 1900). And it wasn't just for Brethren; in fact, it had a much broader appeal.

So, what was an *inglenook* anyway, and how did this name stick? In its debut issue, editor Howard Miller described the building where all the printing and publishing of the church was done. In the room where *The Inglenook* editorial staff worked, he pointed out an open fireplace—"the Inglenook of the Editor" (April 7, 1900). He reminded readers that *inglenook* means "fireside or chimney corner." The magazine's masthead depicted a homey scene of a man—the editor perhaps—sitting by a blazing fire, with a black cat by his side. In many ways the name signifies hospitality, warmth, and comfort.

The Inglenook featured a wide variety of material—book and literature reviews, brief sermons and devotional material, counsel on managing life at home, commentary on current events, educational articles on nature, travel, and history, and short stories in serial format. It had witty segments called "Funnygraphs" and a "Question

& Answer" section. There were advertisements for an array of products and services—from the most innovative balms and elixirs for whatever ails you to real estate schemes enticing readers to go west to places like Colorado and California. *The Inglenook* also contained recipes and helpful household and cooking tips.

As an attractive feature, the magazine began publishing one recipe a week from some sister, "giving the details of a dish within reach of the average reader, and which she *knows* to be all right by trial" (Dec. 15, 1900). The editorial staff endorsed this heartily: "The paper has been good for the head and the heart, and now it proposes to set forth things fit for a king." *The Inglenook* had it all, for one dollar a year.

1901—The First Cookbook

Starting December 22, 1900, recipes were published within a column titled "Our Cooking School." They were submitted by Brethren women only, and the magazine promised: "It is a Dunker method [of cookery] that will be presented, and . . . these recipes will make a collection that cannot be equaled for excellence and practical results in any cookbook to be bought anywhere." Steeped in the Pennsylvania Dutch culinary tradition, many Brethren women submitted favorites like "Good Fried Mush," "Snits and Knepp," "Baked Apple Dumplings," and "Shoo-Fly Pie." But other kinds of recipes were published, too, such as "New England Layer Cake," "Macaroni with Cheese," and "Maryland Biscuits."

The popularity of this column grew, and readers began asking the editor to compile all these great recipes into book form. The editor seemed to like the idea, and put a little buzz in the readers' minds in the February 23, 1901, issue: "Don't cut your '*Nooks* to get the recipes. Who knows but one of these days, when they are all in, these recipes will blossom out in book form—but then this is confidential. Don't tell." In the June 15, 1901, issue it was announced that a cookbook would be created. And it would be given as a gift only to subscribers of the magazine: "It can be had in no other way for love or money. It will not be put on the market, and he or she who wants it must be a '*Nooker*." As readers began asking what the cookbook would be like, the editor said the two greatest features in the cookbook would be the facts that each recipe had been submitted, endorsed, and tested by a sister, and that the recipes were practical and contained common ingredients that any cook had on hand.

The Inglenook Cook Book was published in October 1901, and contained one thousand choice recipes from Brethren women all across the country. It set itself apart from popular cookbooks published in the late nineteenth and early twentieth century, most notably those that came out of the prestigious Boston Cooking School—Mary J. Lincoln's *Mrs.*

Lincoln's Boston Cook Book (1884) and Fannie Farmer's *Boston Cooking-School Cook Book* (1896). One Pennsylvania sister wrote: "I have a good many cook books, but the *Inglenook Cook Book* seems different from all, in that the recipes have such a home-like flavor. The cooking-school books are so high-toned and citified, while this reminds one of the old homestead and the things Mother used to make" (*The Inglenook,* Nov. 30, 1901). This was a cookbook for the common cook, and for the workaday lives of farm people and all those who chose to live simply in relationship to the land. "This book ought to be in every family and this might be one way of letting our light shine to the world," wrote Sister Annie B. Barhhizer (Dec. 14, 1901).

The original cover was plain, with just the title, but the title page was graced with a photograph of a young woman dressed in typical Brethren fashion. Lovingly called "Miss Inglenook," this woman has become synonymous with the Inglenook brand. In the 1980s, Kermon Thomasson, the editor of our denominational magazine *Messenger*, put out a call to learn her identity and quickly learned through multiple readers that she was Anna Evans Wilson of Missouri (February 1985).

This first edition of the *Inglenook Cook Book* has been reprinted many times over the years, most recently in 1981 with a new cover and all the original advertisements.

1902—The Inglenook Doctor Book

The cookbook had such widespread success that the magazine decided to publish another premium for subscribers: an *Inglenook Doctor Book*. In Inglenook fashion, the magazine asked readers to submit their domestic remedies and practical wisdom for what to do in emergencies. Anything for any type of ailment would be considered, but the sender needed to ensure the remedies had been "tried and proven valuable." Only Brethren women were allowed to contribute recipes to the cookbook, but this book would be different and allow anyone—"men as well as women, and outsiders as well as Brethren"—to contribute (*The Inglenook*, July 19, 1902).

The *Inglenook Doctor Book* was published in January 1903 and contained 916 home remedies for common problems such as colic and tonsillitis to more serious illnesses such as cholera morbus and neuralgia. It was not nearly as popular as the cookbook and, once the stock was exhausted, was not available again until a paperback edition was reprinted many years later in 1975 by Brethren Press and Pyramid Publications.

1911—Revised and Expanded

Throughout the first decade of the twentieth century, the *Inglenook Cook Book* continued to be reprinted and was eventually sold in the general marketplace. Advertisements from 1905 show the cookbook being offered for twenty-five cents in paperback and thirty-five cents in oil cloth. In 1907, the magazine expanded its reach beyond the Brethren market by soliciting salesmen and women to sell cookbooks on commission, earning from two to five dollars a day.

As that first decade neared its end, the publishing house decided to revise and expand the 1901 cookbook, which had sold remarkably well, and again offered it to its readers as an incentive for subscribing. In the June 28, 1910, issue of *The Inglenook*, the magazine announced the new edition and promised to include most of the recipes from 1901 along with many more new ones. The sisters were urged to submit their recipes and to make sure the directions were plain, "so that one who has had little experience in the art of cooking may follow them with confidence and fair success." The contributors were reminded to keep three things in mind when submitting recipes: palatability, wholesomeness, and simplicity. And finally, names and addresses would continue to be published next to recipes to give it a personal element.

As the cookbook was coming together, readers submitted their recipes along with suggestions on how to make this revised edition better. One housekeeper suggested adding a few blank pages at the end of each chapter to allow cooks to write or paste in recipes gleaned from other sources. Another cautioned against increasing the size, suggesting cutting out duplicates or combining them with similar recipes. Others criticized the large number of recipes "which require much work and care for their preparation, are of questionable value as healthful, nourishing foods, and which contradict our claim to the simple life" (Aug. 2, 1910). Another reader claimed that too much space was dedicated to simple instructions, things "any housewife ought to know."

Staff took many of these suggestions and criticisms to heart. The editor agreed with many of the critiques but balked at one: "Let the experienced cook pass over the directions accompanying a recipe if she is certain her own way is better than any other, but let us have them for the beginners and those of our number who believe there is still room for improvement in their methods of doing even the simplest things" (Aug. 2, 1910).

The new cookbook was finally published early in 1911. This revised and expanded *Inglenook Cook Book* continued its appeal to Brethren families, still mostly rural, who wanted substantial meals simply prepared. It had almost twice as many pages as the 1901 edition, contained 1,664 recipes, and featured menus for various occasions, simple home remedies, blank pages for pasting or writing notes or new recipes, and a general introduction to each chapter. Again it was offered to subscribers of *The Inglenook*—a one-year magazine subscription and a cookbook for one dollar.

Despite some initial criticism, the revised and expanded edition became even more popular than the 1901 edition. Both editions were considered "bestsellers" of their time, selling more than 100,000 copies combined. The 1911 edition has been reprinted many times over the years, with the most recent reprints coming in 1970, 1974 (as a mass market paperback), and 1981.

1942—The Granddaughters' Cookbook

By 1940 the next generation was ready for its own cookbook—one that reflected practical experience and included recipes fit for modern diets. There was a growing concern, even among Brethren, that increased urbanization coupled with technological advancements in farming were causing a deficiency in the nutritious and simple diet many Americans were used to. H. A. Brandt, assistant editor of the *Gospel Messenger*, addressed this concern September 27, 1941: "Life on the farm is not what it used to be. Machinery in the field and home has lightened the toil and made less necessary some of the heavier foods. . . . It is not that there is any less need for wholesome foods. With many taking somewhat less exercise, the problem of balance in diet is intensified."

Brandt then asked the daughters and granddaughters of the women who made the original *Inglenook Cook Book* how they were adapting to these cultural and societal changes in their kitchens. "Are they adjusting time-honored recipes to the requirements of the times? In many a Brethren kitchen some good cook must be experimenting to find what is best in foods and their preparation. Then why not collect the proven recipes of this sort and bring out a Granddaughter's Inglenook Cook Book?"

Response was positive, and plans were quickly put into place to create a committee, which consisted of Brandt, chairman, Genevieve Crist, editor, and Elizabeth Weigle, assistant editor. A call for recipes was sent out in the fall of 1941. Publishing house staff began addressing many of the current health concerns in their solicitations and recipes. An advertisement from the November 1, 1941, *Gospel Messenger* encouraged folks to make a difference by contributing to a new cookbook: "Many Americans are literally starving in the midst of plenty because they are not giving attention to wholesome economical cooking. We believe the practical cooks in our church can make a contribution toward a more nourishing diet." Another advertisement extolled those who submit "recipes using farm products; recipes using honey, maple syrup or sorghum instead of so much commercial sugar; new ways of preparing the usual vegetables, home-ground cereals and their uses" (Nov. 15, 1941).

Recipes started trickling in—less than a thousand by the end of the year—and then an avalanche hit by the March 1, 1942, deadline. Staff had hoped to get two thousand recipes, but received well over five thousand. This overwhelming response forced the cookbook committee to revise its original plan. In order to keep the cookbook at one dollar, two independent committees, composed of ten women with practical knowledge of cooking, were set up to select the best of the recipes offered. Their evaluation was based on the merits of the recipes, without any name attached. They also consolidated similar materials by presenting basic recipes with important variations indicated. This work became a time-consuming and expensive task (*Gospel Messenger*, Jan. 23, 1943).

Although it took much longer than anticipated, in November 1942 the *Granddaughter's Inglenook Cookbook* was published. It contained fifteen hundred recipes and several new features—charts and tables providing guidelines for such things as measuring food, distin-guishing between cuts of meat and how to cook them, and determining processing times for canning various foods. It also had an extensive index. The response was overwhelm-ing, and within a month staff realized the initial print run of five thousand would be gone in no time. Due to paper rationing during World War II it was impossible to keep copies in stock. Things eased as the war ended, and the printing of cookbooks continued through-out the postwar era.

The cover has changed over the years, from the original plaid one of 1942 to the color-ized drawing of the rural farmstead of the 1970s. Variations of this edition have been released to the general public by Harper and Brothers in 1948 and by Two Continents in 1976. It continues to be reprinted, with the most recent reprint coming in 2006.

INGLENOOK TODAY

So much has changed in the seventy-plus years since Brethren Press last published a cookbook. The way food is grown, processed, distributed, marketed, and sold has evolved dramatically, with most of us now disconnected from the sources of our food. Cooking has been made easier with new kitchen appliances and gadgets, but we also make more use of fast food and take-out restaurants because of our busy schedules. It's harder to find time for family meals.

While our fast-paced lives have complicated the way we prepare food and eat together, there is a growing desire to go back to the basics, to the simple ways of cooking and eating.

It's a hopeful sign. People do still cook, love food, and want to eat healthfully. This movement has inspired Brethren Press to reclaim our own culinary tradition and create a new cookbook for a new generation of cooks. Here's how it happened.

The New Inglenook Cookbook

A few years ago several people suggested that Brethren Press publish a new Inglenook cookbook. Coincidentally, these suggestions came after conversations within the publishing house to see whether there was new life to be breathed into the old Inglenook name. This seemed to be an idea whose time had come.

The first official planning meeting was held October 9, 2010. The next step was to create a website that allowed us to collect recipes and transfer them easily to a database. The database allowed us to track everything we ever wanted to know about each recipe—the contributor, the tester, the test results, comments, and where it was in the overall editorial and production process.

From the very beginning, Brethren Press decided to reclaim the long-standing Inglenook philosophy that recipes should be simple, made with wholesome ingredients, and come from the tried-and-true kitchens of ordinary cooks. Although we accepted all recipes for consideration, we communicated that the recipes in this new cookbook would be mostly "from scratch," avoiding prepackaged foods such as cake mixes and limiting ingredients such as canned soups and gelatin.

We launched *The New Inglenook Cookbook* website at the Church of the Brethren Annual Conference in 2011. Through online forms, people submitted recipes, shared stories or memories about preparing or sharing a meal, and applied to be volunteer recipe testers.

It was important that the testing be as impartial and scientific as possible. Each recipe was rated from one to ten (ten being the best) in six categories: appearance, completeness of instructions, taste, preparation, mass appeal, and cost and availability of ingredients.

Brethren Press received about twenty-five hundred recipes through mid-October 2011, and tested them from April through November 2012. The first task for Karen Crim Dillon, who had volunteered to coordinate all the testing, was to review each recipe, giving it an initial rating based on our cookbook philosophy, handle duplicates, and prepare recipes for the testing phase. Testers, who were assigned three to six recipes at a time, were not given the submitter's name or any other information about the recipe's origin. They had three weeks to make the recipes and submit evaluations using an online form, on which they were encouraged to provide comments, note errors, suggest improvements, and say whether they would make the recipe again. More than one hundred volunteer testers helped evaluate more than sixteen hundred recipes.

Once testers submitted their evaluations, those recipes with a rating of seven or higher were moved to the next phase. Determining the final list of recipes was probably the most challenging part of this project. The selection process was driven primarily by test results, but we also were conscious about *balance*—not only as it related to recipe categories, but also in the location, age, and sex of the submitter. After many drafts, a consensus was finally reached, and we were pleased to see how closely the recipes reflect what was submitted and the breadth of the denomination.

Return to Simple Living

Reinvigorating the Inglenook cookbook tradition is deeply connected to the Church of the Brethren values of simple living and community. As noted back in 1901, this lifestyle is one way of "letting our light shine to the world." How timely that today others are also seeking a return to nutritious meals, practical recipes, shared conversations, and connecting over a meal with family and friends. *The New Inglenook Cookbook* is a nod to the past, but also a look to a hopeful future.

As people of faith, we believe that all we have been given—especially the land, its resources, and the bounty we share—is a gift from God. Our desire is for you to find something within these pages to make, share, and give thanks for. May these new recipes become heirlooms, used by generations to come and cherished for the value and memories they carry with them.

—James Deaton
Managing Editor

RECIPE GUIDELINES

This cookbook comprises over four hundred recipes that were submitted by cooks with varied writing styles and cooking assumptions. Throughout the editorial process we developed a *recipe style*—the way things are worded and presented on the page—that sought clarity, consistency, and conformity with cookbooks published today. For example, in most cases measurements for ingredients are spelled out instead of abbreviated, which employs a modern cookbook convention used for clarity.

Another intentional decision was to write recipe instructions with the novice cook in mind, removing the guesswork when a recipe was complicated or used techniques unfamiliar to inexperienced cooks. Above all, we wanted straightforward recipes so that everyone might feel confident to make these recipes. We hope these added explanations and notes will make the recipes accessible to more people.

Accuracy of Recipes and Nutritional Information

We have made every effort to ensure the accuracy of all the recipes included here through various rounds of testing and detailed editing. (The only exceptions are the classic Inglenook recipes reprinted as is from the early editions.) However, we cannot assume responsibility for the success of the recipes. Use your best judgment when preparing the dishes.

Recipes that generally fit into three nutritional classifications—gluten free, vegetarian, and vegan—have been designated with a special symbol (see below). Where appropriate, we've also listed simple ingredient substitutions or variations to make other recipes more accommodating.

Although we've noted these classifications for certain recipes, detailed nutritional information and expert dietary guidance are beyond the scope of this book. Consult with your physician or a dietitian if you require a special diet or need guidance with regard to specific food allergies or restrictions.

Symbol Definitions

The recipe classifications and symbols described here were created to help you quickly assess whether or not a recipe is right for you, but they are general guidelines based on the opinion of the editors.

The first two recipe classifications primarily relate to the time and expense involved in preparing the recipe. The last three classifications are related to nutritional content and particular food restrictions. Please note that some packaged foods you purchase at the grocery store may not meet the nutrition standards assumed by our gluten-free, vegetarian, and vegan designations. Carefully read each recipe prior to making it, to make sure all the ingredients are appropriate for your family's diet and lifestyle, and, most importantly, double-check the labels on packaged food before purchasing them.

Quick and easy recipes take minimal time to prepare: about 30 minutes of preparation and cooking. Some of these recipes may look complicated, but they are really easy.

Special occasion recipes are usually more involved, more expensive, and good for celebrations.

Gluten-free recipes exclude foods containing the protein gluten, which is found in wheat, barley, and rye. Most flours contain gluten, so avoid breads, cookies, crackers, croutons, and pastas unless specified gluten-free. Many seasoned and processed foods such as salad dressings, condensed soups, soy sauce, snack foods, and cereals may contain gluten as well, so it is important to check the packaging to ensure the product is gluten free.

Vegetarian recipes exclude meat, seafood, and animal-based broths. Butter, eggs, cheese, and other dairy products are acceptable.

Vegan recipes exclude all animal-derived foods, including meat, seafood, animal-based broths, as well as butter, cheese, eggs, and milk.

Serving Sizes and Ingredient Assumptions

Each recipe contains a yield or serving size, which is based on an average adult's appetite. Some recipes have a serving range, to accommodate larger or smaller gatherings or to make a recipe that's typically served during a particular period of a meal fit in another part. For example, some soup recipes could be used as a starter or appetizer but may be just as appropriate as a main dish, served alongside a hearty salad or bread. We've tried to be as flexible as possible with the serving sizes for these kinds of recipes.

For simplicity's sake we have made some assumptions with some of the ingredients. Unless otherwise noted, the flour is all-purpose flour, the sugar is granulated white sugar, the eggs are large, and the milk is 2% or whole milk.

BREAKFAST AND BREADS

Whether at a fine table or
breakfast in bed—
you might try these fresh morsels
instead of a cold bowl of sugary shapes
that make you forget
what you just ate.

Any one of these spoon-licking treats
will make smiles on faces
the next time you meet with
the family and friends you love.
Sweet peaches, fine grains,
and blueberries, too,
will find their way into a story
of time made more special
by the food on the plate.

—Dena Lee
Churchill, Ontario

QUICK
& EASY

SPECIAL
OCCASION

GLUTEN
FREE

VEGETARIAN

VEGAN

Peanut Butter Granola

Often I will clip recipes from the newspaper, stick them away, and never actually try them. However, this recipe was from our local newspaper. We tried it immediately and have been using it ever since.

Makes 6 cups

   4 tablespoons unsalted butter
   1 cup peanut butter, creamy or crunchy
   ½ cup honey
   ⅓ cup packed brown sugar
   1 teaspoon vanilla
   ½ teaspoon salt
   4 cups rolled oats

- Preheat oven to 375°F.

- Line a baking sheet with parchment paper or grease it with oil or butter.

- Combine the butter, peanut butter, and honey in a large glass mixing bowl. Microwave on high for 1 minute, then stir. The mixture should be smooth and thick; if needed, microwave on high for 30-second increments until smooth.

- Add the brown sugar, vanilla, and salt to the peanut butter mixture. Stir until smooth, then add the oats and mix until they are evenly coated.

- Spread the oat mixture on the baking sheet and bake for 10 minutes.

- Remove the granola from the oven and reduce the temperature to 300°F. Stir the granola on the baking sheet to break it up and turn it. Return it to the oven for another 30 minutes at the lower temperature. Check it after 20 minutes to make sure it's not getting too brown. It should be lightly browned when done.

- When the granola is done remove it from the oven and allow it to cool on the baking sheet. It should be crunchy. Break the granola into bite-size pieces and store in an airtight container or bag at room temperature.

—Bev Anspaugh
Rocky Mount, Virginia

JOY IN EATING LOCALLY

Have you ever had performance anxiety in the kitchen? I get ridiculously nervous when it's time to make items for a family reunion or anything for a church potluck, to say nothing of communion bread! Breakfast can be another occasion when we set unrealistically high expectations for ourselves. It's the most important meal of the day, we're told, and so getting it right is important. The virtuous woman in the book of Proverbs "rises while it still night and provides food for her household" (31:15, *NRSV*). Jesus reminds us, though, not to worry about what we'll eat or drink but to live for today in the loving care of our Creator. Our meal at the dawn of the day, like the day itself, is full of possibilities. Breakfast is a great time to take what we have, give thanks for it, and see what happens.

Good breakfast preparation was once a labor-intensive process. I recently made Susie Forney Puterbaugh's "Breakfast Mush" from the 1911 *Inglenook Cook Book* (p. 92), and working my way through that recipe helped me reflect on the experience of cooks in times past and the conveniences I now enjoy. I quickly came to be grateful for all the things I didn't have to do, for all the things I didn't have to procure myself. I was not personally involved in the butchering of bacon I fried for grease, sowing, reaping, or grinding corn, churning butter, gathering eggs, or chopping firewood. My husband wouldn't stay out of the bacon, but at least I wasn't trying to care for any children while the

grease sizzled and spattered. I gave hearty thanks for my dial-controlled gas stovetop as I imagined trying to cook over an unpredictable fire. The mush fried up well, and I was surprised by how satisfyingly robust the mush cakes felt as I chewed. They tasted all the sweeter for their careful preparation, and thanks to a little maple syrup.

Maple syrup is an important part of breakfast in my part of the country, as a locally sourced food. Syrup making is a labor of love, since thirty to forty gallons or more of sap boil down to just a gallon of syrup. I never cared for syrup as a child, refusing even maple sugar candy. I learned to douse my pancakes in cinnamon applesauce at the Sunfield Church of the Brethren's pancake suppers. Now that my tastes have changed, I can fully appreciate maple syrup and its place in local traditions. My grandmother, Joyce Hoover Snavely, remembers syrup as an important source of calories for her family during the Great Depression. She was eleven in 1940, when the community of Vermontville, Michigan, held its first syrup festival and her family sold surplus syrup there.

Breakfast is big business here in Michigan. Battle Creek is known as the Cereal City, the birthplace of Kellogg's and Post. At Camp Brethren Heights in the 1990s, where we had from-scratch French toast one morning and oatmeal another, cereal dispensers offered an ever-present alternative. Familiar flakes were just the turn of a dial away. When I arrived at Manchester University, I felt close to home when I saw the variety of cereal dispensers filling most of a countertop.

Kathe E. Ward's "Maple-Nut Granola" recipe is bound to be one of my new favorite treats. I use dried Michigan cherries and maple syrup made by a cousin's grandparents. I am happy to have found a local store's countertop mill for freshly milled oats. Pecans and pepitas combine nicely for a crunchy, delicious granola. It's very shelf stable, and can be enjoyed for breakfast or a hearty, mid-morning snack. Seek out local ingredients to add and enjoy your own version—with no worries!

—Beth Allen DuBois
Charlotte, Michigan

BREAKFAST MUSH

Put 1½ cups of water, 1½ cups of sweet milk, a piece of butter the size of an egg, and salt to taste, in a pan. Let come to a boil, then stir in corn meal to make a soft mush easily dropped with a spoon; cook a few minutes, then add 2 eggs, beat well, cook a minute or two longer. Have the pancake griddle hot, with a liberal supply of butter and meat fryings melted. Drop the mush in by the spoonful and fry brown on both sides. Serve hot.

—Sister Susie Forney Puterbaugh, Kidder, Missouri

Maple-Nut Granola

Makes about 8 cups

¼ cup vegetable oil
¼ cup pure maple syrup (grade B for strongest flavor)
¼ cup honey
1 tablespoon maple sugar or light brown sugar
1 teaspoon ground cinnamon
¼ teaspoon salt
3 cups rolled oats
1 cup pepitas (shelled pumpkin seeds) or sunflower seeds
1 cup slivered almonds or pecans
2 cups sweetened dried cherries

■ Preheat the oven to 350°F. Line a large baking sheet or shallow roasting pan with a nonstick baking mat or parchment paper.

■ Combine the oil, syrup, honey, maple sugar, cinnamon, and salt in a medium bowl and stir.

■ In a large bowl, combine the oats, pumpkin seeds, and almonds. Pour the oil mixture over the oat mixture and toss until evenly coated. Spread the granola evenly in the prepared pan and bake for 15 to 20 minutes, or until a deep golden brown.

■ Reduce the temperature to 300°F and leave the oven door ajar to bring the temperature down while you use a spatula to gently turn the granola, trying not to break up the clumps. Bake for another 8 to 10 minutes until the granola is toasty brown, but watch carefully to make sure it does not burn.

■ Transfer the pan to a wire rack to cool completely. Break into chunks and then mix in the dried fruit.

■ Store in an airtight container.

Notes: You can use quick-cooking or gluten-free oats, but don't use instant oatmeal. And feel free to use whatever nuts or dried fruit you prefer. This recipe can be easily doubled.

—Kathe E. Ward
Troy, Ohio

Kathe Says . . .

My daughter, Ellen Fox, was raised in Ohio but now lives in Vermont and works for Shelburne Farms. She gave me the cookbook *Cooking with Shelburne Farms* by Melissa Pasanen with Rick Gencarelli, which inspired this recipe. It is a wonderful blend of flavors. We eat it as a snack. I also sometimes use other dried fruits, but the cherries make it special. And my husband and I like our granola to have clumps, so we use some honey and turn the mixture carefully just once during cooking and let it cool completely before touching it. Just a pinch of salt really brings out the other flavors.

Baked Oatmeal with Peach Topping

I helped my business partner, Sue Richards, serve this breakfast dish to many guests at our bed and breakfast, The RidgeRunner, in Middlesboro, Kentucky, in the 1990s and 2000s.

Serves 6

BAKED OATMEAL
⅓ cup vegetable oil
½ cup sugar
1 large egg, beaten
2 cups quick-cooking oats
1½ teaspoons baking powder
½ teaspoon salt
¾ cup milk

PEACH TOPPING
1 cup sugar
2 tablespoons cornstarch
2 cups fresh peaches, diced

- Preheat the oven to 350°F. Grease an 8-inch square baking pan and set aside.

- For the oatmeal, mix the vegetable oil, sugar, and egg in a bowl.

- In a separate bowl, combine the oats, baking powder, salt, and milk and stir to mix. Add the egg mixture and stir until the batter is well combined. Pour the batter into the prepared pan. Bake for 25 to 30 minutes.

- Meanwhile, make the peach topping. Combine the sugar, cornstarch, and 2 cups water in a saucepan and bring to a boil over medium-high heat. Reduce the heat to medium low and cook until the mixture is clear and thickened, about 10 minutes.

- Remove the saucepan from the stove and mix in the fruit.

- Serve either hot or cold over the baked oatmeal.

—Irma C. Gall
Walker, Kentucky

Mom's Apple Rings

My mother, Margaret Holley, found this recipe about twenty-five
years ago in the Sullivan County (Tenn.) newspaper. Since then,
I have made it scores of times, especially in years when apples are
plentiful, and I always get rave reviews. Don't worry about how
the rolls look going in; it will all even out in the end.

Serves 14 to 16 (if you can eat just one)

> **½ cup butter, melted**
> **2 cups sugar**
> **1½ cups self-rising flour**
> **½ cup shortening**
> **⅓ cup milk**
> **2 cups peeled and finely chopped apples**
> **1 teaspoon ground cinnamon**

- Preheat the oven to 350°F. Spread the butter in a 13 x 9-inch baking dish and set aside.

- Heat the sugar and 2 cups water in a medium saucepan over medium heat, stirring until the sugar dissolves.

- Put the flour in a large mixing bowl and cut in the shortening using a pastry blender or two knives until it forms coarse crumbs. Add the milk and stir until all the flour is mixed into the milk. Turn onto a floured surface and roll out into a large rectangle ¼ inch or less thick. Arrange the apples evenly over the dough and sprinkle cinnamon over the apples. Roll the dough lengthwise as for a jelly roll. It is okay if some of the apples poke out.

- Slice the roll into 14 to 16 slices, ½ inch thick. Place the slices into the prepared dish and then pour the sugar syrup over the rolls. It may look like too much water, but the crust will absorb it.

- Bake for about 45 minutes.

—Deanna H. Carey
Gray, Tennessee

Sweet Tea Ring

This recipe has been served at Fairview Church of the Brethren for over fifty years. It's always a favorite for church carry-in dinners. You will need to choose one of the filling options for this recipe.

Serves 8 to 10

DOUGH
2 (.3-ounce) packages active dry yeast
1½ cup warm milk
½ cup sugar
½ cup shortening
1 teaspoon salt
2 eggs
4 cups flour or more, divided

CINNAMON-RAISIN FILLING
2 tablespoons butter, softened
½ cup packed brown sugar
2 teaspoons ground cinnamon
½ cup raisins

APRICOT-CHERRY FILLING
½ cup finely chopped dried apricots
½ cup finely chopped maraschino cherries

DATE FILLING
1 cup chopped dates
¼ cup sugar
⅓ cup coarsely
   chopped nuts

GLAZE
1 cup powdered sugar
1 tablespoon milk
½ teaspoon vanilla

- Grease a large baking sheet and set aside. Dissolve the yeast in ½ cup warm (70°F) water in a large bowl. Stir in the milk, sugar, shortening, salt, eggs, and 2 cups of the flour. Beat until smooth.

- Mix in enough remaining flour to make the dough easy to handle. Turn the dough onto a lightly floured surface and knead until smooth and elastic, about 5 minutes.

- Grease a glass or ceramic bowl with shortening or oil. Place the dough in the greased bowl and turn it over to coat. Cover the bowl and let the dough rise in a warm place until it doubles in size, about 1½ hours. (The dough is ready if an indentation remains when touched.)

- Punch down the dough and divide into two pieces. Roll one piece into a 15 x 9-inch rectangle on a lightly floured surface.

- **If using the cinnamon-raisin filling**, spread the butter over the dough and then sprinkle with brown sugar, cinnamon, and raisins.

- **If using the apricot-cherry filling**, combine the apricots and maraschino cherries in a bowl, mix well, and then spread on the rolled-out dough.

- **If using the date filling**, cook the dates, sugar, and $\frac{1}{3}$ cup water in a saucepan over medium heat, stirring constantly, until thickened. Stir in the nuts and then let cool. When cool spread the mixture over the dough.

- When the filling is made and spread on the dough, tightly roll the dough lengthwise and pinch the edge of the dough to seal well. Stretch the roll to make it an even diameter. With the sealed edge down, shape the dough into a ring on the prepared baking sheet. Pinch the ends together.

- With scissors, make cuts two-thirds of the way through the ring at 1-inch intervals. Turn each section on its side, keeping it in a ring shape. Let rise until double, about 40 minutes.

- Preheat the oven to 375°F. Bake until golden brown, 25 to 30 minutes. If the tea ring browns too quickly, cover it loosely with aluminum foil.

- While the tea ring is baking, make the glaze. Combine the powdered sugar, milk, and vanilla in a bowl and mix until the glaze is smooth and of desired consistency, adding more milk to make it creamier or more sugar to make it thicker.

- When the tea ring is done, remove it from the oven and let it cool slightly. While still warm, spread the glaze on top and, if desired, decorate with any leftover nuts or cherries.

Notes: After kneading the dough, it can be covered and refrigerated in a greased bowl for up to 4 days. If using self-rising flour, omit the salt.

—Helen Schwarten
Cordova, Maryland

BLUEBERRY BUCKLE

This recipe is in memory of my mother, Leona Ober Buterbaugh.

Serves 6 to 8

DOUGH
¾ cup sugar
¼ cup shortening
1 egg
½ cup milk
2 cups flour
2 teaspoons baking powder
½ teaspoon salt
2 cups blueberries

TOPPING
½ cup sugar
½ teaspoon ground cinnamon
⅓ cup flour
¼ cup butter, softened

- Preheat the oven to 375°F. Grease a 9-inch square pan with shortening or butter. Add a ¼ cup flour and shake to coat entirely. Discard any leftover flour. Set the pan aside.

- To make the dough, combine the sugar, shortening, egg, and milk in a bowl and mix thoroughly.

- In a separate bowl, sift together the flour, baking powder, and salt. Add to the sugar and milk mixture and stir to mix well. Stir in the blueberries carefully to keep from smashing the fruit.

- Spread the batter into the prepared pan.

- For the topping, combine the sugar, cinnamon, flour, and butter and mix with a pastry blender or two knives into fine crumbs. Spread evenly over the top of the cake batter.

- Bake for 45 to 50 minutes, or until a toothpick inserted into the center comes out clean. Serve warm or cold.

Note: If you use frozen berries, add 5 to 10 minutes to the baking time.

—Mona Irwin
Clymer, Pennsylvania

QUICK COFFEE CAKE

This recipe was given to me as a wedding gift in 1972. It was in a box of recipes that was found in the kitchen of Chicago First Church of the Brethren. The church also gave me a hand grinder from the kitchen.

Serves 9

DOUGH
1½ cups flour
2 teaspoons baking powder
½ teaspoon salt
½ teaspoon ground mace or nutmeg
6 tablespoons sugar
2 tablespoons shortening
1 egg
½ cup milk or water

TOPPING
4 tablespoons sugar
2 tablespoons flour
¼ teaspoon ground mace or cinnamon
1 teaspoon butter

- Preheat the oven to 375°F. Grease a 9-inch square baking dish with shortening or butter.

- For the dough, sift the flour, baking powder, salt, mace or nutmeg, and sugar into a large bowl. Cut in the shortening with a pastry blender or two knives to form fine crumbs. Add the egg and milk or water and stir to form a smooth dough. Pour into the prepared dish.

- For the topping, combine the sugar, flour, mace or cinnamon, and butter in a bowl. With a fork mix until thoroughly combined. Sprinkle over the top of the coffee cake.

- Bake for 25 minutes.

Note: Whole wheat flour can be used for half the flour in the recipe. It calls for milk or water, so it can be dairy free.

—Mary Kay Snider Turner
Gettysburg, Pennsylvania

CRUMBS OR NO CRUMBS

When I was growing up, coffee cake meant a special occasion— overnight guests, a family weekend on the bay, a snowy day. And coffee cake was synonymous with Crusty Coffee Cake, from the *Granddaughter's Inglenook Cookbook* (p. 27). Because everyone liked it did not mean we all agreed—the great debate was crumbs or no crumbs. My aunt stirred all the crumbs into the batter rather than leaving some for the top. The rest of us conspired to be sure she was never the one making it for a family gathering. We thought the crumbs were the best part.

—Kathie Kurtz
Manassas, Virginia

	Yield (Loaf Pan*)	Shortening	Sugar	Eggs	Dry Ingredients	Wet Ingredients
Apple Orange Jill L. Keeney (Durham, Maine)	3	⅓ c + 2 T oil	2 c	4	4 c flour, 2 tsp baking powder, 1½ tsp baking soda, 1 tsp salt	⅔ c orange juice, 1 ripe banana, 1 tsp lemon extract
Butterscotch Nut**	1	1½ T	1 c brown	1	2 c flour, ¾ tsp baking powder, ½ tsp baking soda, ¼ tsp salt	1 c buttermilk
Date Nut**	1	1 T	1 c brown	1	1 c flour, 1 tsp baking powder, 1 tsp baking soda, ⅛ tsp salt	1 tsp vanilla
Lemon Connie Fletcher (Denton, Md.)	1	½ c	1 c	2	1½ c flour, 1 tsp baking powder, ½ tsp salt	½ c milk
Lemon Poppy Seed Betty L. Breidenstine (Hummelstown, Pa.)	2	1½ c oil	2¼ c	3	3 c flour, 1½ tsp baking powder, 1½ tsp salt	1½ c milk, 1½ tsp vanilla, 1 tsp lemon extract, ½ tsp almond extract
Mango Nut Peggy Holupka (Dundalk, Md.)	1	½ c oil	1½ c	3	2 c flour, 1 tsp baking soda, ½ tsp salt, ½ tsp cinnamon	1 tsp vanilla
Oatmeal Honey Shirley Pennington (Ironton, Mo.)	1	¼ c butter, melted		1	1 c flour, 1 T baking powder, ½ tsp salt, 1 c quick-cooking oats	1 c milk , ¼ c honey
Pumpkin Pauline Fillmore (Live Oak, Calif.)	3	1 c oil	1½ c + 1½ c brown		5 c flour, 4 tsp baking soda, ½ tsp salt, 1 tsp each cinnamon, cloves, ginger, nutmeg	3 c cooked pumpkin, 1 tsp vanilla
Rhubarb Nut Janet Duane Click (Harrisonburg, Va.)	2	⅔ c oil	1½ c brown	1	2½ c flour, 1 tsp baking soda, 1 tsp salt	1 c buttermilk, 1 tsp vanilla
Triple Chocolate Eric Yager (Columbia City, Ind.)	1 to 2	½ c butter	⅔ c brown	2	2½ c flour, 1 tsp baking soda, 1 tsp salt	1 c mini chocolate chips, melted, 1½ c unsweetened applesauce, 2 tsp vanilla
Whole Wheat Banana Ruby M. Hineline (Rice Lake, Wis.)	2	⅔ c oil	1½ c	4	1½ c flour, 1½ c whole wheat flour, ½ tsp baking powder, 1 tsp salt, 1 tsp pumpkin pie spice	2 c mashed banana, 1 tsp vanilla
Zucchini Bev Anspaugh (Rocky Mount, Va.)	2	1 c oil	1¼ c	3	2 c flour, ¼ tsp baking powder, 2 tsp baking soda, ¾ tsp salt, 1 T cinnamon	1 T vanilla
Zucchini Chocolate Chip Ben Brubaker (South Bend, Ind.)	2	1 c oil	2 c	3	3 c flour, 1 tsp baking powder, 1 tsp baking soda, 1 tsp salt, 2 tsp cinnamon	1 T vanilla

- Bring ingredients to room temperature. Preheat the oven.
- To make the batter, cream the shortening, butter, or oil and sugar until light and fluffy. Continue beating as you add eggs one at a time.
- Mix the dry ingredients in a separate bowl.

*Loaf pans vary in size, so begin checking the bread after 30 minutes to prevent burning.

Try one of these thirteen classic quick breads. Find one you like, read across the row, left to right, to determine the list of ingredients, and then follow the general directions found below the chart.

Special Ingredients	Baking Instructions/Glaze or Topping
Finely chop in a blender or food processor: 2 large unpeeled apples, cored and quartered, 1 large unpeeled orange, seeded and quartered, and 1½ c raisins; 1 c chopped nuts (optional)	Bake at 350°F for 50 to 55 minutes.
½ c chopped nuts	Bake at 350°F for 45 to 55 minutes.
1 c chopped dates soaked in 1 cup hot water, ½ c chopped nuts	Bake at 350°F for 45 to 55 minutes.
Grated rind from 1 lemon	Line pan with greased wax paper. Bake at 350°F for 40 to 50 minutes. After baking, top with glaze. For the glaze, combine juice from 1 lemon with ¼ c sugar. Spoon over hot bread, and pierce top with toothpick. Let cool completely; remove from pan. Allow to season a day.
1½ tsp poppy seeds	Bake at 325°F for 60 to 70 minutes. After baking, top with glaze. For the glaze, heat and stir, until clear, ¼ c orange juice, ¾ c sugar, ½ tsp vanilla, ¼ tsp almond extract, ¼ tsp lemon extract.
2 c chopped fresh mango, ½ c chopped nuts	Bake at 350°F for 30 to 35 minutes.
	In an 8- or 9-inch square pan, bake at 400°F for 15 to 20 minutes.
1 c raisins, 1 c chopped nuts	Bake at 350°F for 30 to 45 minutes.
1½ c chopped rhubarb, ½ c chopped nuts	For the topping, combine ½ c sugar, ½ tsp cinnamon, 1 T butter, melted. Sprinkle on top of batter, and bake at 325°F for 50 to 60 minutes.
½ c chocolate chips	Bake at 350°F for 35 to 45 minutes. After baking, top with glaze. For the glaze, melt ½ c mini chocolate chips and 1 T butter, and then stir in 2 to 3 T milk. Remove from heat and stir in ½ c powdered sugar, ½ tsp vanilla.
	Bake at 350°F for 50 to 60 minutes. Note: Use 3 c whole wheat flour instead of half all-purpose and half whole wheat.
2 c shredded zucchini, 1 c chopped nuts	Bake at 350°F for 50 to 60 minutes.
2 c shredded zucchini, ½ c mini chocolate chips, ½ c chopped nuts (optional)	Bake at 325°F for 50 to 60 minutes.

■ Gradually add the dry ingredients to the batter alternately with the wet ingredients. Fold in any special ingredients at the end.

■ Pour into greased loaf pans, and bake as specified until an inserted toothpick comes out clean.

■ Let the bread cool for 10 minutes before removing from the pan. Spread optional glaze over warm bread.

**Adapted and modernized from the Granddaughter's Inglenook Cookbook (p. 36).

CLOUD BISCUITS

These biscuits are very light and tender.

Makes about 8 large biscuits

2 cups flour
4 teaspoons baking powder
1 tablespoon sugar
¼ teaspoon salt
½ cup shortening
1 large egg, beaten
⅔ cup milk

■ Preheat the oven to 450°F. Lightly grease a baking sheet and set aside.

■ Combine the flour, baking powder, sugar, and salt in a bowl. Add the shortening and blend with a pastry blender or two knives until the mixture resembles coarse crumbs.

■ Make a well in the center of the mixture. Add the egg and milk. Mix with a fork until the dough pulls away from the sides of the bowl.

■ Turn the dough onto a lightly floured surface. Knead the dough until it forms a ball. With a floured rolling pin, gently roll out the dough to ½ to ¾ inch thickness. Cut out biscuits with a 2½-inch biscuit cutter; do not twist the cutter.

■ Place the biscuits on the prepared baking sheet about 2 inches apart and bake for 12 to 15 minutes, until golden brown.

—Grace Caplinger
Eaton, Ohio

SWEET POTATO BISCUITS

These biscuits are a favorite among the Joyfield Farm residents in North Manchester, Indiana. You can easily substitute white flour if you don't like whole wheat.

Makes about 8 large biscuits

1 cup mashed cooked sweet potato
¼ cup shortening, melted
1½ cups whole wheat flour
1 tablespoon baking powder
Dash of salt
3 tablespoons milk (optional)

■ Preheat the oven to 350°F. Lightly grease a baking sheet and set aside.

■ Combine the sweet potato and shortening in a bowl and stir. Add the flour, baking powder, and salt. Stir until just combined. For a softer dough add the milk, 1 tablespoon at a time, until the desired consistency. Stir with a wooden spoon until well mixed.

■ Transfer the dough to a floured board and pat or roll until about ½ inch thick. Using a 2- to 3-inch biscuit cutter, cut the dough into biscuits and arrange them on the prepared baking sheet about 2 inches apart.

■ Bake for 8 to 10 minutes.

—June Kindy
North Manchester, Indiana

	Yield (Muffin*)	Dry Ingredients	Wet Ingredients	
Apple Bacon**	12	2 c flour, 1 T sugar, 4 tsp baking powder, 1 tsp baking soda, 1 tsp salt	1 egg, 1 c milk, 2 T shortening	
Blueberry or Other Fruit *Barb Coffman (Phoenixville, Pa.)*	12	1¾ c flour, ¼ c granulated sugar, ¼ c brown sugar, 1 tsp baking soda, 1 tsp cinnamon	1 egg, 1 c plain yogurt (or sour cream), ¼ c oil	
Bran *Cheryl A. Johnson (Perrysburg, Ohio)*	42 to 48 regular	5 c flour, 3 c sugar, 5 tsp baking soda, 2 tsp salt, 2 tsp allspice, 1 15-oz box raisin bran cereal	4 eggs, 4 c buttermilk, 1 c oil, 2 tsp vanilla	
Bumper Crop Zucchini *Judy Steckly (Fort Wayne, Ind.)*	12	1½ c flour, 1 c sugar, ½ tsp baking powder, ½ tsp baking soda, ½ tsp apple pie spice	2 eggs, ½ c oil, ½ tsp vanilla, 1 c shredded zucchini	
Oat Apple *Karen Crim Dillon (Vandalia, Ohio)*	24	1½ c flour, 1½ c brown sugar, ½ tsp baking soda, ½ tsp salt, 1 tsp cinnamon, 1 pinch nutmeg, 1 c rolled oats	2 eggs, 1 cup milk, ½ c butter, 1 tsp vanilla	
Oat Bran *Retta Jean Reinoehl (Olathe, Kans.)*	6	¾ c flour, 2 T brown sugar, ½ tsp baking soda, ½ tsp salt, 1 c oat bran, ½ tsp cinnamon (optional), ¼ tsp nutmeg (optional)	1 egg, 1 c buttermilk, 2 T oil	
Pumpkin Oat *Raechel L. Sittig-Esser (Waterloo, Iowa)*	12 jumbo or 30 to 36 regular	3 c flour, 2¼ c brown sugar, 1 T baking powder, 1½ tsp baking soda, 1½ tsp salt, 2 c rolled oats, 2 c quick-cooking oats	3 eggs, ¾ c milk, 1½ c oil, 1 T vanilla, 29 oz canned pumpkin	
Raisin Wheat**	12	1 c flour, 1 c whole wheat flour, 2 T brown sugar, 4 tsp baking powder, ½ tsp salt	1 egg, 1 c milk, 3 T shortening	
Savory Zucchini *Judy Steckly (Fort Wayne, Ind.)*	12	2½ c flour, 1 T sugar, 2 tsp baking powder, 1 tsp baking soda, ¼ tsp salt, 1 to 2 tsp black pepper, ½ c grated Romano cheese	2 eggs, 1 c milk, ¼ c olive oil, 1 c shredded zucchini	
Sour Cream**	12	2⅔ c flour, ¼ c sugar, 2 tsp baking powder, 1 tsp baking soda, 1 tsp salt	2 eggs, 2 c sour cream, 3 T shortening	

- Bring ingredients to room temperature. Preheat the oven.

- Mix and/or sift all the dry ingredients in a bowl.

- Mix the wet ingredients in a separate bowl.

- Pour the combined wet ingredients all at once into the dry ingredient mixture. Stir only enough to combine all. The batter will be lumpy.

- Fold in any special ingredients at the end.

- Fill greased or paper-lined muffin tins ⅔ full.

- Bake as directed, until an inserted toothpick comes out clean.

Try one of these ten classic muffin recipes. Find one you like, read across the row, left to right, to determine the list of ingredients, and then follow the general directions found below the chart.

Special Ingredients	Baking Instructions
	Layer 1 T batter, 1 T applesauce, 1 T batter in muffin cup. Crumble 1 tsp crisp bacon on top. Bake at 350°F for 15 to 20 minutes.
1 c blueberries or other fruit	Bake at 400°F for 15 to 20 minutes.
	Bake at 375°F for 18 to 20 minutes. Batter can be transferred to an airtight container and kept in the refrigerator for up to 6 weeks. When ready to bake, do not stir batter when dipping out to fill muffin pan.
½ c chopped nuts	Bake at 350°F for 18 to 20 minutes.
3 c chopped apples, ¾ c chopped nuts, ¾ c raisins	Bake at 350°F for 20 to 25 minutes.
½ c chopped fruit and/or nuts (use optional spices, based on the kind of fruit you use)	Bake at 350°F for 15 to 20 minutes. Note: Substitute 1 c wheat bran for oat bran.
Optional spices: 1 tsp cinnamon, ½ tsp nutmeg, ½ tsp ginger	Sprinkle a few rolled oats on top of batter, if desired. Bake at 400°F for 30 minutes (jumbo) or 25 minutes (regular). These freeze well.
½ c chopped raisins	Bake at 350°F for 15 to 20 minutes.
	Sprinkle a little Romano cheese on top of batter, and bake at 400°F for 22 to 25 minutes.
	Bake at 350°F for 15 to 20 minutes.

*Muffin pans vary, but regular-size muffin pans typically hold 12; jumbo muffin pans hold 6, and mini muffin pans hold 24. Adjust baking time for larger or smaller muffin cups.

**Adapted and modernized from the Granddaughter's Inglenook Cookbook (p. 32).

APRICOT SCONES

Makes 16 scones

SCONES
2 cups flour
½ cup sugar
1 tablespoon baking powder
½ teaspoon salt
⅓ cup cold butter
½ cup chopped dried apricots
½ cup chopped pecans
1 teaspoon grated orange peel
1 cup plus 2 tablespoons whipping cream, divided

DEVONSHIRE CREAM
3 ounces cream cheese, softened
1 tablespoon powdered sugar
½ teaspoon vanilla extract
⅓ to ½ cup whipping cream

- Preheat the oven to 375°F. Lightly grease a baking sheet and set aside.

- For the scones, combine the flour, sugar, baking powder, and salt in a bowl. Cut in the butter with a pastry blender or two knives until the mixture resembles fine crumbs.

- Add the apricots, pecans, and orange peel. Add 1 cup of the whipping cream and rapidly stir with a fork just until moistened.

- Turn the dough onto a floured surface and knead 5 or 6 times. Divide in half and roll each half into balls. Flatten each ball into a 6-inch circle and cut each circle into 8 wedges.

- Brush each wedge with some of the remaining 2 tablespoons of whipping cream.

- Place the scones on the prepared baking sheet (or you can use a baking stone) and bake for 13 to 15 minutes, or until a toothpick comes out clean.

- While the scones are baking make the Devonshire cream. Combine the cream cheese, powdered sugar, and vanilla extract in a small mixing bowl and beat until fluffy. Gradually beat in enough whipping cream to achieve a spreading consistency. Cover and chill at least 2 hours.

Notes: You can serve the scones with Devonshire cream and a jam of your choice, or they are great just plain. If you want smaller scones, divide the dough into fourths before rolling into balls. This will give you 32 wedges. You will need to reduce the baking time by a few minutes.

—Elsie M. Holderread
McPherson, Kansas

CRANBERRY SCONES

Makes 12 scones

3 cups flour
½ cup sugar
2½ teaspoons baking powder
½ teaspoon baking soda
½ teaspoon salt
6 tablespoons cold butter
1 cup dried cranberries
⅔ cup white chocolate chips
1 cup vanilla yogurt mixed with ¼ cup milk

- Preheat the oven to 350°F. Line a baking sheet or jelly-roll pan with parchment paper.

- Combine the flour, sugar, baking powder, baking soda, and salt in a mixing bowl. Cut in the butter with a pastry blender or two knives until the mixture resembles coarse crumbs. Stir in the cranberries and white chocolate chips.

- Make a deep well in the flour mixture and pour in the yogurt mixture. Stir just until moistened.

- Divide the dough in half, pat or roll each half into a 7-inch circle, and then cut each circle into 6 wedges (like a pie). Place the wedges on the prepared pan. Brush the tops with a bit of milk and bake for 16 minutes.

Variations: You may use dried pineapple, dried cherries, or dried apricots in place of the cranberries.

—Betty Folkens Thill
Stockton, Illinois

Gluten-Free Scones

Serves 16 to 32

1½ cups gluten-free sorghum flour
½ cup gluten-free tapioca flour
1½ teaspoons cream of tartar
½ teaspoon baking soda
1 teaspoon xanthan gum
½ teaspoon salt
¼ cup sugar
4 tablespoons cold butter (cut into ½-inch slices)
1 large egg, lightly beaten
⅔ cup low-fat plain yogurt or ½ cup nondairy milk
½ cup chopped pecans
½ cup chopped dried apricots

- Preheat the oven to 400°F. Coat a baking sheet with cooking spray and set aside.

- Combine the flours, cream of tartar, baking soda, xanthan gum, salt, and sugar in a food processor or mixing bowl. Pulse on and off to combine the ingredients or stir to mix. Add cold butter and pulse about 15 times or cut in the butter with a pastry blender until the mixture resembles coarse crumbs.

- Combine the egg and yogurt or nondairy milk in a bowl and then add to the flour mixture and process for about 10 seconds or stir with a wooden spoon until the dough forms large curds.

- If using a food processor, at this point transfer the dough to a bowl. Gently fold in the pecans and apricots or whatever nuts and fruit you might be using.

- Divide the dough in half and roll each piece into balls. Flatten the balls into circles about ½ inch thick. Brush each circle with a little milk if you wish and then cut into 8 wedges.

- Transfer the scones to the prepared baking sheet (or you can use a baking stone) and bake for 15 to 20 minutes.

Note: If you want smaller scones, divide the dough into fourths before rolling into balls and cutting into wedges. This will give you 32 wedges. You will need to reduce the baking time by a few minutes.

—Elsie M. Holderread
McPherson, Kansas

OLD-FASHIONED DOUGHNUTS

This recipe was passed from my grandmother to my mother and now to me. It's in memory of Charlene Long and Dasie Click Long. My father loves these heavy doughnuts dunked in coffee.

Makes 3 dozen doughnuts

4 cups flour
⅔ teaspoon salt
3 teaspoons baking powder
¾ cup sugar
1 teaspoon ground nutmeg

1 egg, beaten
1 cup milk
½ cup plus 2 tablespoons
   shortening, divided
Powdered sugar

- Sift the flour, salt, baking powder, sugar, and nutmeg in a mixing bowl.

- Combine the egg, milk, and 2 tablespoons of the shortening in a separate bowl. Add to the flour mixture. Stir with a wooden spoon to combine.

- Transfer the dough to a lightly floured surface. Using a floured rolling pin, roll the dough to about ½-inch thickness. Using a 2-inch cookie cutter, cut as many circles as possible from the dough. Using a ½-inch cookie cutter, cut out the centers of the larger circles. (Alternately, use a special doughnut cutter that removes the center automatically.) Reroll the centers and cut as many more doughnuts as possible.

- Heat about 2 tablespoons of the remaining shortening in a large skillet over medium-high heat. Add as many doughnuts as possible without crowding them and fry for about 3 minutes, turning once, until nicely browned. Add more shortening for each batch, if necessary, making sure to wait until the shortening is hot before adding more doughnuts. When the doughnuts are done, roll them in the powdered sugar and put them on a platter to cool, although they are best eaten warm.

—Linda Q. Long
Mount Solon, Virginia

CREAM CHEESE BRAIDS

When left on the front porch or office desk early in the morning, this recipe is extremely effective in brightening a pastor's day.

Makes 4 (12-inch) loaves

DOUGH
8 ounces sour cream
½ cup sugar
½ cup (1 stick) butter, melted
1 teaspoon salt
2 (.3-ounce) packages active dry yeast
2 eggs, beaten
4 cups flour

FILLING
2 (8-ounce) packages cream cheese, softened
¾ cup sugar
1 egg, beaten
⅛ teaspoon salt
2 teaspoons vanilla extract

GLAZE
2 cups sifted powdered sugar
¼ cup milk
½ teaspoon almond extract

■ To make the dough, combine the sour cream, sugar, butter, and salt in a bowl; mix well.

■ Dissolve the yeast in ½ cup warm (105 to 115°F) water in a large mixing bowl; stir in the sour cream mixture. Then add the eggs and stir.

■ Gradually stir in the flour; the dough will be soft. Cover tightly with plastic wrap and chill for 1 to 2 hours or overnight.

■ Meanwhile make the filling. Combine the cream cheese, sugar, egg, salt, and vanilla extract in a food processor or mixing bowl. Process in a food processor or beat with a handheld electric mixer until well blended.

■ Grease two baking sheets and set aside. Divide the dough into 4 equal portions. Turn each portion out on a heavily floured surface, and knead 4 or 5 times.

- Roll each portion into a 12 x 8-inch rectangle. (You may need to prepare one at a time if you don't have a lot of work space.) Spread a quarter of the filling (about ½ cup) over each rectangle, leaving a ½-inch margin around the edges. Carefully roll the dough lengthwise like a jelly roll. Firmly pinch the edge and ends to seal. Carefully place the rolls, seam side down, on the prepared baking sheets, two to a sheet.

- Make 6 equally spaced X-shaped cuts across the top of each loaf. Cover and let rise in a warm (85°F) place free from drafts until double in bulk, about 1 hour.

- Preheat oven to 375°F and bake for 15 to 20 minutes.

- While the braids are baking, prepare the glaze. Combine the powdered sugar, milk, and almond extract and mix well. When the braids are finished baking, remove from the oven and spread the glaze over the tops while warm.

—Helen Schwarten
Cordova, Maryland

BIND US TOGETHER

As a young female pastor at the Palmyra Church of the Brethren, I was invited to join the deacon women to make communion bread for love feast. The dough was divided into twelve separate balls. Twelve women gathered around a table and began to knead the dough, singing hymns while they worked. Every five minutes the balls of dough were passed to the right to ensure consistency in spite of different handling techniques and different hand temperatures. It was a genuine and powerful act of communion—with Christ and with one another.

—Rhonda Pittman Gingrich
Minneapolis, Minnesota

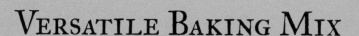

VERSATILE BAKING MIX

Whenever a recipe calls for a commercial mix, like Bisquick, just use this in the same measurement. It can last several months in the refrigerator or longer in the freezer without additives or preservatives. This baking mix easily makes pancakes, muffins, biscuits, even cookies or cakes.

Makes approximately 15 cups

10 cups flour
½ cup baking powder
1 tablespoon salt
1 tablespoon cream of tartar
½ cup sugar
2¼ cups (4½ sticks) butter

■ Sift the flour, baking powder, salt, cream of tartar, and sugar at least three times to make sure the ingredients are well mixed. Cut in the butter until the mixture is like coarse meal. Keep in the refrigerator or freezer in an airtight container until needed.

Pancakes

Mix together 3 cups baking mix, 2½ cups milk, and 1 egg until just moistened. Batter will be lumpy. Pour batter on a hot, oiled griddle. Flip when bubbles appear and continue baking until golden. Makes 18 pancakes.

Biscuits

Preheat the oven to 450°F. Stir ⅔ cup milk into 3 cups baking mix and stir just until moistened. Knead on lightly floured surface for 1 minute or less. Roll or pat the dough ½ inch thick and cut into biscuits or drop by spoonful on a greased baking pan. Bake for 9 to 11 minutes. Makes 18 biscuits.

Coffee Cake

Preheat the oven to 425°F. Combine 3 cups baking mix, ½ cup sugar, 1 egg, and ¾ cup milk in a medium bowl. Stir until well mixed. Pour into a greased 8-inch pan.

Mix ½ cup brown sugar, ¼ cup flour, ¼ cup (½ stick) butter, and ½ teaspoon ground cinnamon to form a crumble and sprinkle over the top of the batter. Dust with more cinnamon or some nutmeg. Bake for 20 minutes or until an inserted toothpick comes out clean.

Quick Yeast Rolls*

Preheat the oven to 400°F. Dissolve 1 (.3-ounce) package yeast in ¾ cup warm (100 to 110°F) water. Stir in 2½ cups baking mix and 1 tablespoon sugar. Knead the dough on a floured surface until smooth. Cut out rolls and place on a greased baking pan. Let the rolls rise for 1 hour. Bake for 10 to 15 minutes or until golden brown. Brush with melted butter. Makes 18 rolls.

Variations

- For sweet rolls, brush with melted butter and sprinkle with cinnamon sugar before baking.
- For garlic rolls, brush with butter and sprinkle with garlic powder before baking.
- For cheesy rolls, add 1 cup Cheddar cheese and 1 teaspoon dried dill to the batter, brush with butter, and sprinkle with Parmesan cheese before baking.

*This recipe was adapted from one submitted by Jane Wolfhope (Johnstown, Pennsylvania).

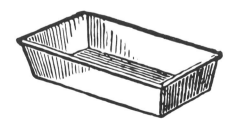

German Pancake

I have eaten this since I was a small child, and I have made it in many different variations for my own children. It can be sweet or savory and goes with any kind of fruit.

Serves 3 to 4

4 eggs, beaten
4 tablespoons flour
1½ tablespoons sugar
1 cup milk
Pinch of salt
¼ cup (½ stick) butter
Juice of 1 lemon
Powdered sugar to taste for dusting
¼ teaspoon ground cinnamon

- Preheat the oven to 425°F.

- Combine the eggs, flour, sugar, milk, and salt in a mixing bowl and stir to combine.

- Melt the butter in a 9-inch cast-iron skillet or 9-inch glass dish in the oven. Make sure the butter does not brown.

- As soon as the butter is melted, remove the skillet or baking dish, add the pancake batter, and bake for 7 minutes. Reduce the heat to 375°F and bake 8 more minutes, or until puffy and slightly browned on top.

- Remove from the oven and brush the lemon juice over the top. Dust with powdered sugar and cinnamon.

Notes: Granulated sugar can be substituted for powdered sugar. This can be served with fruit jam and sour cream, blackberry syrup, or many other sweet accompaniments.

—Stephanie Ann Sappington
Brentwood, Missouri

PERFECT BUTTERMILK PANCAKES

Our family has a tradition of having cooked breakfasts on Sunday morning. The batter for these pancakes can be mixed on Saturday night for a warm, quick Sunday breakfast.

Serves 4 to 6

> **2 cups flour**
> **2 tablespoons baking powder**
> **¼ cup sugar**
> **2 large eggs**
> **2 tablespoons canola oil**
> **2 cups buttermilk**

- Combine the flour, baking powder, sugar, eggs, oil, and buttermilk in a large bowl and stir just until blended.

- Heat a large skillet over medium heat. Coat with cooking spray, and when hot, pour about ⅓ cup batter into the hot skillet. Cook until bubbles form on the outer edges of pancakes, about 3 minutes. Flip the pancakes and cook for about 2 minutes more. Transfer to a plate in a warm (175°F) oven and continue cooking pancakes until the batter is used up.

- Serve the warm pancakes with maple syrup and butter. Makes about 8 pancakes.

Notes: Regular milk may be substituted for the buttermilk, and this recipe may be halved.

—Dianne Gleim Bowders
York, Pennsylvania

OATMEAL WAFFLES

These waffles are hearty. For a nuttier flavor, substitute steel-cut oats for the rolled oats.

Serves 6 to 8

1 cup all-purpose flour
½ cup whole wheat flour
1 cup rolled oats
3 teaspoons baking powder
½ teaspoon ground cinnamon
2 eggs, lightly beaten
1½ cups milk or buttermilk
6 tablespoons butter, melted
2 tablespoons brown sugar

■ Combine the flours, oats, baking powder, and cinnamon in a large bowl and set aside.

■ In a small bowl, combine the eggs, milk, butter, and brown sugar and whisk to mix. Add to the flour mixture and stir until well blended.

■ Preheat waffle iron. Pour batter onto lightly greased waffle iron (amount will vary with size of the waffle iron). Close the lid and bake until golden and crisp.

—Donna E. Stiver
Roann, Indiana

BAKED FRENCH TOAST

Campers at Camp Ithiel, in Gotha, Florida, ask for this breakfast by name every summer. This is a great recipe for group cooking, and it is delicious and high in sugar!

Serves 12

- 10 eggs, beaten
- 2 cups orange juice
- 1 cup (2 sticks) butter, melted
- 1½ cups sugar
- 1¼ teaspoons ground cinnamon
- 24 slices thick-sliced crusty bread

- Preheat the oven to 325°F.

- Combine the eggs and orange juice and stir to combine.

- Combine the butter, sugar, and cinnamon and divide between two 13 x 9-inch baking dishes. Spread the butter mixture around to thoroughly coat the bottoms.

- Dip the bread in the egg mixture, turning to coat thoroughly. Lay the bread in the dishes.

- Bake for 25 minutes. When ready to serve, flip the bread pieces over so the glaze is on top.

—Mike Neff
Gotha, Florida

BAKED APPLE FRENCH TOAST

This is a wonderful brunch recipe that will have your guests asking for seconds. It takes only about twenty minutes of prep time the day before. I used it for a Christmas brunch.

Serves 10

20 (1-inch) slices French bread, divided
1 (20-ounce) can apple pie filling
8 eggs
2 cups milk
2 teaspoons vanilla
½ teaspoon ground cinnamon
½ teaspoon ground nutmeg
1 cup packed brown sugar
½ cup (1 stick) cold butter, cubed
1 cup chopped pecans
2 tablespoons corn syrup

■ Coat a 13 x 9-inch baking dish with butter or oil. Arrange 10 slices of bread in the baking dish. Spread the pie filling over the bread slices and top with the remaining bread.

■ Combine the eggs, milk, vanilla, cinnamon, and nutmeg and whisk to combine. Pour over the bread. Cover and refrigerate for 8 to 10 hours or overnight.

■ When ready to bake, remove the French toast from the refrigerator and let sit for 30 minutes before baking. Preheat the oven to 350°F.

■ Meanwhile, place the brown sugar in a small bowl. Cut in the butter with a pastry blender or two knives until the mixture resembles coarse crumbs. Stir in the pecans and corn syrup. Sprinkle over the French toast and bake, uncovered, for 35 to 40 minutes, or until a knife inserted near the center comes out clean. Serve hot.

—Vivian S. Ziegler
Lancaster, Pennsylvania

Stuffed French Toast

Serves 8

16 (1-inch) slices French bread
¼ cup cream cheese at room temperature, divided
¼ cup fruit preserves, divided
6 eggs
1½ cups milk
1½ teaspoons vanilla
1½ teaspoons ground cinnamon
1½ teaspoons ground nutmeg
6 tablespoons butter, divided

- Cut pockets into the crust of each slice of bread, but not all the way through.

- Insert 1 teaspoon of the cream cheese and 1 teaspoon of the preserves into each pocket.

- Combine the eggs, milk, vanilla, cinnamon, and nutmeg and whisk to combine.

- Heat 1 teaspoon of the butter in a skillet over medium heat. Dip the filled bread slices into the batter and brown in the butter about 2 minutes on each side.

Note: Texas toast or homemade bread can be substituted for French bread.

—Mandi Kae Brous
Hays, Kansas

Food, an Equalizer

Whatever the region, culture, ethnicity, or family configuration, cooking and eating are equalizers. All people have traditions and favorite foods, and I have found that we all become equal with our needs when we sit around a dinner table. Acceptance, kindness, and friendship are evident through sharing food, even when language isn't common. It has been my privilege to cross many cultural divides at my dinner table, and I have found it impossible to hate or even dislike people when you have shared a meal together and looked into their hearts.

—Janet E. Whetzel
Dayton, Virginia

Ham and Cheese Crêpes

Makes 12 to 15 crêpes

CRÊPES
½ cup flour
½ teaspoon salt
4 eggs
1 cup milk, divided
2 tablespoons butter,
  melted and slightly cooled

1 pound deli ham, cut in ¼-inch
  strips
1 (7-ounce) can mushroom stems and pieces

SAUCE
5 tablespoons butter
5 tablespoons flour
2½ cups hot milk
½ teaspoon dry mustard
1 teaspoon salt
1 teaspoon pepper
1½ cups Cheddar cheese

- To make the crêpes, combine the flour and salt in a large mixing bowl. Add eggs and ½ cup of the milk; beat until smooth. Add the remaining ½ cup milk and butter and beat again. Cover and let rest in the refrigerator for about 1 hour.

- To a crêpe pan over medium heat, add ⅛ cup batter and quickly tilt and swirl to coat the entire pan. Cook for about 1 minute and then, using a rubber spatula, carefully flip the crêpe and cook for 30 seconds more. Continue making crêpes until all the batter is used.

- To make the sauce, melt the butter in a saucepan over low heat. Stir in the flour and cook, stirring constantly, for about 1 minute. Remove from the heat.

- Stir in the milk, mustard, salt, and pepper. Return the pan to medium heat and cook, stirring constantly, until the sauce boils and thickens.

- Add the cheese and stir until melted.

- Preheat the oven to 350°F. Coat a 13 x 9-inch and an 8 x 8-inch baking dish with butter or oil.

- To assemble, add a little ham and mushrooms to each crêpe and roll up. Place the crêpe seam side down in the prepared baking dishes. Repeat with the remaining crêpes, using the remaining ham and mushrooms.

- Pour the cheese sauce over the crêpes and bake for 25 to 30 minutes.

—Helen Wagoner Wenger
Anderson, Indiana

BREAKFAST ENCHILADAS

Chorizo is a Mexican sausage that gives this dish an authentic flavor, but any spicy sausage can be used.

Serves 8

1 pound chorizo
1 (4-ounce) can green chilies
½ cup chopped green onions
½ cup chopped green bell pepper
¼ teaspoon garlic powder
2 drops Tabasco sauce (optional)
2 cups shredded Cheddar cheese, divided
8 (7-inch) flour tortillas
6 eggs
2 cups half-and-half
1 tablespoon flour
¼ teaspoon salt

■ Coat a 13 x 9-inch baking dish with butter or oil and set aside.

■ Combine the chorizo, chilies, onions, pepper, garlic powder, and Tabasco and mix well.

■ Place ⅓ cup chorizo mixture and 3 tablespoons shredded cheese in each tortilla. Roll up the tortillas and place them seam side down in the prepared dish.

■ Beat the eggs with the half-and-half, flour, and salt. Pour over the enchiladas in the dish. Cover and refrigerate for 8 to 10 hours or overnight.

■ When ready, remove the enchiladas from the refrigerator and let sit while you preheat the oven to 350°F. Then bake, covered, for 45 to 50 minutes. Remove the cover, sprinkle the remaining cheese on top, and bake for 10 more minutes.

—Maria Garza-Huber
Goshen, Indiana

THE AMAZING EGG

I grew up a "city girl" in a rural county, and I frequently spent time on farms owned by family or church members. Over the years, agribusiness moved into the county, including an industrial egg plant. It didn't take long before we figured out that the life of the chickens at the egg plant was vastly different from the life of the chickens on the family farms. And somewhere along the line the eggs themselves seemed to change. Eggshells got too thin to easily peel off boiled eggs. (In my mind that accounts for the shrinking number of deviled eggs platters we see at church potlucks!) Suddenly salmonella became a threat if you ate raw eggs. Long gone were the days of licking the cake batter bowl or of mixing up raw-egg protein shakes à la Rocky Balboa. Then doctors began to warn of the cholesterol in eggs being detrimental to our health. Activists started clamoring about the need for chickens to be free-range.

The chickens I knew most personally belonged to Sister Nancy. They not only were free-range, but they ran the range, or at least the driveway! They were territorial and noisy, but oh so charming. Such coops of chickens used to be a mainstay of rural Brethren life. Accordingly, earlier editions of the Inglenook cookbook were filled with egg-based recipes of all kinds. Eggs from family coops provided fresh, economical food for cooking and an extra stream of income. In fact, most of the items that I liked best from Sister Nancy's kitchen—chicken with homemade egg noodles and lemon meringue pie—were directly from her chickens in one way or another. I also was the beneficiary of their feed sacks, which were made of one square yard of calico material that would get passed on to my mother. Unbeknown to my city peers, many of my play clothes were made from those colorful feed sacks.

I feel sorry for kids today who can't eat raw cookie dough. They also probably have no idea what adults are talking about with all those chicken idioms about ruling the roost, strutting around like a banty rooster, not counting your chickens before they hatch, being a tough old bird, or the gruesome but colorful, running around like a chicken with your head cut off.

However, there is good news for the amazing egg. The American Egg Board reports that the cholesterol level in eggs has dropped, and therefore our guilt in eating them can drop, too. Eggs are still an amazing and inexpensive source of protein, with an average of six grams of protein plus vitamin D and other nutrients, for only 70 calories. Raising chickens at the local level—especially free-range and organic—is becoming popular throughout the country. Why, where I live in Denver folks are even starting to keep chicken coops in the city.

So please enjoy the great new egg recipes presented here. I especially like Anna Lee Peterson's "Spicy Sausage Quiche," because it's healthful and quick and easy. And, if you cheat like I do and buy the precooked sausage crumbles at the grocery store, then all that you have to do is measure and bake! How great is that?

I've also included an old-timey recipe from the 1911 *Inglenook Cook Book* for "Pickled Eggs" (p. 58). This colorful dish from Sister J. E. Keeny was part of the Pennsylvania Dutch tradition of serving seven sweets and seven sours. It's a bit of Brethren cooking lore to make you smile.

—Sarah Leatherman Young
Denver, Colorado

PICKLED EGGS

Boil eggs ½ hour, then place them in cold water so that the shells may be easily removed. Put them into a jar and cover with vinegar in which red beets have been previously pickled; add 1 tablespoonful of sugar. After allowing them to remain in this liquid for 24 hours, they will be ready for use.

—Sister J. E. Keeny, Natchitoches, Louisiana

Spicy Sausage Quiche

I have been making this family favorite since my three children were babies. It is easy and can be enjoyed any time of day. The variations are a nice way to keep it interesting and provide veggies for the family.

Serves 6

1¼ cups skim milk
4 large eggs
¼ teaspoon salt
¼ teaspoon pepper
2 cups shredded Cheddar or Swiss cheese
2 tablespoons flour
½ pound spicy sausage, cooked and crumbled
1 frozen (9-inch deep-dish) piecrust

- Preheat the oven to 350°F.

- Combine the milk, eggs, salt, and pepper in a large bowl. Mix well and set aside.

- In a medium bowl, toss the cheese with the flour and add to the egg mixture. Add the sausage and stir to combine thoroughly. Pour into the piecrust and bake on the middle oven rack for 40 to 45 minutes, or until a toothpick inserted into the center comes out clean.

Variations: If you like vegetables, consider adding ¼ cup finely diced onions, mushrooms, broccoli, and/or spinach.

—Anna Lee Peterson
Frederick, Maryland

Spinach Quiche in No-Roll Piecrust

My mother adapted this recipe for our family while we were living in Nigeria, where she and my father served as Church of the Brethren mission workers. She made her own yogurt made of powdered milk, because American-style dairy products weren't available. The piecrust is so simple and trouble free that I have never learned to make a real one!

Makes 1 (9-inch) pie, about 6 servings

CRUST
1½ cups sifted flour
1 teaspoon salt
⅓ to ½ cup vegetable oil
2 tablespoons cold milk

FILLING
½ small onion, chopped
1 cup shredded Cheddar cheese
1 cup yogurt
1 teaspoon salt
1 tablespoon flour
2 eggs
¼ teaspoon pepper
Dash of ground nutmeg
1 cup cooked spinach

- Preheat the oven to 450°F.

- For the crust, sift together the flour and salt and pour into a 9-inch pie pan.

- Whisk together the oil and milk in a small bowl or cup, using a fork.

- Pour the oil and milk mixture over the flour mixture and stir with a rubber spatula until just combined.

- Press the dough to the shape of the pan and flute the edges of the crust.

- Sprinkle the onion and cheese over the crust.

- In a large bowl combine the yogurt, salt, flour, eggs, pepper, nutmeg, and spinach and mix well. Pour into the piecrust over the onion and cheese and bake for 15 minutes. Reduce the temperature to 350°F and bake for another 30 minutes.

—Cheryl Brumbaugh-Cayford
Elgin, Illinois

EGG STRATA

Serves 6 to 8

6 slices bread, divided
1 pound bacon, cooked, divided
3 tablespoons butter, melted
3 eggs
½ teaspoon dry mustard
½ teaspoon salt
2 cups milk
½ pound grated Cheddar cheese

■ Trim the crust off the bread. Grease a 1½ quart casserole dish and arrange one layer of the bread slices in the dish. Sprinkle ⅓ of the bacon on top. Pour 1 tablespoon butter over the bacon.

■ Combine the eggs, mustard, salt, and milk in a bowl and stir to mix. Pour ⅓ of the egg mixture over the bacon and butter. Add ⅓ of the cheese and then repeat the layers until all the ingredients are used.

■ Put the strata in the refrigerator for at least 3 hours to let the flavors meld. When ready to bake, preheat the oven to 350°F. Bake, covered, for 1 hour.

Notes: This can be made the night before, and you can use ham or sausage instead of the bacon if you prefer.

—Marilyn D. Gryder
Tallmadge, Ohio

SAUSAGE BREAKFAST CASSEROLE

This can be stored in the refrigerator for a few days before baking. I prepare and take this to the bereaved.

Serves 18 to 20

> 2 pounds sausage
> 4½ cups cubed day-old bread
> 2 cups shredded sharp Cheddar cheese
> 10 eggs
> 4 cups milk
> 1 teaspoon dry mustard
> 1 teaspoon salt
> Pepper to taste
> ½ teaspoon onion powder

- Coat two 13 x 9-inch baking dishes with butter or oil and set aside.

- Brown the sausage in a skillet over medium heat, breaking it into small pieces as it cooks. Drain and set aside.

- For each of the two prepared baking dishes, arrange the bread cubes on bottom, add a layer of sausage, and then a layer cheese on top.

- Combine the eggs, milk, mustard, salt, pepper, and onion powder in a bowl and whisk to mix well; pour over top of each baking dish. Refrigerate overnight.

- When ready to cook, remove the dishes from the refrigerator and preheat the oven to 325°F. Bake, uncovered, for about 1 hour. Tent with foil if the casseroles begin to burn.

Notes: You can substitute ham or sausage for the bacon. If you like it spicier, try adding ½ cup chopped onion, green pepper, or chilies for added flavor.

—Joyce I. Bybee-Brown
Warsaw, Missouri

SPOONBREAD

This is an elegant, soufflé-like breakfast item from my husband's family. It is easy to assemble and can bake while you prepare fruit or other breakfast items. My father-in-law always put grape jelly or apple butter on his spoonbread. Most of us just melt a little butter on it, but it is also good plain.

Serves 4

½ cup cornmeal
1 teaspoon salt
¼ teaspoon baking soda
1 teaspoon baking powder
2 eggs, separated
1 cup milk
1 cup buttermilk
1 tablespoon melted butter

■ Preheat the oven to 400°F. Grease an 8- or 9-inch baking dish and set aside.

■ Combine the cornmeal, salt, baking soda, and baking powder in a large bowl and set aside.

■ Beat the egg whites until stiff and set aside.

■ Beat the egg yolks thoroughly. Add the milk and buttermilk. Slowly add the cornmeal mixture while stirring with a wooden spoon. Add the melted butter. Fold in the egg whites and then pour into the prepared baking dish. Bake for about 25 minutes, or until the edges are lightly toasted.

Notes: If you don't have buttermilk, add 1 teaspoon vinegar to milk and let sit for 2 minutes. Low-fat milk works as well as whole milk in this recipe.

—Sharon Bunch Helbert
Broadway, Virginia

EARLY COLONIAL BREAD

Makes 2 loaves

½ cup yellow cornmeal
½ cup brown sugar
1 teaspoon salt
¼ cup vegetable oil
2 (.3-ounce) packages active dry yeast
¾ cup whole wheat flour
½ cup rye flour
4¼ cups all-purpose flour

■ Combine the yellow cornmeal, sugar, and salt in a large bowl. Add 2 cups boiling water and the oil and stir to thoroughly combine. Cool to lukewarm.

■ Soften the yeast in ½ cup lukewarm water (100 to 110°F). Stir the yeast mixture into the cornmeal mixture.

■ Stir in the flours to make a moderately stiff dough. If necessary, add a little more all-purpose flour until the right consistency. Knead well on a floured board. Divide the dough in half and let it rest for 10 minutes. Then shape the pieces into two loaves.

■ Grease two 9 x 5 x 3-inch loaf pans. Put each piece of dough into a loaf pan and let rise until double in size, about 30 minutes.

■ Preheat the oven to 350°F and bake for 45 to 50 minutes. The bread should sound hollow when tapped. Remove from the pans and cool on a rack.

—Kathryn (Burkholder) Schoppers
Preston, Minnesota

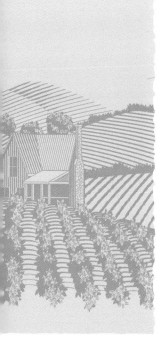

No-Knead French Bread

My eleven-year-old granddaughter, Cortland, and I love making this *for family dinners. Make it early in the day or later to serve it warm.*

Makes 2 loaves

- 1 (.3-ounce) package active dry yeast (2¼ teaspoons)
- 1 tablespoon sugar
- 2 teaspoons salt
- 4 cups bread flour
- 1 tablespoon cornmeal
- 2 tablespoons butter, melted

■ Add the yeast to 2 cups lukewarm (100 to 110°F) water in a large bowl. Add the sugar and salt and stir until dissolved.

■ Stir in the flour all at once and mix until well combined. Coat a second mixing bowl with oil or butter. (Or you can turn the dough onto a floured dinner plate and wash and grease the bowl used to mix the dough.)

■ Transfer the dough to the prepared bowl, adding a little more flour if it's sticky. Cover with a damp towel and let rise in a warm place for 45 minutes or until double in size.

■ Grease a French bread pan or baking sheet. Flour your hands and divide the dough in half. Shape it into long loaves. Place the loaves onto the prepared pan or baking sheet and let rise for 45 minutes.

■ Preheat the oven to 425°F. Brush the tops of the loaves with melted butter and bake for 10 minutes. Lower the temperature to 375°F and bake another 20 minutes.

■ Remove from the oven and again brush with butter. Cool on a baking rack.

—Carolyn Yates Seidel
Clifton, Virginia

Breaking Bread Together

Communion bread is perhaps the most universal of Brethren foods. Yet each congregation and gathering has its own recipe or adaptation, along with a host of shared practices and memories.

The congregation I grew up in had special forks with a specific number of tines that were used to prick the pieces of unleavened bread, leaving twelve marks—one for each of Jesus' disciples. There was often disagreement over whether it was a four-tined fork pricked three times, or a three-tined fork pricked four times. Other congregations prick the bread once with a five-tined fork to represent the five wounds in Jesus after his crucifixion. Some congregations have specific baking sheets and rulers used exclusively for the preparation of communion bread. As women across the denomination gather to prepare communion bread for love feast, held the Thursday before Easter, traditions meld and stories are shared as their hands turn and knead the dough. It is thought that the varying temperatures of the sisters' hands as they trade balls of dough ensure a perfect outcome. Across the denomination the preparation of the bread is almost as sacred as the act of breaking it together.

Tradition surrounds the various ingredients, too. Some use whole milk, some heavy cream, others reduced-fat milk. Some recipes, like Betty Godsey's recipe, use sugar but no salt, which created quite a kerfuffle at our love feast because I didn't make the "right" bread. One recipe from the 1911 *Inglenook Cook Book* from Sister Emma Click, of Tekoa, Washington, calls for graham flour and bolted flour, ingredients that most modern cooks are unfamiliar with (p. 122). Over time, some recipes and traditions have been adapted slightly to accommodate available ingredients, tools, and necessity. My current congregation celebrates communion weekly because we have a shared history with the Christian Church (Disciples of Christ). We have also started making gluten-free communion bread so that all members of our congregation can partake. While the flours—usually a mix of brown rice, corn, soy, and garbanzo beans—can be a challenge to work with at first and give the communion bread a slightly different flavor, the ability for everyone to participate fully is something very important to us.

The only practice that is nearly universal among Brethren of all traditions and generations is snacking on communion bread remnants. Fresh out of the oven, it is a luxurious snack to reward those who knead the dough. Growing up, my siblings and I would sneak into the kitchen and steal bites of communion bread left over after worship. Communion bread right out of the oven is still one of my favorite treats, though pieces snuck from the freezer are tasty, too. There is something about the flaky, buttery, richness that is more satisfying than a cracker and much more decadent than any cookie.

When we gather at the communion table to share the bread and cup, we are gathering at a table that extends beyond our sanctuary, our districts, even our denomination. As we reach across the table and break bread together, we are inextricably linking our lives together with Christians all over the world. The same is true when we prepare communion bread. My mother and I often make it together in her kitchen. As we knead, roll, measure, and prick, I know that I am partaking in a sacred practice that generations of Brethren women have experienced. Communion bread becomes the thread that binds us together, connecting us to that first communion where Jesus called us to follow him in life and practice.

Unleavened Bread or Communion Bread

Sift for 2 or 3 times 3 parts of graham flour and 1 part of bolted flour; stir into it with a spoon 1 pint of sweet cream. When as stiff as can be stirred, remove to kneading board and knead well; bake in a moderate oven. This is sufficient for 50 communicants.

—Sister Emma Click, Tekoa, Washington

—Elizabeth Ullery
Olympia, Washington

Communion Bread

This recipe was given to me by Esther Dodson in 1946. It had been given to Esther by Stella Amos.

Serves 50

2 cups flour
2 tablespoons sugar
½ cup cold butter
½ cup cream

- Preheat the oven to 375°F.

- Combine the flour and sugar in a bowl. Cut in the butter until the mixture resembles coarse crumbs. Add the cream and mix until the dough is smooth and the flour is incorporated.

- Transfer the dough to a lightly floured surface and, using a lightly floured rolling pin, roll the dough as thin as possible. Cut into 1-inch wide strips. Using a dinner fork prick the strips at 1-inch intervals. Place on a baking sheet and bake until just starting to brown, about 15 minutes.

- Remove from the oven and let cool on the baking sheet. Break into serving size pieces at the fork pricks.

—Betty E. Godsey
Independence, Kansas

Tips for Making Gluten-Free Communion Bread

When making gluten-free communion bread, follow your traditional recipe with a few modifications. Add ¼ teaspoon xanthan gum for each cup of gluten-free flour. This helps the dough hold together, giving it the ability to stretch. Gluten-free dough tends to be stickier than traditional dough, so it's helpful to roll it out between two pieces of parchment paper to keep it from clinging to the rolling pin.

—Elizabeth Ullery
Olympia, Washington

Kneading Dough

I remember spending the day at Aunt Bea's house, the Ikenberry homeplace, where the church women gathered to make communion bread. I would help mix the ingredients and shape the dough into a ball. One hour of kneading the dough was forever for a young child! I was fascinated by my grandmother's marker that was laid on the dough to mark the rows so they could be evenly cut. I couldn't wait to taste the bread when it came out of the oven, and even now, years later, that taste makes these memories come alive.

—Suzanne Ikenberry Rhoades
Daleville, Virginia

DILLY BREAD

Makes 1 loaf

1 (.3-ounce) package yeast
1 cup creamed cottage cheese
2 tablespoons sugar
1 tablespoon minced onion
1 tablespoon butter, softened
2 tablespoons dill seed
1 teaspoon salt
½ teaspoon baking soda
1 egg, beaten
2¼ to 2½ cup flour

■ Add the yeast to ¼ cup lukewarm (100 to 110°F) water in a large bowl. Heat the cottage cheese in a saucepan over medium heat until just warm. Add to the water. Then add the sugar, onion, butter, dill seed, salt, baking soda, egg, and flour and stir until well combined.

■ Cover and let rise for 1 hour.

■ Preheat the oven to 350°F.

■ Grease a 9 x 5 x 3-inch loaf pan. Place the dough in the prepared pan and bake for 30 to 40 minutes. Remove the pan from the oven and brush the bread with melted butter and sprinkle with salt.

Note: If you can't find creamed cottage cheese, whole milk cottage cheese will work too.

—Sheila Foltz
Cranberry Township, Pennsylvania

Light and Tasty Whole Wheat Crescents

Serves 24

2 (.3-ounce) packages active dry yeast or 1½ tablespoons bulk
yeast

1 cup milk, scalded

½ cup butter, softened

1 cup instant potato flakes

½ cup brown sugar

1 teaspoon salt

2 eggs

2 cups whole wheat flour

2 cups bread flour

- Dissolve the yeast in ½ cup warm (100 to 110°F) water and set aside. Grease a large bowl and set aside.

- Combine the scalded milk, butter, potato flakes, brown sugar, and salt in the work bowl of a stand mixer or a large mixing bowl. When the milk mixture is lukewarm, add the yeast mixture and eggs. Beat well.

- Add the whole wheat flour and mix with the dough hook attachment for 3 minutes, or use a wooden spoon. Add the bread flour to make a soft dough. Knead with the dough hooks 3 minutes longer or by hand for 5 to 8 minutes. Turn the dough out into the prepared bowl, turning to grease all sides. Cover and let rise in a warm place for 1½ hours or until doubled in size. Line 4 baking sheets with parchment paper and set aside.

- When the dough is ready, divide it into three equal portions and transfer to a floured surface. Roll each portion into a 12-inch circle. Spread a thin layer of butter over the circle. Using a sharp knife, cut each circle into 8 wedges. Roll each wedge into a crescent shape, starting at the long end and curving the edges inward while rolling.

- Place the crescents on the prepared baking sheets at least 2 inches apart. Cover and let rise another 45 minutes to 1 hour.

- When ready to bake, preheat the oven to 350°F and bake the crescents for 8 to 10 minutes until nicely browned. You may need to do this in a couple of batches.

- Cool the crescents on the pans for 3 minutes before transferring to a wire rack to finish cooling. Brush the hot crescents with melted butter before serving.

—Fancheon J. Resler
Albion, Indiana

Fancheon Says . . .

This is a recipe I use when teaching young people—and sometimes older ones—how to work with yeast. I do workshops with 4-H members and other groups, and I always tell them not to rush the process. I say, "Do the laundry, mow the yard, clean the house. Get lots of work done while the dough rises." Or better yet, study your Sunday school lesson! Yeast breads are my specialty, but this is my best and more often used bread recipe. I have shared it with many people and serve it at nearly every company meal in our home. Everyone experiences success with this recipe.

Perfectly Easy Dinner Rolls

Makes 24 rolls

 2 (.3-ounce) packages active dry yeast
 ½ cup (1 stick) butter, melted
 ½ cup sugar
 3 eggs
 1 teaspoon salt
 4 to 4½ cups unbleached all-purpose flour

■ Add the yeast to 1 cup warm (105 to 115°F) water in a large bowl. Let the mixture stand until yeast is foamy, about 5 minutes.

■ Stir in the butter, sugar, eggs, and salt. Beat in the flour, 1 cup at a time, until the dough is too stiff to mix (some flour may not be needed). Cover and refrigerate for 2 hours or up to 4 days.

■ Grease a 13 x 9-inch baking dish.

■ Turn the chilled dough out onto a lightly floured board. Divide the dough into 24 equal-size pieces. Roll each piece into a smooth round ball. Place balls in even rows in the prepared pan. Cover and let the dough balls rise until double in volume, about 1 hour.

■ Preheat the oven to 375°F.

■ Bake the rolls until golden brown, 15 to 20 minutes. Brush the warm rolls with melted butter, if desired. Break them apart to serve.

—Janice Parsons Paulus
Muskegon, Michigan

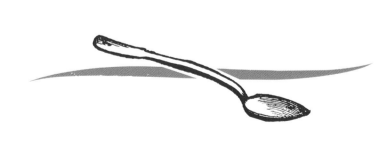

WHOLE WHEAT ROLLS

This recipe can make whole wheat bread too. Just divide the dough in half and bake in two loaf pans at 350°F for about forty-five minutes.

Makes 30 to 36 rolls

> 2 (.3-ounce) packages active dry yeast
> ⅓ cup butter
> ⅓ cup honey
> 3 tablespoons sugar
> 1 tablespoon salt
> 2 cups warm milk
> 4 cups whole wheat flour
> 2 to 3 cups all-purpose flour

- Dissolve the yeast in ½ cup warm (100 to 110°F) water.

- Combine the butter, honey, sugar, and salt in a large mixing bowl. Add the warm milk and stir with a wooden spoon to combine. Add the yeast mixture to the milk mixture.

- Then stir in the flour. Gradually add enough all-purpose flour until the dough is stiff enough to knead, at least 2 cups. Knead for about 10 minutes, until smooth and elastic.

- Grease a large mixing bowl with butter or oil. Put the dough in the bowl and turn to coat with the butter or oil. Cover with plastic wrap and allow the dough to rise until double in size, about 1 hour.

- Shape into 1½-inch balls (golf ball size). Put on a greased baking sheet 2 to 3 inches apart and allow to double in size, 1 to 1½ hours.

- Preheat the oven to 350°F and bake for 20 to 25 minutes, until golden brown.

Variation: For a slightly different whole wheat roll recipe, substitute ¼ cup vegetable oil for the butter and use 3 cups whole wheat flour to 3 to 4 cups all-purpose flour. Use water instead of milk. Thanks to Mary (Kitty) W. Reish from Dayton, Virginia.

—June L. Craun
Bridgewater, Virginia

BRAN ROLLS

My grandmother learned this recipe in a cooking class before my mother was born. These rolls became my mother's staple carry-in dish. Now I frequently make them myself for family reunions and carry-in dinners. The dough needs to be sticky or the rolls will be hard. It may be kept in the refrigerator up to one week before using. This is a light dough and rises rapidly.

Makes 48 rolls

1 cup vegetable oil
½ cup brown sugar
1 cup bran flake cereal
1½ teaspoons salt
2 eggs, beaten
1 tablespoon yeast or 2 (.3 ounce) packages
6½ cups flour

■ Combine the oil, brown sugar, cereal, and salt in a large mixing bowl. Add 1 cup boiling water. Let cool to room temperature.

■ In a small bowl pour 1 cup lukewarm (100 to 110°F) water and add the yeast. Mix until dissolved. Let rest until the yeast starts to bubble, about 5 minutes.

■ Add the eggs and yeast to the bran mixture. Stir $3\frac{1}{4}$ cups of the flour and beat until smooth. Add the remainder of the flour until the dough is stiff but still a little sticky. Cover the bowl and refrigerate overnight or until ready to use.

■ When ready to use, remove the dough from the refrigerator and divide into three to four pieces. Roll out on a lightly floured surface to about 14 inches in diameter. Cut into 16 pie-shaped wedges. Roll each wedge into a crescent shape by starting at the large end and ending with the tip which should be tucked under the roll. Place on a lightly oiled or parchment paper-lined baking sheet. Let the crescents rise until double, about 1 hour.

■ Preheat the oven to 400°F and bake for 9 to 12 minutes. These are best warm.

—Jennifer L. Allison
Doylestown, Ohio

Oatmeal Dinner Rolls

Makes 18 rolls

1 cup quick-cooking oats
3 tablespoons butter
1 (.3-ounce) package dry active yeast
⅓ cup packed brown sugar
1 tablespoon granulated sugar
1 teaspoon salt
4¾ to 5¼ cups flour, divided

- Bring 2 cups of water to boil in a saucepan over high heat. Add the oats and butter. Bring back to a boil, reduce the heat to medium high, and cook for 1 minute more, stirring frequently. Remove from the heat and let cool.

- In a large bowl dissolve the yeast in ⅓ cup of warm (100 to 110°F) water. Add the cooled oats, sugars, salt, and 4 cups of the flour. Beat until smooth. Add enough flour to form a soft dough.

- Turn onto a floured surface; knead for 6 to 8 minutes, kneading in more flour as necessary until smooth and elastic.

- Grease a large mixing bowl with butter or oil. Put the dough in the bowl and turn to coat with the butter or oil. Cover with plastic wrap and let rise in a warm place until doubled, about 1 hour.

- Punch the dough down and let it rest for 10 minutes. Grease a 13 x 9-inch baking dish with butter or oil and set aside.

- After the dough has rested, divide it into 18 pieces and roll into balls. Place the balls of dough into the prepared baking dish, cover, and let rise until doubled in size, about 45 minutes.

- Preheat the oven to 350°F and bake for 20 to 25 minutes, until golden brown. Remove from the baking dish and transfer to a wire rack to cool.

—Mary (Kitty) V. Reish
Dayton, Virginia

Peace at the Table

A meal of bread and water in contented peace is better than a banquet spiced with quarrels.

—Proverbs 17:1
The Message

ANNE'S MOLASSES WHEAT BREAD

This recipe was given to me by Anne, one of my high school students when I taught English at Wenatchee High School. We named the recipe for her. I was only six years older than most of my students, and many of them are still my friends. You may spread butter on the tops of the baked loaves while they are still warm to give a softer crust.

Makes 2 loaves

- 1 (.3-ounce) packet active dry yeast
- 2¾ cups whole wheat flour, divided
- 4¾ cups all-purpose flour, plus extra for kneading
- ⅓ cup rolled oats
- ⅓ cup wheat germ
- ⅓ cup cornmeal
- ⅓ cup cracked wheat (or 4-grain cereal)
- ⅓ cup molasses
- 1 tablespoon salt
- 3 tablespoons vegetable oil

■ Dissolve the yeast in 1 cup warm (100 to 110°F) water in a large bowl. Combine ¾ cup of the whole wheat and ¾ cup of the all-purpose flour and add to the water. Stir until a thick batter forms. Allow to rise 45 minutes in a warm place.

■ Add 2 cups warm (100 to 110°F) water and stir. Add the rolled oats, wheat germ, cornmeal, cracked wheat, molasses, salt, oil, and the remaining 2 cups whole wheat flour. Work in enough all-purpose flour to make an elastic dough you can handle. Knead for 5 to 10 minutes. Cover and let rise for 1 hour or until doubled.

■ Grease two 9 x 5 x 3-inch loaf pans. Divide the dough into two equal pieces. Form each piece into a loaf, place in the prepared loaf pans, and let rise 1 hour more.

■ Put into the oven without preheating and bake at 375°F for 50 minutes, or until golden brown.

—Merry Christina Roy
East Wenatchee, Washington

PUMPERNICKEL BREAD

Makes 1 loaf

1 (.3-ounce) package active dry yeast
1 cup large-curd creamed cottage cheese
2 tablespoons sugar
1 tablespoon minced onion
1 tablespoon butter
2 teaspoons dill or caraway seeds
1 teaspoon salt
½ teaspoon baking soda
1 egg, beaten
2¼ to 2½ cups flour

- Sprinkle the yeast over ½ cup lukewarm (100 to 110°F) water. Stir until dissolved.

- Heat the cottage cheese until lukewarm, and combine in mixing bowl with sugar, onion, butter, dill or caraway seeds, salt, baking soda, egg, and yeast mixture.

- Add the flour a little at a time, stirring after each addition, to make a stiff batter. Cover and let rise in a warm place until double in size, 50 to 60 minutes.

- Grease a 1½-quart round casserole dish with butter or oil. Then stir down the risen dough with 25 vigorous strokes and turn into the prepared casserole dish.

- Cover and let rise in warm place until double in size, 30 to 40 minutes.

- Preheat the oven to 350°F and bake for 40 to 50 minutes. Cover with foil for the last 15 minutes of baking if necessary to prevent burning.

Note: If you can't find creamed cottage cheese, whole milk cottage cheese will work too.

—Janet Duane Click
Harrisonburg, Virginia

BREAD FOR EVERY BELLY

When we stepped into the house, the aroma of Grandpa's freshly baked whole wheat bread would greet us every time we'd visit. He would usually have oatmeal raisin cookies for us, too—tasty after-dinner treats. We could smell the love in the air, from a day spent in the kitchen preparing for the granddaughters' visit.

Favorite foods like these have great power to conjure nostalgia. Certain smells invoke sweet memories of childhood innocence. Specific tastes remind us of being nurtured and fed by loved ones. As sweet as the memories may be, we know that those early experiences of food can never be re-created exactly. This reality is heightened for folks with dietary restrictions that place once-favorite ingredients off-limits.

It seems that we are more and more aware of the unique dietary needs of different bodies, breaking down any notion of one unifying diet across a culture. Many of my friends are intolerant to gluten, that core element of wheat, barley, and rye. It seems like such a sacrifice.

GLUTEN 101

Gluten is a very useful nutrient. It's great at sticking foods together and helping breads rise. So it's more common than you might think. Gluten is found primarily in products made with wheat, barley, and rye. Other grains and legumes like rice, quinoa, beans, and corn are great for gluten-free folks. But gluten also pops up in other surprising places, such as packaged seasoning mixes and salad dressings, soy sauce, many vegetarian alternatives to meat proteins, and even some ice cream.

Some people are gluten-sensitive and experience indigestion from gluten contamination in their food. Others must avoid wheat products specifically, including skin contact. Celiac disease is the most severe form of gluten intolerance. Some people have skin reactions after eating gluten products; some find gluten impairs their energy level; others simply avoid gluten as a personal health choice.

No more will Grandpa's whole wheat bread soothe their bellies—just the opposite, in fact!

But all is not lost. Cooking gluten-free, dairy-free, vegetarian, or to meet other dietary needs actually encourages the cook to be more creative in many ways. It makes the cook work harder to get the same result—perhaps extracting a greater commitment in the process. A cook might even get to know the recipe better. It pushes him to make the recipe his own: adjusting quantities, playing around with flavors, tweaking the timing. It's still his great-aunt's recipe, but it's also his, now.

And it drives the cook to greater consciousness of the food, to ask broader, more existential questions of her cooking: What is the defining essence of this food? Where do these ingredients come from? What is the taste and texture of the end result? What is the recipe's heritage? How do you experience the love with which it is stirred, poured, and served?

Like any valuable tradition, the survival of a recipe rests not only on the purity with which is it repeated, generation after generation, but with its adaptability in the face of new needs. The recipe's survival also rests on the devotion of the cooks who keep returning to it, and who then share it with others. A recipe that excludes people from eating it will soon fall out of a cook's repertoire, if folks cannot enjoy her culinary creations.

When Grandpa's bread recipe is made with rice flour and sorghum instead of Kansas wheat, it just might nourish even more bellies as it's passed on to new generations. The smell of warm bread can still greet my grandchildren when they come for a visit, from a gluten-free cornbread with tasty kernels crunching against their teeth.

Get started on shaping the traditions you'll pass on to the next generations by trying Marcella Huet's "Gluten-Free Sour Cream Cornbread" recipe. Plain yogurt works in place of sour cream, and any frozen or canned corn offers the tasty crunch. A little extra brown sugar or honey never hurt, either! It's gluten-free, quick to make, and tasty for every belly. Yum.

—Audrey deCoursey
Portland, Oregon

GLUTEN-FREE SOUR CREAM CORNBREAD

Serves 8 to 10

1 (8½-ounce) can cream-style corn
8 ounces sour cream
2 eggs
½ cup vegetable oil
1 cup cornmeal
3 teaspoons baking powder
½ teaspoon baking soda
1 teaspoon salt

■ Preheat the oven to 400°F. Coat an oven-safe 10-inch skillet with butter or oil.

■ Combine the corn, sour cream, eggs, and oil in a bowl and beat until well mixed.

■ Combine the cornmeal, baking powder, baking soda, and salt in a separate bowl. Add to the corn mixture and stir until well mixed. Pour into the prepared skillet and bake for 30 minutes, until the edges start to brown.

—Marcella Huet
Johnstown, Pennsylvania

HOSPITALITY TIPS FOR DIETARY NEEDS

The top tip is always communication. When you're inviting over new friends for a meal, try to remember to ask if they have any dietary needs for you to take into account. If you want to accommodate this into your menu for the meal, great! Your guest might be able to suggest a good recipe if you need one. But don't be afraid to be honest if you can't or just rather wouldn't change your menu. You can ask your guest to provide an ingredient or dish to meet their particular need; most guests are more appreciative of your friendship than being served a perfect meal. Talking this through ahead of time takes extra planning, but shows your thoughtfulness.

—Audrey deCoursey
Portland, Oregon

CORN STICK CORNBREAD

*My sister, Miriam Zumbrun, and I baked this when we were
children, and then baked it for our own children. This was from
the recipe box of our mother, Mary Senger Swinger. The optional
additions are my updated version.*

Makes 12 to 15 corn sticks

½ cup sugar
½ cup shortening
1 egg
1 cup cornmeal
1 cup milk
1 cup flour
2 teaspoons baking powder
½ teaspoon salt
1 cup corn (optional)
1 cup grated sharp Cheddar cheese (optional)
1½ teaspoons finely chopped jalapeño peppers (optional)

■ Preheat the oven to 350°F. Grease two 7-stick or three 5-stick cast-
iron corn stick pans and put in the oven while heating.

■ Beat the sugar and shortening until creamy. Beat in the egg. Add
the cornmeal and mix. Slowly add the milk, stirring constantly.

■ Add the flour, baking powder, and salt. Mix well. Add the corn,
cheese, and jalapeño peppers, if using, and stir to mix. Pour the
batter into the corn stick wells, filling each section half full.

■ Bake for 10 to 15 minutes, or until lightly browned. When done,
let the corn sticks cool a few minutes before cutting.

Note: If you don't have a corn stick pan, you can use an 8- or 9-inch baking
pan. Just don't preheat it, and increase the baking time to 25 to 30 minutes.

—Martha Swinger Burkholder
Verona, Pennsylvania

CHEESE STUFFED BREADSTICKS

I entered this recipe in my first 4-H Foods Review. It was a great experience. This is excellent served with marinara sauce.

Serves 12

> 1 tablespoon yeast
> 1 teaspoon sugar
> 1 cup whole wheat flour
> 1½ cup all-purpose flour
> 1 teaspoon salt
> 2 tablespoons olive oil
> 12 ounces mozzarella cheese
> Garlic powder to taste
> ⅓ cup butter, melted

- Add the yeast and sugar to 1 cup warm (100 to 110°F) water. Let it sit for a few minutes to activate the yeast.

- Combine the whole wheat flour, all-purpose flour, salt, and oil. Add the yeast mixture and knead into a soft dough. Let it rest for 5 to 10 minutes. Then separate the dough into 12 balls. Roll each dough ball into a breadstick. Flatten the breadsticks with a rolling pin.

- Preheat the oven to 450°F.

- Slice the cheese into 12 strips. Lay 1 slice of cheese on each breadstick. Sprinkle with garlic powder. Fold the dough around the cheese and seal well.

- Brush melted butter on each breadstick. Sprinkle with garlic powder again. Allow to rise 5 to 10 minutes and then bake for 12 minutes. Brush on more melted butter and serve warm.

—Emilie M. Deffenbaugh
Johnstown, Pennsylvania

SOFT PRETZELS

Makes 12 to 15 pretzels

1 tablespoon yeast
¼ cup sugar
¼ cup instant nonfat powdered milk
2 eggs, beaten, divided
¼ cup vegetable oil
¾ teaspoon salt
3 to 4 cups flour
2 tablespoons kosher salt

■ Grease or line a baking sheet with parchment paper.

■ Add the yeast and sugar to ¾ cup lukewarm (100 to 110°F) water. Let rest until the mixture starts to bubble, about 15 minutes.

■ Combine the powdered milk, 1 of the beaten eggs, and oil in a large bowl. Add the yeast mixture. Stir in flour 1 cup at a time to make a stiff dough. Turn out onto a floured surface and knead for 3 to 4 minutes. Cover with a towel and let rise for 1 hour.

■ Cut the risen dough into 12 to 15 balls. Roll each ball into an 18- to 24-inch-long rope. Shape each rope into a pretzel and place on a baking sheet. Brush the pretzels with the second beaten egg. Sprinkle with kosher salt. Let rise until double in size, about 45 minutes.

■ Preheat the oven to 400°F and bake the pretzels for 15 minutes or until golden brown.

—Norma J. Riley
Goshen, Indiana

APPETIZERS, SNACKS, AND BEVERAGES

Answer the door. Greet
guests. Take coats. Offer
a drink—hot or cold,
depending on the weather.
Lead the way to living
room or dining room,
wherever you have
arranged an artful
array of appetizers:
tiny meatballs,
stuffed mushrooms,
antipasto, a few
hot, bubbly dips,
a platter of crudite,
a tray of luscious cheeses.
Yet even if it is
as simple as a bowl
of olives, a toss of
tomatoes atop toasted bread,
the meaning is clear:

Friends,
I am glad you are here.
Each of you
is special to me.
Now let us enjoy
one another's fine
company. The evening
is young, and we
have all the time
in the world.

—Karen Allred McKeever
Elgin, Illinois

QUICK
& EASY

SPECIAL
OCCASION

GLUTEN
FREE

VEGETARIAN

VEGAN

PIMENTO CHEESE SPREAD

Serves 8 to 10

½ cup mayonnaise
¾ cup grated sharp Cheddar cheese
1 small onion, grated
1 cup pimentos, drained
½ cup salad olives, diced
Hot sauce to taste (Tabasco is preferred)

■ Combine the mayonnaise, cheese, onion, pimentos, olives, and hot sauce in a bowl. Mix all the ingredients together with a fork.

■ Spread on crackers or brown bread.

—Benjamin F. Simmons
Hershey, Pennsylvania

WARM HAM AND CHEESE SPREAD

Serves 18 to 20

4 cups cooked ground ham
1 cup shredded Swiss cheese
1 cup shredded Cheddar cheese
1 cup shredded American cheese
¼ to ⅓ cup mayonnaise
½ teaspoon ground mustard or 1 teaspoon spicy brown mustard

■ Preheat the oven to 350°F.

■ Combine the ham, cheeses, mayonnaise, and mustard. Spread in 13 x 9-inch baking dish. Bake uncovered for 15 to 20 minutes or until bubbly.

■ Serve with chips or crackers.

Notes: You may need more mayonnaise if ground ham is too dry. A couple of tablespoons of spicy brown mustard instead of ground mustard is good and provides more moisture.

—Anita K. Heatwole
Waynesboro, Virginia

White Cheddar Spread

This spread was inspired by a white Cheddar spread from Langensteins' Grocery in New Orleans. Leftovers make good sandwiches.

Serves 8 to 10

2 cups shredded white Cheddar cheese (sharp is best)
½ bunch green onions, white and green parts chopped
½ cup finely chopped walnuts
½ cup mayonnaise, divided (no substitutes)
Dash garlic salt
¼ teaspoon cayenne pepper

■ Combine the cheese, onions, walnuts, ⅓ cup of the mayonnaise, garlic salt, and cayenne pepper. Mix everything together, adding more mayonnaise until you achieve a spreadable consistency.

■ Serve with crackers or rye bread.

—Gail C. McGlothin
Tyler, Texas

Hot Artichoke Dip

Serves 4

1 cup mayonnaise
1 cup grated Parmesan cheese
2 (6½-ounce) jars marinated artichoke hearts, drained and coarsely chopped
2 cups shredded mozzarella cheese
1½ teaspoons garlic powder
Paprika for garnish

■ Preheat the oven to 350°F.

■ In a large bowl, combine the mayonnaise, Parmesan cheese, artichokes, mozzarella cheese, and garlic powder and mix well. Transfer to an 8 x 8-inch baking dish. Bake for 30 minutes or until surface is lightly browned and bubbly.

■ Sprinkle with paprika and serve warm with pita chips, crackers, or bread.

—Chris Fogerty and JoAnn Myers
North Manchester, Indiana

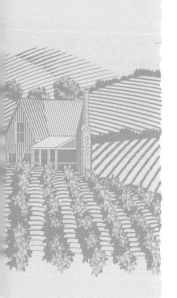

STUFFED MUSHROOMS

Leftover filling can be used as a sandwich or cracker spread.

Serves 10 to 12

    1 pound fresh whole mushrooms
    2 tablespoons butter, divided
    9 ounces cream cheese
    1 teaspoon chopped chives
    6 to 8 pieces cooked bacon
    ½ teaspoon garlic salt
    Shredded Cheddar cheese

- Preheat the oven to 375°F. Lightly grease a 13 x 9-inch baking dish and set aside.

- Wash the mushrooms in cold water and remove the stems. Chop about half the stems. Heat a saucepan over medium-high heat. Melt 2 teaspoons of the butter and sauté the chopped stems. Remove from the heat.

- Combine the cream cheese with the chives and add to the chopped mushroom stems.

- Crumble the bacon and add it to the cream cheese mixture. Add the garlic salt.

- Stuff the cream cheese mixture into the mushroom caps.

- Melt the remaining butter in a small dish. Dip the bottom of the mushroom caps in the melted butter and then place in the prepared baking dish. Top each mushroom with some of the shredded cheese.

- Bake for 15 minutes or until bubbly.

—Margaret A. Wolfe
Waterloo, Iowa

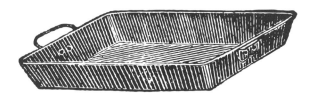

BASIC CHEESE BALL

Serves 8 to 10

▪ Form 8 ounces softened cream cheese into a ball and roll into one of the following:

- 1 cup chopped nuts (almonds, pecans, walnuts, pine nuts)
- 1 cup sunflower seeds
- ½ cup chopped parsley or chives
- 1 (4-ounce) package dried beef, chopped
- 1 cup shredded coconut
- 1 cup shredded cheese
- ½ cup chocolate shavings

▪ Cover and chill in the refrigerator for at least 2 hours. Serve with crackers, pita chips, or for the sweet options, butter cookies or graham crackers.

Pecan and Beef Cheese Ball

Mix 8 ounces cream cheese with 1 tablespoon onion soup mix, $\frac{1}{3}$ cup mayonnaise, and 8 ounces grated sharp Cheddar cheese. Form into a ball and roll in 1 cup chopped pecans or finely chopped dried beef. Cover and chill for at least 2 hours.

Glenna W. Trimmer, Carlisle, Pennsylvania

Chocolate Cheese Ball

Mix 8 ounces cream cheese with $\frac{1}{2}$ stick butter (soft), and $\frac{1}{4}$ cup creamy peanut butter. Add $\frac{3}{4}$ cup powdered sugar, 3 tablespoons cocoa powder, $\frac{1}{2}$ cup chopped peanuts, and $\frac{1}{2}$ cup chocolate chips. Form into a ball and chill for 2 hours. Then roll in $\frac{2}{3}$ cup chopped pecans. Cover and chill for at least 2 hours.

Miriam Headley, Hutchinson, Kansas

Pineapple Pecan Cheese Ball

Mix 24 ounces cream cheese with 30 ounces crushed, drained pineapple, 1 to 2 diced green bell pepper, 1 diced onion, 1 teaspoon seasoned salt, and 1 cup chopped pecans. Form into two balls. Roll the balls in 1 cup chopped pecans. Cover and chill for at least 2 hours.

Virginia Reed, Indianapolis, Indiana

Holiday Ham Cheese Ball

Mix 8 ounces cream cheese with $\frac{1}{2}$ cup grated Cheddar cheese, $4\frac{1}{2}$ ounces canned deviled ham, hot sauce to taste, and 2 tablespoons chopped chives. Form into a ball and roll in $\frac{1}{2}$ cup grated Cheddar cheese. Cover and chill for at least 2 hours.

DeeDee Schaefer, Ashland, Ohio

The Perfect Vegetable Cheese Ball

Mix 16 ounces cream cheese with $\frac{1}{2}$ cup whipped salad dressing, $\frac{1}{4}$ teaspoon bacon fat, hot sauce to taste, $\frac{1}{3}$ cup grated Parmesan cheese, $\frac{1}{2}$ teaspoon minced chives, $\frac{1}{4}$ cup minced vegetables (carrots, bell pepper, broccoli, green onion), and 10 strips crumbled cooked bacon (optional). Form into a ball and roll in $\frac{1}{2}$ cup shredded Cheddar cheese. Cover and chill for at least 2 hours

DeeDee Schaefer, Ashland, Ohio

Ham and Olive Cheese Ball

Mix 24 ounces cream cheese with 16 ounces grated sharp Cheddar cheese, 9 ounces canned deviled ham, $\frac{1}{2}$ teaspoon chopped chives, $\frac{1}{4}$ cup chopped green olives with pimento, $\frac{1}{2}$ teaspoon celery seed, $\frac{1}{2}$ teaspoon cayenne pepper, $\frac{1}{2}$ teaspoon salt, and 2 tablespoons prepared mustard. Form into a ball. Cover and chill for at least 2 hours.

Marilyn D. Gryder, Tallmadge, Ohio

Onion Cheese Ball

Mix 8 ounces cream cheese with 12 ounces grated sharp Cheddar cheese, $\frac{1}{3}$ cup Parmesan and Romano cheese blend, 1 teaspoon Worcestershire sauce, 2 to 4 drops hot sauce (Tabasco), $\frac{1}{4}$ cup ($\frac{1}{2}$ stick) butter (soft), $\frac{1}{3}$ cup chopped pecans, $\frac{1}{2}$ cup minced onion. Form into a ball and roll in a mixture of $\frac{1}{2}$ cup chopped pecans and 2 tablespoons dried parsley. Cover and chill for at least two hours.

Drusilla L. Pasley, Boones Mill, Virginia

Spicy Mexican Cheese Ball

Toast $\frac{2}{3}$ cup chopped pecans in 275°F oven for 20 minutes or till fragrant. Toss with 1 tablespoon melted butter and a dash of salt. Mix 16 ounces cream cheese with 4 chopped green onions, $\frac{1}{2}$ cup shredded Cheddar cheese, $\frac{1}{4}$ cup taco seasoning, and $\frac{1}{4}$ cup mild picante sauce. Form into a ball and roll in the toasted pecans. Garnish with fresh parsley. Cover and chill for at least 2 hours.

Sandra T. Carroll, Salem, Virginia

Hearty Cheese Ball

Mix 16 ounces cream cheese with 16 ounces shredded sharp Cheddar cheese, 1 teaspoon Worcestershire sauce, 1 teaspoon lemon juice, and $\frac{1}{2}$ jar pimento cheese. Form into a ball and roll in chopped nuts or chopped dried beef. Cover and chill for at least 2 hours.

Kathe E. Ward, Troy, Ohio

Chicken Cheese Ball

Mix 16 ounces cream cheese with 1 cup chopped cooked chicken, $\frac{3}{4}$ cup minced onion, and 1 tablespoon Worcestershire sauce. Form into a ball and roll in chopped pecans. Cover and chill for at least 2 hours.

Pamela J. Cota, Troy, Ohio

SWEET AND SOUR HAM BALLS

Serves 10

2 slices bread
1 teaspoon salt
1 tablespoon dried parsley
1 tablespoon prepared mustard
¾ cup milk
1 pound ground ham
1 pound ground pork
1 tablespoon cornstarch
1½ cups light brown sugar
1 teaspoon dry mustard
½ cup apple cider vinegar

■ Preheat the oven to 350°F. Grease a 13 x 9-inch baking dish or baking sheet with sides and set aside.

■ Tear the bread into small pieces into a mixing bowl. Add the salt, parsley, mustard, and milk. Stir until the milk and mustard have been absorbed by the bread.

■ Add the ham and pork. Mix well and form into 30 small balls. Place in a single layer in the prepared dish or baking sheet.

■ Bake for 1 hour. Pour off the fat and discard.

■ Meanwhile, prepare a sauce. Combine the cornstarch, brown sugar, dry mustard, vinegar, and 1¼ cups water in a saucepan and mix well. Bring to a boil over high heat. Reduce the heat to medium and stir until the mixture is clear, about 10 minutes.

■ When the meatballs have cooked for an hour, remove from the oven, pour the sauce over them and bake for 45 minutes more.

—Arlene Werking Barney
North Manchester, Indiana

Tomato and Goat Cheese Crostini

Serves 20

2 large tomatoes, seeded and diced
⅛ teaspoon salt
2 tablespoons plus 1 teaspoon olive oil, divided
2 (3-ounce) logs herb-flavored goat cheese, crumbled
2 tablespoons chopped fresh basil
¼ teaspoon black pepper
12-ounce French baguette
2 tablespoons olive oil
2 garlic cloves, halved
2 teaspoons chopped fresh parsley

■ Stir together the tomatoes, salt, and 1 teaspoon of the oil in a bowl; set aside.

■ Combine the cheese, basil, and pepper in a bowl; stir and set aside.

■ Cut the baguette diagonally into 20 ½-inch-thick slices. Brush both sides evenly with the remaining 2 tablespoons olive oil.

■ Toast the bread in 300°F oven for 2 minutes on each side, until golden brown. Rub cut slices of garlic over the toasted bread slices; spread about ½ tablespoon cheese mixture evenly over each bread slice. Top with tomato mixture, and sprinkle each with parsley.

—Kay S. Tipton
San Antonio, Texas

Texas Caviar

This can be used on anything calling for salsa, or even as a side salad. It's colorful, yummy, and healthy!

Serves 12

1 (15-ounce) can black beans, drained
1 (15-ounce) can black-eyed peas (optional)
2 (14½-ounce) cans corn
1 large onion, chopped
1 green bell pepper, coarsely chopped
1 red bell pepper, coarsely chopped
1 (14-ounce) can sliced black olives, drained
½ bunch fresh parsley, finely chopped
½ bunch fresh cilantro, finely chopped
Juice of ½ lime
Salt to taste
Black pepper to taste

- Combine the black beans, peas (if using), corn, onion, bell peppers, olives, parsley, cilantro, lime juice, salt, and pepper in a large mixing bowl. Mix all the ingredients together.

- Serve with tortilla chips (multigrain are especially good).

Notes: I prefer Italian (flat-leaf) parsley, but other kinds are fine too. A 14-ounce can of diced tomatoes can also be added for juicier texture and color contrast.

—Rebecca Golladay
Harrisonburg, Virginia

Hot Corn Dip

This is a family favorite. I make it for every family gathering.
You can make this in a slow cooker if you'd like.

Serves 40

1 (15-ounce) can white corn, drained
1 (15-ounce) can yellow corn, drained
1 (10-ounce) can diced tomatoes with green chilies, undrained
1 (8-ounce) package cream cheese, diced
½ teaspoon chili powder
½ teaspoon garlic powder
Chopped fresh cilantro to taste

■ Preheat the oven to 350°F.

■ In an 8 x 8-inch baking dish, combine the corn, tomatoes, cream
cheese, chili powder, garlic powder, and cilantro and mix well.
Bake for 30 minutes or until hot and bubbly.

■ Serve with tortilla chips

—Kristi Houck Gordon
Frederick, Maryland

LOVING AND SERVING THROUGH FOOD

It seemed to happen overnight—this sudden regard for salsa. Think about it. How many restaurants now tempt our taste buds with complimentary baskets of chips and bowls of salsa, while we wait for our "real" meal to be delivered from the kitchen? How many gatherings with friends and family have included some sort of salsa dip?

Sometime in the 1990s, salsa surpassed ketchup as one of America's favorite condiments. And its popularity is easy to understand. Salsa is simple to prepare, and it's healthful. Especially when using fresh ingredients, the sweet corn and the biting onion mixed together with the bright cilantro and sour lime blend to create an appetizer that's hard to resist. But there's more to salsa than its tastiness and accessibility. It can also symbolize the true meaning of fellowship: coming together in love.

As Brethren, we are accustomed to the idea of coming together for fellowship around food. It's hard for any Brethren to pass up a good ice cream social. And our potlucks are almost legendary.

But as the years have progressed, the food around our fellowship tables might look a little different these days. Sure, the traditional German-influenced foods are still around. Our potlucks wouldn't be the same without at least one scalloped potato dish or green bean casserole.

But, in our global society, we continue to incorporate more international influences in our cuisine. Sandwiches are now wrapped in flour tortillas. Vietnamese pho may be the next chicken noodle soup. Strained (or Greek) yogurt is a popular substitute for sour cream (not to mention "regular" yogurt). Instead of macaroni and cheese, Mediterranean couscous or South American quinoa might be served as a side dish.

In many cultures, food symbolizes love—love for your family, your friends, your community. You can show this love and affection through the way you prepare your food, the quality of your food, and the bright flavors in your food. It's an act of service for those who mean the most to you—and a gift given to the people who are blessings in your life.

I've experienced this love every day in my own multicultural home. I grew up eating traditional Vietnamese fare (with a smattering of good old German Anabaptist food, too). During my college years, my friends and I found ample opportunities to share a large pizza or a generous serving of chips and salsa. Now, in my adult life, my husband's family is introducing me to their African American soul food traditions. Despite the differences in all these meals, one thing is always the same: the love—the gift of preparing and sharing the food, together.

This type of fellowship sounds familiar, doesn't it? For generations—regardless of where we called home—Brethren and other Anabaptists have lived in community, serving each other as brothers and sisters in Christ. Perhaps this service happens during a family dinner, a youth workcamp, love feast, or a church potluck. Or, maybe this service happens over a bowl of salsa, with a side of chips. When you think about it, many times this service—this gift of love—happens around tables complete with food that is made and shared from the heart. Over this food, we are building strong, lasting relationships with each other.

Salsa as we define it today is not found in any of the previous Inglenook editions, but here's a classic recipe from the 1911 cookbook (p. 316) that shares similar ingredients.

CHILI SAUCE

Take 12 ripe tomatoes, 2 onions, 2 bunches of celery cut fine, sweet and sharp peppers, 1 cup cider vinegar, a little salt, and cinnamon if liked. Boil all together not too soft.

—Sister Lizzie Pehlman, Millersville, Pennsylvania

—Madalyn Metzger
Bristol, Indiana

Sweet Corn Salsa

Serves 10

1 cup frozen whole kernel corn
¼ cup finely chopped red bell pepper
¼ cup finely chopped green bell pepper
2 tablespoons finely chopped red onion
1 tablespoon chopped fresh cilantro
1½ teaspoons lime juice
¼ teaspoon salt
⅛ teaspoon black pepper

- Combine the corn, bell pepper, onion, cilantro, lime juice, salt, and black pepper in a serving bowl. Mix all the ingredients together.

- Cover and let stand at room temperature for 30 minutes, or up to 1 hour in the refrigerator.

- Serve with tortilla chips.

—Carrie Lynn Bush
Kokomo, Indiana

SALSA, MI AMOR

When it comes to salsa, many in our fast-paced society opt for the premade, bottled variety that lines grocery store shelves. Bottled salsa is usually a form of *pico de gallo* or *salsa cruda*. Not surprisingly, some salsa aficionados don't consider the bottled variety to be authentic—but its long shelf life and widespread availability have helped spread its popularity. This popularity became apparent in the 1990s, when salsa sales in the United States surpassed ketchup, taking the lead over one of our society's favorite condiments. But, did you know that neither salsa nor ketchup reigns supreme? Mayonnaise actually takes the title of America's most favorite condiment (based on retail sales).

—Madalyn Metzger
Bristol, Indiana

Strawberry and Mango Salsa

Serves 10 to 12

2½ to 3 cups strawberries, chopped
1 to 2 mangos, chopped
1 large red onion, chopped
1 green bell pepper, chopped
1 yellow bell pepper, chopped
1 orange or red bell pepper, chopped
1 to 2 jalapeño pepper, chopped, seeded
   or unseeded according to heat level
¼ cup chopped fresh parsley
¼ cup chopped fresh cilantro
1 to 2 teaspoons black pepper
Salt to taste
⅓ cup fat-free Catalina Dressing

■ Combine the strawberries, mangos, onion, bell peppers , jalapeño pepper, parsley, cilantro, pepper, salt, and dressing in a large bowl.

■ Mix well and enjoy with tortilla chips, eggs, fish, or just about anything.

Notes: I prefer using the Italian flat-leaf parsley. Using lime juice for the dressing is good too.

—Rebecca Golladay
Harrisonburg, Virginia

HUMMUS

This recipe came from a friend of mine from Turkey. You can add a lot more garlic than the recipe states. Greek yogurt makes a very smooth texture.

Serves 8 to 10

> 1 (15-ounce) can chickpeas, rinsed and drained
> 1 teaspoon minced garlic
> ¼ cup lemon juice
> 3 tablespoons tahini
> 1 teaspoon cumin
> ¼ cup plain yogurt
> 2 tablespoons olive oil
> Salt to taste

- Combine the chickpeas, garlic, lemon juice, tahini, cumin, yogurt, oil, and salt in the work bowl of a food processor and blend until smooth.

- Transfer to a nice dish and serve with pita or tortilla chips.

—Carolyn S. Willoughby
Johnstown, Pennsylvania

White Bean Dip with Pita Chips

Serves 6

1 (15-ounce) can white beans, rinsed and drained
2 garlic cloves, minced
Juice of ½ a lemon
¾ cup olive oil, divided
¼ cup loosely packed chopped Italian parsley
Freshly ground black pepper
1 tablespoon dried oregano or Italian seasoning, divided
6 pitas

■ Preheat the oven to 400°F. Lightly grease 2 baking sheets and set aside.

■ Combine the beans, garlic, lemon juice, $\frac{1}{3}$ cup of the olive oil, and parsley in the work bowl of a food processor. Pulse the mixture until coarsely chopped. Transfer to a mixing bowl and season with the pepper to taste and 1 teaspoon of the oregano or Italian seasoning. Stir to mix.

■ Brush each pita with the remaining olive oil and sprinkle with pepper to taste and the remaining oregano or Italian seasoning. Cut the pitas in half, and then into triangles.

■ Arrange the pita pieces on the prepared baking sheets and bake for 8 to 12 minutes, until lightly toasted.

—Jennifer Hausfeld
Troy, Ohio

ZUCCHINI PIZZA BITES

Serves 14 to 18

4 cups shredded unpeeled zucchini, drained and squeezed dry
1 cup shredded Cheddar cheese, divided
1 cup shredded mozzarella cheese, divided
2 eggs, beaten
1 pound ground beef
1 medium onion, chopped
¼ teaspoon salt
¼ teaspoon garlic salt
1 (8-ounce) can tomato sauce
2 teaspoons dried oregano
1 medium green bell pepper, julienned
5 medium fresh mushrooms, sliced
⅓ cup grated Parmesan cheese

- Preheat the oven to 400°F. Grease a 15 x 10-inch baking dish and set aside.

- In a large bowl, combine the zucchini, ½ cup of the Cheddar cheese, ½ cup of the mozzarella cheese, and the eggs. Mix well. Press the mixture onto the bottom and up the sides of the prepared baking dish.

- Bake for 20 to 25 minutes or until the crust is set and lightly browned.

- Combine the beef, onion, salt, and garlic salt in a skillet over medium heat. Brown the beef until it is no longer pink, about 10 minutes. Drain. Stir in the tomato sauce and oregano. Mix well. Spoon over the crust. Sprinkle with bell pepper, mushrooms, Parmesan cheese, and remaining Cheddar and mozzarella cheeses. Bake for 15 minutes more, or until golden brown.

- Let stand 5 minutes before cutting. Cut into 2-inch squares.

—Jennifer Klinedinst
Walkerton, Indiana

THE OLD COOKBOOK

My kitchen bookshelf holds a 1911 edition of the *Inglenook Cook Book*. I don't know how or when it appeared. It just showed up one day when I was looking for another book. The flyleaves are covered with handwritten recipes and home remedies, and the book is stuffed with them, even one for the treatment of rheumatism, along with fliers for livestock sales in Mount Joy, Pa., and in Sunnyside, N.J. It is well worn and the spine is gone, but it bespeaks a family's love of good food.

—David L. Farmer
Elizabethtown, Pennsylvania

Tijuana Tidbits

This is great to give in bags to friends at Christmas.

Serves 14 to 18

4 cups tortilla chips, broken into 1½-inch pieces
3 cups square rice or corn cereal
1 (3- to 3½-ounce) package microwave popcorn, or 8 to 9 cups
popped
12 ounces mixed cocktail nuts
½ cup light corn syrup
½ cup (1 stick) butter
½ cup firmly packed brown sugar
1 tablespoon chili powder
⅛ teaspoon ground cinnamon
⅛ to ¼ teaspoon ground red pepper (optional)

■ Preheat the oven to 250°F.

■ Toss the tortilla chips, cereal, popcorn, and nuts in large roasting pan.

■ Combine the corn syrup, butter, brown sugar, chili powder, cinnamon, and red pepper, if using, in small saucepan over medium-high heat. Bring to a boil, stirring until all the ingredients are dissolved and well mixed. Pour over the cereal mixture in the pan, stirring to coat.

■ Bake for 1 hour, stirring every 20 minutes. Remove from the oven and turn onto a large sheet of wax paper to cool. Once cool, break up and store in an airtight container. Will keep for up to 2 weeks.

Note: This could be gluten free if you use gluten-free tortilla chips.

—Irma N. Varner
Bassett, Virginia

CARAMEL CORN

Feeds 10 hungry kids or 20 adults

- 1 cup (2 sticks) butter
- 2 cups packed brown sugar
- ½ cup light corn syrup
- 1 teaspoon salt
- 1 teaspoon vanilla
- 1 teaspoon baking soda
- 3 (3- to 3½-ounce) packages microwave popcorn, or 24 cups popped
- 2 cups peanuts

- Preheat the oven to 250°F.

- Combine the butter, sugar, corn syrup, and salt in a large, heavy saucepan over medium-high heat and boil for 5 minutes, stirring only until the mixture starts to boil. Remove from the burner and add the vanilla and baking soda. The mixture will expand quite a lot.

- Put popped popcorn and peanuts in a large roaster. Pour the corn syrup mixture over the popcorn and peanuts. Mix thoroughly.

- Bake for 1 hour, stirring every 15 minutes. Lay out on wax paper to cool. Once cool, break it apart and store in airtight containers at room temperature. It will keep for about 2 months.

—Nancy L. Brooks
Topeka, Kansas

CARAMEL CASHEW CEREAL MIX

This can be made without the nuts, and the corn cereal can be replaced with other crunchy cereals.

Serves 12 to 14

  1 (21-ounce) box square corn cereal, about 10 cups
  1 to 1½ cups cashew halves and pieces
  1 cup (2 sticks) butter
  2 cups packed brown sugar
  ½ cup light corn syrup
  1 teaspoon baking soda
  1 teaspoon vanilla

- Place the cereal and cashews in a brown paper grocery bag and set aside.

- Melt the butter in a saucepan over medium-high heat. Add the brown sugar and corn syrup and stir to mix. Bring to a boil and cook for 2 minutes, stirring frequently.

- Remove from the heat and add the baking soda and vanilla. Stir until the mixture lightens in color and becomes foamy.

- Pour the mixture over the cereal and cashews in the paper bag. Fold over the top of the bag and shake well.

- Place the bag in the microwave and cook on high for 1 minute. Remove the bag from the microwave and shake well. Repeat two more times.

- Spread the hot mixture on parchment paper-lined baking sheets, stirring occasionally until cool. Store in an airtight container at room temperature. This will keep for a couple of months.

—Raechel L. Sittig-Esser
Waterloo, Iowa

RUSSIAN TEA

I have made this tea almost every Christmas for the last fifty years. It's so good with Christmas cookies or for any winter entertainment. It can also be served chilled.

Serves 8

- 4 tea bags or 1 tablespoon loose tea
- 1 teaspoon whole allspice
- 1 teaspoon whole cloves
- 1 cinnamon stick
- ½ cup sugar
- 1 cup frozen orange juice, concentrated
- 2 cups pineapple juice
- Juice of 1 lemon

- Steep the tea in 5 cups of very hot water for 5 minutes.

- Heat another 5 cups of water to boiling in a saucepan over high heat. Add the allspice, cloves, cinnamon stick, and sugar. Reduce the heat to medium low, and simmer for 5 minutes. Pour the spice mixture through a fine sieve into a large pot. Add the tea. Add the sugar and stir to dissolve.

- Add the concentrated orange juice, pineapple juice, and lemon juice and stir. Add more sugar if desired. Heat to almost boiling; serve hot.

—Margaret R. Witmer
Oxford, Ohio

CHRISTMAS PUNCH

The original recipe called for ½ cup sugar. I like my punch a little sweeter, so I changed it to ¾ cup sugar. Put in whatever you like.

Serves 10 to 12

   32 ounces cranberry juice cocktail
   46 ounces unsweetened pineapple juice
   2 cups orange juice
   ⅔ cup lemon juice
   1 to 2 teaspoons almond extract
   ¾ cup sugar
   3 (12-ounce) cans ginger ale

■ Combine the cranberry juice, pineapple juice, orange juice, lemon juice, almond extract, and sugar in a large bowl. Stir until the sugar is dissolved and then chill.

■ Just before serving add the ginger ale and stir.

—Emily A. Bell
Ravenna, Ohio

BERRY GOOD PUNCH

My family liked this recipe the first time I served it, and now they expect it every winter for the holidays.

Serves 10 to 12

   6 cups orange juice
   2 cups cranberry juice cocktail
   2 (10-ounce) packages frozen strawberries
   3 cups ginger ale

■ Combine the orange and cranberry juices in a large serving bowl. Purée the strawberries and add to the juices.

■ Add the ginger ale just before serving.

—Shirley A. Barnhart
New Carlisle, Ohio

EGGNOG

I always make six times the recipe for our church's New Year's Eve party. It is a favorite holiday recipe. Serve in a slow cooker to keep warm, and if you want to cut the fat use 1% or nonfat milk.

Serves 4 to 6

> 4 cups milk, divided
> 3 to 4 eggs, separated
> ½ cup sugar
> 1 to 2 teaspoons pure vanilla
> Pinch of salt
> 2 to 3 maraschino cherries (optional)
> Fresh grated nutmeg

- Combine ¼ cup of the milk with the egg yolks and sugar in a saucepan. Cook over medium-low heat, stirring constantly to avoid cooking the egg, for about 2 minutes. Add the remainder of the milk and cook, stirring constantly until warm, but not boiling.

- Strain into a serving bowl, just in case any egg cooked. Stir in the vanilla.

- Combine the egg whites and salt in a bowl and beat with an electric mixer until stiff. Place on top of the eggnog and dot with maraschino cherries, if using. Top with fresh grated nutmeg.

—Pauline Fillmore
Live Oak, California

SPICED APPLE CIDER

This is a fall campfire favorite of our Sunday school class. You can use apple juice instead of apple cider if you'd like. If you don't have cheesecloth, you can strain it through a coffee filter.

Serves 8

8 cups apple cider
¼ cup packed brown sugar
6-inch cinnamon stick
1 teaspoon allspice
1 teaspoon whole cloves
1 teaspoon shredded orange peel
8 thin orange wedges (optional)
Whole cloves (optional)

- In a large saucepan, combine the cider and brown sugar.

- For the spice bag, place the cinnamon stick, allspice, cloves, and orange peel in the center of a double-thick, 6-inch square of cheesecloth (can substitute coffee filters for the cheesecloth). Tie closed with clean kitchen string. (Using a tea ball and floating the cinnamon stick works well, too.) Add the bag to the saucepan with cider.

- Bring to boiling; reduce heat. Simmer, covered, for 10 minutes.

- Meanwhile, if desired, stud orange wedges with cloves.

- Discard spice bag or remove tea ball and cinnamon stick. Serve cider in mugs. Garnish with orange wedges, if using.

—Jenni Godfrey
Goshen, Indiana

Hot Grape Punch

My grandfather, David Preston Sherfy (1839-1921), planted Concord grapes years ago. We can lots of juice every year, and the good strong grape flavor is very satisfying and nutritious, especially around the holidays or in the dead of winter. This recipe can be easily doubled to serve a large family or church gathering.

GF 🥕 Ⓥ

Serves 16 to 18

- 1 cup sugar
- 1 cinnamon stick
- 10 whole cloves
- 1 quart (4 cups) grape juice
- ¼ cup lemon juice
- 1 cup orange juice

■ Combine the sugar, cinnamon stick, and cloves in a cheesecloth square or large coffee filter. Tie off at the top with kitchen twine. Placing the spices in a metal tea ball or diffuser will work as well.

■ Combine the grape juice, lemon juice, orange juice, and 8 cups of water in a large pot. Add the spice mixture and heat over medium heat, but do not boil. This can be kept warm in a slow cooker on low for easy serving.

—Margaret S. Holley
Johnson City, Tennessee

Chai (Tea Mix)

Serves 4

- 3 cups nonfat powdered milk
- 1½ cups sugar
- 1 cup unsweetened instant tea
- ¾ cup vanilla-flavored powdered creamer
- 1½ teaspoons ground ginger
- 1½ teaspoons ground cinnamon
- ½ teaspoon ground cardamom
- ½ teaspoon ground cloves

■ Combine the powdered milk, sugar, tea, powdered creamer, ginger, cinnamon, cardamom, and cloves and store in an airtight container at room temperature.

■ Use 3 tablespoons of the mix to ¾ cup boiling water or to taste.

—Norma J. Riley
Goshen, Indiana

Soups and Stews

He sat at the dinner table there,
With discontented frown.

The potatoes and steak are underdone,
And the bread was baked too brown.
The pie was sour, the pudding too sweet,
And the mince meat much too fat.
The soup was greasy, too, and salt—
'Twas hardly fit for a cat.

"I wish you could taste the bread and pies
I have seen my mother make;
They were something like, and 'twould do you good
Just to look at a slice of her cake."
Said the smiling wife: "I'll improve with age,
Just now, I'm but a beginner.
But your mother called to see me to-day,
And I got her to cook the dinner."

—Woman's Life
The Inglenook magazine (Sept. 18, 1906)

QUICK
& EASY

SPECIAL
OCCASION

GLUTEN
FREE

VEGETARIAN

VEGAN

Lentil and Sausage Soup

Serves 8 to 10

½ to 1 pound sausage
1 large onion, chopped
1 celery rib, chopped
1 cup shredded carrots
1 tablespoon garlic, chopped
1 (16-ounce) package dry lentils, rinsed
2 (15-ounce) cans chicken broth
1 (15-ounce) can diced tomatoes
1 tablespoon garlic powder
1 tablespoon dried parsley
2 bay leaves
½ teaspoon dried oregano
¼ teaspoon dried thyme
¼ teaspoon dried basil
1 tablespoon salt
½ teaspoon black pepper

■ Brown the sausage in a heavy saucepan over medium heat. When done transfer to a large soup pot, and sauté the onion, celery, and carrots in the pan with the sausage drippings. Cook for about 4 minutes and add the garlic. Continue cooking until the onions are translucent and the celery is soft, about 3 more minutes.

■ Add the vegetables to the soup pot. Put the pot over heat and add the lentils, chicken broth, tomatoes, garlic powder, parsley, bay leaves, oregano, thyme, basil, salt, and pepper. Bring to a boil, and then reduce the heat to medium low. Simmer for 2½ to 3 hours, or until the lentils are tender.

Notes: You can add your favorite pasta or green peas during the last 15 to 20 minutes of cooking if you'd like. Feel free to adjust the spices to your taste.

—Rebecca L. Ebie
Mogadore, Ohio

BLACK BEAN SOUP

This is a great standard bean soup. If the soup is too thick for your tastes, thin it with more water or chicken stock. If you prefer more vegetables, add a can of drained corn about ten minutes before finishing. **(GF)**

Serves 6 to 8

1½ pounds (24 ounces) dried black beans, soaked overnight and drained (about 3½ cups soaked)
1 pound smoked ham hock or shank
4 or 5 small bay leaves
1¼ teaspoons salt plus more to taste, divided
⅛ teaspoon baking soda
½ cup olive oil
2 medium onions, finely chopped
2 to 3 celery ribs, finely chopped
1 to 2 carrots, finely chopped
2 medium sweet potatoes, chopped into ½-inch pieces
2 teaspoons chili powder
2 tablespoons ground cumin
6 medium garlic cloves, minced
4 cups chicken stock
2 tablespoons molasses
1 to 2 red bell peppers, chopped
4 tablespoons lime juice
1 (15-ounce) can corn, drained (optional)
⅓ cup sour cream
1 avocado, peeled and chopped
Chopped fresh cilantro to taste

- Place the soaked beans and ham pieces in a large thick-bottomed pan over high heat. Add 6 cups of water. Add the bay leaves, $^{3}/_{4}$ teaspoon of the salt, and the baking soda. Bring to a boil and then reduce the heat to low. Cover and let simmer for about $1^{1}/_{2}$ hours or until the beans are tender.

- Remove the ham and set aside. Remove the bay leaves, any bones and fat, and discard them.

- Heat the olive oil in a large frying pan on medium heat. Add the onions, celery, carrots, sweet potatoes, and the remaining $^{1}/_{2}$ teaspoon salt. Sauté until the vegetables are soft and lightly browned, about 15 minutes.

- Add the chili powder, cumin, and garlic and sauté for 2 to 3 more minutes. Add the chicken stock, molasses, and bell pepper. Stir and cook for another 15 to 20 minutes.

- Add the reserved ham and optional corn to the soup. Add the lime juice and cook for a few minutes until heated through. Pour the soup into bowls and top each bowl with a spoonful of sour cream, some chopped avocado pieces, and cilantro to taste.

—Marty Barlow
Dayton, Virginia

BROCCOLI SOUP

Serves 3 to 4

3 cups broccoli or 2 (10-ounce) packages frozen broccoli
½ cup diced celery
½ cup chopped onion
1 cup low-sodium chicken broth
2 cups milk
2 tablespoon cornstarch
¼ teaspoon salt
Black pepper to taste
Thyme to taste
¼ cup shredded Cheddar cheese

- Place the broccoli, celery, onion, and chicken broth in a large saucepan over high heat. When boiling, reduce the heat to medium low, cover, and cook until tender, about 18 minutes.

- Stir together the milk, cornstarch, salt, pepper, and thyme in a bowl and then add to the soup. Increase the heat to medium high and cook, stirring constantly, until the soup is thickened and the mixture begins to boil. Remove from the heat. Add the cheese and stir until melted.

Note: This could be a vegetarian dish if you use vegetable broth instead of chicken broth.

—Rebecca L. Ebie
Mogadore, Ohio

WEDDING SOUP

Serves 10 to 12

1 pound lean ground beef
1 pound Italian sausage
½ cup grated Romano cheese
½ cup grated Parmesan cheese
½ cup Italian bread crumbs
2 eggs, well-beaten
1 to 2 garlic cloves, minced
Salt to taste
Black pepper to taste
3 quarts (12 cups) chicken broth
1 pound chopped fresh spinach or frozen and drained
¾ cup acini di pepe pasta, uncooked, or 2 cups cooked rice

■ Combine the ground beef, Italian sausage, Romano cheese, Parmesan cheese, bread crumbs, eggs, garlic, and salt and pepper to taste in a large bowl. Mix well with a wooden spoon. Roll tablespoons of the mixture into small meatballs and place them in a large cast-iron skillet or a large baking sheet coated with olive oil.

■ Preheat the broiler to high and broil the meatballs until brown on all sides, turning regularly, about 10 minutes. Drain the meatballs on a paper towel-lined plate.

■ Pour the chicken broth into a large stock pot and bring to a slow simmer over medium heat. Add the meatballs, spinach, and pasta or rice. Bring back to a slow simmer, reduce the heat to medium low, and cook until the meatballs float to the top and the pasta is al dente, about 25 minutes.

—Janis Sauro
Johnstown, Pennsylvania

CHEESEBURGER SOUP

Serves 6 to 8

½ pound ground beef
¾ cup chopped onion
¾ cup diced celery
¾ cup shredded carrots
1 teaspoon dried basil
1 teaspoon dried parsley
4 tablespoons butter, divided
3 cups chicken broth
4 cups peeled, diced potatoes
¼ cup flour
2 cups cubed American cheese
1½ cups milk
¾ teaspoon salt, or to taste
¼ to ½ teaspoon black pepper
¼ cup sour cream

■ Brown the ground beef in a saucepan over medium heat for about 8 minutes. Drain and set aside.

■ In same pan, sauté the onion, celery, carrots, basil, and parsley in 1 tablespoon of the butter over medium heat until the vegetables are tender, about 10 minutes.

■ Add the broth, potatoes, and beef and bring to a boil over high heat. Reduce the heat to medium low, cover, and simmer for 10 to 12 minutes, until potatoes are tender.

■ Meanwhile, in a small skillet, melt the remaining 3 tablespoons of butter over medium heat. Briskly stir in the flour and cook for 3 to 5 minutes, or until bubbly.

■ Increase the heat under the soup to medium high. Add the flour mixture and bring back to a boil. Cook for 2 minutes, stirring constantly. Reduce the heat to low. Add the cheese, milk, salt, and pepper; stir until cheese melts. Remove from the heat and then blend in the sour cream.

—Wendy Martin
Myerstown, Pennsylvania

Gazpacho

Historians believe this recipe, although Spanish in origin, may have Roman roots. This soup is served chilled and is most delicious in summer when garden vegetables are at their ripest. We have had this soup at a wonderful restaurant in Barcelona (El Pintor) with Manchester University students who are with BCA Study Abroad.

Serves 6

> 5 to 6 cups chopped tomatoes (2 28-ounce cans whole tomatoes work in a pinch)
> 1 (32-ounce) bottle vegetable juice
> 2 peeled cucumbers, chopped
> 1 green bell pepper, chopped
> 1 large sweet onion, chopped
> 2 large celery ribs, chopped
> 3 garlic cloves, finely minced
> 2 slices white bread, torn into pieces
> 1 tablespoon extra virgin olive oil
> 1 tablespoon balsamic vinegar (optional)
> 1 tablespoon cider vinegar
> 1 teaspoon salt
> ½ teaspoon pepper
> 1 teaspoon hot sauce

■ Combine the tomatoes, vegetable juice, cucumbers, bell pepper, onion, celery, garlic, bread, oil, vinegars, salt, pepper, and hot sauce in the bowl of a food processor or blender. Process or chop for 45 to 60 seconds, until very fine. Serve chilled.

Notes: All of the ingredients can be adjusted to taste. For added texture and punch you can add sour cream or extra chopped cucumber, bell pepper, or onion to the blended soup.

—Jo Young Switzer
North Manchester, Indiana

Keeping Your Pantry Small

To keep my pantry small, I buy one kind of pasta (thin noodles or spaghetti) and use it for all my dishes that call for pasta—spaghetti and meatballs, macaroni and cheese, soup, in broth as a side dish, with mushroom gravy and beef. Use your imagination.

—Anna L. Swindell
Everett, Pennsylvania

Peanut Butter Pumpkin Soup

This is a great fall soup. If you prefer winter squash, substitute that for pumpkin.

Serves 8 to 10

4 tablespoons butter
3½ to 4 cups puréed cooked pumpkin
⅓ cup sugar
1 teaspoon pumpkin pie spice
2 cups puréed cooked sweet potatoes
1 cup peanut butter
6 cups chicken broth
1 teaspoon salt
1 teaspoon black pepper
Sour cream for garnish (optional)
Chives for garnish (optional)

■ Melt the butter in a large pot over medium-high heat. Add the pumpkin, sugar, pumpkin pie spice, sweet potato, and peanut butter. Stir until well mixed.

■ Add the chicken broth, salt, and pepper and stir until smooth. Bring to a boil then reduce the heat to medium low and simmer for 20 minutes.

■ Garnish each bowl with a dollop of sour cream and a few chopped chives, if desired.

Note: Make this vegetarian by substituting vegetable broth for the chicken broth.

—Waneta I. Benson
Mechanicsburg, Pennsylvania

Feasting of Community

We met together for soup and bread to celebrate the baptism of one of our members. It nourished our bodies as only simple foods can. The aromas permeated the house as bodies perched on every chair, couch, and ledge. Laughter bubbled up amid connections of our spirits. We all departed hours later, our bellies full, and our hearts satisfied. The food was fundamental, but the feasting was in the gathering.

—Lori Steiner Jans
Tipp City, Ohio

Butternut Squash–Chipotle Soup

Serves 6

1 medium butternut squash
3 tablespoons olive oil, divided
1½ cups chopped onion
½ cup chopped celery
½ cup chopped carrot
2 garlic cloves, minced
4 to 6 cups chicken or vegetable broth
Salt and pepper to taste
2 teaspoons chipotles in adobo sauce, minced
½ cup sour cream, divided (optional)

■ Preheat the oven to 400°F.

■ Cut the squash in half lengthwise. Scoop out and discard the seeds and stringy pulp.

■ Grease a 12 x 7-inch glass baking dish with 1 tablespoon of the oil. Place the squash in dish cut side down, and pierce it all over with a fork. Bake the squash for 45 minutes or until tender. Let cool.

■ Heat the remaining 2 tablespoons oil in a large, heavy soup pot over medium-high heat. Sauté the onion, celery, and carrot for 10 minutes. Add the garlic and cook for 2 minutes more.

■ Scoop the flesh of the squash into the pot and stir. Add 4 cups of broth and bring to a boil. Reduce the heat to medium low and simmer, covered, for 30 minutes, or until the vegetables are very tender. Season with salt and pepper and add the chipotle peppers.

■ Purée the soup in batches in a blender or food processor, adding more broth if necessary to reach your desired consistency.

■ Ladle into bowls and top each bowl with a dollop of sour cream, if desired.

—Susan Kinsel Fitze
New Lebanon, Ohio

SNOW DAY HAM AND POTATO SOUP

This was always a favorite "snow day" supper when my kids were young. For an accompaniment, I baked "cornsticks" (cornbread in pans shaped like individual ears of corn).

Serves 4

   4 cups chicken broth
   1 cup dried green split peas
   1 medium onion, chopped
   1 to 2 cups chopped ham
   ½ teaspoon salt
   ¼ teaspoon freshly ground black pepper
   3 medium potatoes, diced
   3 medium carrots, sliced

■ Combine chicken broth, peas, onion, ham, salt, and pepper in a large soup pot over medium-high heat. Bring to a boil and reduce the heat to low. Cover and simmer for 1 hour, stirring occasionally.

■ Add the potatoes and carrots and continue simmering for 20 minutes, or until the potatoes and carrots are soft.

—Sylvia M. Hess
Xenia, Ohio

SIMPLE SOUPS, WORLDS APART

Much has changed in the last one hundred years with regard to our tastes and culinary habits, yet simple, flavorful soups still hold a special place on our tables. Whether you're feeding a crowd of dinner guests or preparing a weeknight meal for the family, there's sure to be a soup you can turn to. From brothy stocks to hearty stews, nearly every culture in the world has its own take on simple soups.

Of course, simple can mean lots of different things in the kitchen. For some of us it refers to fast and easy. For others simple might mean using few processed, hard-to-find, or expensive ingredients, sticking to plain, classic flavors, or not using meat or animal products.

Traditionally, soups were simple because they were based on what was grown in the garden plot or available from nearby farms. Nowadays, we might practice various expressions of simplicity for numerous reasons. Soups are often the simplest way to focus on eating seasonally, to create a hospitable meal for varied diets, or to experience the flavors of another culture.

Leafing through the pages of the soup chapter of the 1911 *Inglenook Cook Book*, I was surprised to see how many variations there are on simple, basic themes. For example, nine of the forty-four recipes are for some version of potato soup! The frequent use of such ingredients is indicative of the small-farm lifestyle many Brethren practiced at that time. One recipe for "Mock Turtle Soup" even calls for "1 calf's head ready cleaned and cracked" (p. 16). It's readily apparent that earlier Brethren found simple, resourceful ways to create soup from whatever they had on hand.

Alongside "Soup Without Meat" and "A Good Soup" can be found one lone entry that claims international heritage: "German Tomato Soup" (p. 14). Of course, many of these classic recipes reflect the Church of the Brethren's German cultural influence, but this is the only one to identify it so clearly. Reading through this recipe now it may not seem anything other than traditional American in style, but originally it evoked the smells and tastes of another part of the world.

Over the past century our ideas of what constitutes a "highly seasoned soup" have evolved quite a bit, along with our interest in cuisine from around the globe. "Dhal" is an excellent example of a simple soup that comes to us from another food culture. A recipe with lentils, coconut milk, and garam masala may seem exciting and exotic to us, but variations on dhal (also spelled dal, daal, or dahl) are as common in Indian cuisine as potato and tomato soup are in ours.

We live in an increasingly multicultural society, and expanding our culinary comfort zones is a great first step toward opening ourselves to more meaningful connections with those whose traditions and experiences are different from our own. Perhaps making one of the many simple, internationally-inspired soups from this chapter will help you to grow a bit closer to sisters and brothers from around the world.

—Matthew E. McKimmy
Richmond, Indiana

GERMAN TOMATO SOUP

Chop fine 1 medium-sized onion, 2 medium-sized carrots, 1 small head of celery, and add to 1 quart of tomatoes. Stew gently for one hour. Remove from the fire, and put through a sieve to remove seeds, pressing as much of the pulp through as possible. Return to the fire, adding salt and pepper to taste and a generous amount of butter. When boiling, stir in 2 tablespoonfuls of flour moistened with water, to the consistency of cream. Stir till boiling and serve immediately. This is excellent for those who like highly seasoned soup.

—Sister Grace Holsinger Butterbaugh, Elgin, Illinois

DHAL

Dhal is a typical main dish in India and Pakistan. It is made *with lentils and a wonderful array of exotic spices. Don't be afraid. The coconut milk softens the spices to give it a nice creamy flavor.*

Serves 4

> 2 tablespoons butter
> 1 onion, chopped
> 2 garlic cloves, finely chopped
> ½ teaspoon turmeric
> 1 teaspoon garam marsala
> ½ teaspoon chili powder
> 1 teaspoon ground cumin
> 2 pounds fresh tomatoes, chopped, or 2 (15-ounce) cans
>   diced tomatoes, strained
> 1 cup dry red lentils
> 2 teaspoons lemon juice
> 2½ cups vegetarian broth
> 1 (14-ounce) can coconut milk (shake the can well)
> Salt and pepper to taste
> Chopped cilantro for garnish
> Lemon slices for garnish

■ Melt the butter in a soup pot over medium heat and sauté the onion for 3 to 4 minutes. Add the garlic and sauté for another 2 minutes. Add the turmeric, garam marsala, chili powder, and cumin and cook for 30 seconds. Stir in the tomatoes, lentils, lemon juice, vegetable broth, and coconut milk and bring to a boil over high heat.

■ Reduce the heat to medium low and simmer for 20 to 30 minutes, or until the lentils are done.

■ Add salt and pepper and garnish with cilantro and lemon slices, if desired.

Notes: This is a great vegan dish if you use oil instead of butter for sautéing the vegetables. Serve it with naan, pita bread, or other hearty bread for a full meal. It may be processed in a blender for a smoother texture.

—April K. McGlothin-Eller
Chicago, Illinois

SIMPLICITY MEETS HOSPITALITY

Every Monday night I host a dinner and conversation get-together that's open to anyone who would like to join us. The menu is typically a vegetarian soup and fresh-baked bread. Making this meal meat-free has been a great way to keep it simple and hospitable for anyone who might show up, while still offering plenty of opportunity to explore flavors from around the world.

—Matthew E. McKimmy
Richmond, Indiana

CREAMY POTATO, BROCCOLI, AND CHEDDAR SOUP

Serves 6

2 cups chicken broth
2 cups diced potatoes (2 large)
½ cup diced carrots (1 large)
½ cup (1 stick) butter
¼ cup chopped onion
1 garlic clove, chopped
⅓ cup flour
2 cups milk
2 cups shredded sharp Cheddar cheese
1 cup cooked cubed ham
½ cup chopped broccoli
Salt and pepper

■ In a large soup pot bring the broth to a boil over high heat. Add the potatoes and carrots and cover. Reduce the heat to medium and simmer for 15 minutes.

■ Meanwhile, make a white sauce. Melt the butter in a skillet over medium heat. Add the onion and sauté for 6 to 7 minutes. Add the garlic and cook for 2 minutes more. Stir in the flour until the mixture is smooth and bubbly. Slowly add the milk while stirring constantly until all the flour is dissolved and the mixture is thickened, about 5 minutes.

■ Add the cheese and stir well until melted. Add the ham and stir until combined. Then pour the cheese mixture into the potato mixture and add the broccoli.

■ Add salt and pepper to taste. Cook for another 10 minutes, but don't bring to a boil.

—Margie Knapp
Bassett, Virginia

LOADED BAKED POTATO SOUP

For a lighter soup, substitute cooked cauliflower for the potatoes.

Serves 8

⅔ cup butter
⅔ cup flour
2 pints (4 cups) half-and-half
3 cups milk
5 to 7 medium baking potatoes, peeled, cooked, and cubed
4 green onions, sliced
10 to 12 strips of bacon, cooked and crumbled
2 cups shredded mild Cheddar cheese
1 cup sour cream
¾ teaspoon salt
½ teaspoon pepper
1 teaspoon garlic powder

■ Melt the butter in a large soup pot over medium heat. Add the flour and stir until smooth and bubbly. Gradually add the half-and-half, stirring constantly, and cook until thickened, about 8 minutes.

■ Add the milk, potatoes, and onions and cook over low heat until thickened, about 10 minutes.

■ Add the bacon, cheese, sour cream, salt, pepper, and garlic powder. Simmer until the cheese is melted. Serve hot.

—Janice Parsons Paulus
Muskegon, Michigan

MINESTRONE

This is a flavorful soup. If you don't have fresh tomatoes, you can always use tomato juice.

Serves 6

3 slices bacon, chopped
1 cup chopped onion
½ cup chopped celery
2 large garlic cloves (optional)
1 (15-ounce) can beef broth
1 (15-ounce) can navy beans
1 (28-ounce) can crushed tomatoes
½ cup uncooked macaroni
½ teaspoon salt
1 cup finely shredded cabbage
1 cup chopped zucchini

■ Cook the bacon in a soup pot over medium heat until brown, about 7 minutes. Add the onion and celery and cook until the onions are translucent and the celery is tender, about 4 minutes. Add the garlic, if using, and cook for 2 minutes more.

■ Stir in the broth, beans, 2½ cups water, tomatoes, macaroni, and salt. Bring to boil over high heat. Cover, reduce the heat to medium low, and simmer for 15 minutes.

■ Remove the lid and add the cabbage and zucchini. Cook for 10 minutes, stirring occasionally, or until the vegetables are tender.

—Grace Caplinger
Eaton, Ohio

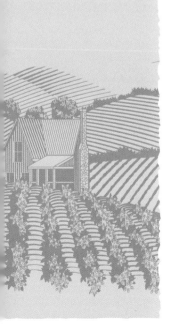

FRESH TOMATO SOUP

Serves 4

½ cup (1 stick) butter
½ cup chopped onion
¼ cup flour
6 medium tomatoes, peeled, seeded, and diced
1 teaspoon salt
½ teaspoon pepper
1 teaspoon sugar
1 tablespoon dried basil or ½ cup fresh, chopped and lightly packed
Lemon slices for garnish (optional)

■ Melt the butter in a 3-quart saucepan over medium heat. Add the onion and sauté until translucent, about 6 minutes. Add the flour and stir until well mixed. Gradually add 1½ cups water, stirring constantly.

■ Add the tomatoes, salt, pepper, sugar, and basil. Bring to a boil over high heat. Reduce the heat to low and simmer for 30 minutes, stirring frequently. If the soup is too thick, add some more water. Serve with lemon slices, if desired.

Note: This can be converted to vegan by using margarine.

—Elsie M. Holderread
McPherson, Kansas

FISH LOVER'S SOUP

This is a great way to add omega-3 fatty acids to your diet. Adding two cups of corn will give it more texture and color.

Serves 6

3 tablespoons olive oil
1 onion, chopped
2 garlic cloves, minced
2 teaspoons salt
¼ teaspoon pepper
1 bay leaf
¼ teaspoon thyme
3½ pounds fish (pollock, red snapper, tilapia, cod or whatever), roughly chopped
1 cup pasta shells or 2 cups diced potatoes
Lemon juice
1 (12-ounce) can evaporated milk
Fresh dill, paprika, or chives for garnish (optional)

■ Heat the oil in a large soup pot over medium heat. Sauté the onion until soft, about 4 minutes. Add the garlic and cook for 2 minutes more. Add the salt, pepper, bay leaf, and thyme and stir to combine.

■ Stir in the fish and cook for 8 to 10 minutes. Add enough water to just cover the fish, increase the heat to high, and bring to a boil. Reduce the heat to medium low and simmer for 10 minutes more.

■ Add the pasta or potatoes and simmer until the pasta is al dente or the potatoes are tender, about 8 minutes for the pasta and 15 for the potatoes. Add the lemon juice to taste.

■ Add the evaporated milk and stir for a few minutes. Discard the bay leaf before serving.

■ Garnish each bowl with a sprinkling of dill, paprika, or chives just before serving, if desired.

Note: This could be gluten free if you use potatoes instead of pasta shells.

—Norma J. Riley
Goshen, Indiana

IRISH POTATO SOUP

There are not a lot of Irish in the Church of the Brethren, so I have taken a few of the best Brethren recipes and built on my own to come up with this variation. Over the years it seems to be a pleasant addition to church luncheons. It's not just a soup; it's dinner in a bowl.

Serves 6 to 8

4 large potatoes, peeled and diced
4 vegetable bouillon cubes
½ teaspoon sea salt
½ teaspoon garlic salt
6 cups milk
½ to 1 cup flour, depending on thickness desired
½ cup chopped mushrooms
1 cup diced or sliced ham
1 cup diced cabbage
4 tablespoons (½ stick) butter

- In a large soup pot, add the potatoes, bouillon cubes, sea salt, garlic salt, and just enough water to cover the potatoes. Bring to a boil over high heat. Reduce the heat to medium high and cook uncovered for 10 minutes.

- Meanwhile, in a large saucepan over medium heat, bring the milk to a gentle simmer, just until small bubbles appear at the edges. Turn the heat to low and transfer 1½ cups of the hot milk to a mixing bowl and add the flour. Gently stir with a fork until all the flour is mixed into the milk.

- Add the mushrooms and ham to the soup, increase to medium-high heat, and cook for 5 minutes. Add the cabbage and butter and cook 5 minutes more.

- When the soup has cooked for the full 20 minutes, add the 4½ cups of hot milk and gently stir, bringing back to a simmer. Then gently pour the thickened milk into the pot and stir until well mixed. Reduce heat to medium low and simmer for 15 to 20 minutes, stirring occasionally.

—Larry O'Neill
Collegeville, Pennsylvania

BREAD OF LIFE

Bread of life, whose body, broken, feeds the hunger of my heart, may the thanks that you have spoken bless each loaf I break apart. Let these hands now calmly folding speak my gratitude for grace, lest the treasure I am holding disappear before my face. Lord, I welcome you to table; grace my supper ever new. With your feast of love enable ev'ry guest to live for you.

—Kenneth I. Morse
Gospel Messenger (1955)

MEXICAN CORN SOUP

We have prepared this soup for as many as one hundred people at a time, though stirring the "white sauce" part was tricky. This recipe can easily be doubled for more servings and can be a vegetarian dish if you use vegetable broth.

Serves 4

3 tablespoons butter
⅓ cup chopped green bell pepper
¼ cup sliced green onion
1 large garlic clove, minced
5 tablespoons flour
¼ teaspoon oregano
¼ teaspoon black pepper
2 cups milk
1 cup chicken or vegetable broth
1 bay leaf
1 (12-ounce) can corn or 1½ to 2 cups frozen corn
1½ cups salsa
1½ cups shredded Monterey Jack cheese
Tortilla chips for garnish
Fresh cilantro for garnish

■ Melt the butter in a heavy 3-quart saucepan over medium heat. Add the bell pepper and sauté for 3 to 4 minutes. Add the green onions and garlic and cook until tender, about 3 minutes more.

■ Stir in the flour, oregano, and pepper, and bring to a simmer.

■ Gradually add the milk and broth and stir to combine. Add the bay leaf. Bring to a boil, stirring constantly, and cook for 1 minute. Remove from the heat.

■ Add the corn, salsa, and cheese and stir. When the cheese is melted, remove the bay leaf.

■ Garnish with tortilla chips and cilantro. Serve immediately.

—Rachel Gross
North Manchester, Indiana

STUFFED PEPPER SOUP

This recipe is a favorite of my regulars in the restaurant where I work. I first made it when we had too many green peppers to use before they went bad. It was a hit with my boss, so we put it on the menu and I now make it once a week.

Serves 12

- 1 pound ground beef
- 1 (28-ounce) can diced tomatoes, undrained
- 1 (28-ounce) can tomato sauce
- 2 cups chopped green bell pepper
- ¼ cup packed dark brown sugar
- 2 teaspoons salt
- 1 teaspoon pepper
- 2 cups long-grain white rice
- 2 beef bouillon cubes

■ Brown the ground beef in a large soup pot over medium heat. Drain the fat and then add the tomatoes, tomato sauce, bell pepper, brown sugar, salt, pepper, rice, bouillon cubes, and 8 cups of water. Bring to a boil over high heat.

■ Reduce the heat to medium and simmer for 30 to 40 minutes, or until the rice is cooked and the peppers are tender.

Note: You can substitute minute rice for the long-grain white rice to save a little time.

—Susie M. Dundore
Myerstown, Pennsylvania

TORTELLINI SOUP

My daughter gave me this recipe. It is a great dish to take to a potluck or to someone who is sick. It is very easy to put together.

Serves 6 to 8

1 pound Italian sausage
2 (14½-ounce) cans chicken or beef broth
3 (14½-ounce) cans diced tomatoes
1 (12-ounce) bag frozen cheese tortellini
Grated Parmesan cheese for garnish

■ Brown the sausage in a soup pot over medium heat. Drain well. Add the broth and tomatoes and let simmer for about 1 hour.

■ Add the tortellini during the last 10 minutes. Ladle into individual bowls and sprinkle Parmesan cheese on top to garnish.

—Marilyn A. Owens
Ashland, Ohio

Zucchini Garden Chowder

This is a great winter chowder, and it freezes well. The zucchini holds its texture after being frozen. Use farm-grown sweet corn that has been frozen, if possible. If you want to triple the batch, it fits into an 8-quart soup pot.

Serves 6 to 8

⅓ cup butter
2 medium zucchini, chopped
1 medium onion, chopped
2 tablespoons minced fresh parsley (or 1 tablespoon dried)
1 teaspoon dried basil
⅓ cup flour
¼ teaspoon pepper
3 chicken bouillon cubes
1 teaspoon lemon juice
1 (14½-ounce) can diced tomatoes, undrained
1 (12-ounce) can evaporated milk
1 (10-ounce) package frozen corn
¼ cup grated Parmesan cheese
2 cups shredded Cheddar cheese

- Melt the butter in a Dutch oven or soup pot over medium heat. Add the zucchini, onion, parsley, and basil and sauté until the vegetables are tender, about 8 minutes.

- Add the flour and pepper and stir until well combined.

- While constantly stirring, gradually add 3 cups of water. Add the bouillon cubes and lemon juice and mix well.

- Bring to a boil over medium-high heat and cook for 2 minutes, stirring frequently.

- Add the tomatoes, evaporated milk, and corn and return to a boil. Reduce the heat to medium low, cover, and simmer for 5 minutes, or until corn is tender.

- Just before serving, stir in the cheeses until melted.

Note: This could be a vegetarian dish if you used vegetable broth instead of chicken bouillon.

—Karen Stocking
South Elgin, Illinois

This is a wonderful way to make your own homemade cream soups. Follow the basic recipe, adding special ingredients to whatever flavored cream soup you'd like to make.

Makes about 2 cups (equivalent of 1 can prepared condensed soup)

¼ cup (½ stick) butter
¼ cup flour
1 cup milk

¾ cup broth (meat-based or vegetarian)
Salt and pepper

- Sauté the onion and garlic and cook any special ingredients, as listed below (except cheese). Make sure the vegetables are tender and the meat is fully cooked. Set aside.

- Melt the butter in a saucepan over medium heat. Stir in the flour and cook for about 2 minutes to make a roux. Add the milk and broth and stir or whisk until completely smooth.

- Add the special ingredients to the saucepan. Bring to a boil, and then reduce the heat and simmer for 5 to 10 minutes. Stir often as the soup will thicken. Add salt and pepper and other seasoning to taste.

Cream of Asparagus — ½ cup diced onion, ½ cup chopped asparagus

Cream of Broccoli — ½ cup diced onion, ½ cup chopped broccoli, ½ cup shredded cheese (optional)

Cream of Celery — ½ cup diced onion, ½ cup chopped celery

Cream of Cheese — ½ cup shredded Cheddar, Swiss, Pepper Jack, Parmesan, Havarti, or American

Cream of Chicken — ½ cup diced onion, ½ cup chopped cooked chicken, 2 garlic cloves, minced

Cream of Corn — ½ cup diced onion, ½ cup corn

Cream of Mushroom — ½ cup diced onion, 2 garlic cloves, minced, ½ cup chopped mushrooms

Cream of Onion — ¾ cup diced onion, 2 garlic cloves, minced

Cream of Potato and Ham — ½ cup diced onion, ½ cup chopped celery, ½ cup chopped carrots, ½ cup chopped cooked potato, ½ cup chopped cooked ham, ½ cup shredded cheese

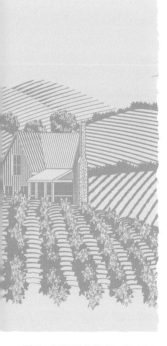

SHRIMP-SCALLOP CHOWDER

This is wonderful seafood chowder. If you like a thicker chowder, add a diced potato or 1/3 cup of potato flakes with the celery soup to thicken it up.

Serves 4 to 6

> 1 tablespoon olive oil
> 1 small onion, chopped
> 1 garlic clove, minced
> 1 (10¾-ounce) can cream of celery soup, undiluted
> 1½ cups milk
> 2 tablespoons fresh basil, chopped (or 1 tablespoon dried basil)
> ½ pound medium fresh shrimp
> ½ pound fresh scallops
> ¼ cup chicken broth
> Salt and pepper to taste
> 1 cooked potato, diced, or ⅓ cup potato flakes (optional)

■ Heat the oil in a large soup pot over medium heat. Add the onion and sauté for about 5 minutes. Add the garlic and cook until the onions are translucent, about 5 minutes more. Add the soup, milk, and basil and bring to a boil over high heat.

■ Reduce the heat to medium and add the shrimp and scallops. Simmer for 3 to 5 minutes or until the shrimp turns pink. Add the chicken broth, salt and pepper, and potato, if using. Bring back to a simmer before serving.

—Anita K. Heatwole
Waynesboro, Virginia

PUMPKIN BEEF STEW

Serves 4 to 6

2 tablespoons vegetable oil, divided
1½ pounds stew beef, cubed
1 medium onion, cut into wedges
1 garlic clove, sliced
2 cups beef broth
½ cup tomato sauce
½ teaspoon ground allspice
Salt and pepper to taste
1 cup sliced carrots, cut ½ inch thick (2 medium carrots)
3 large potatoes, peeled and roughly chopped
1 (10- to 12-pound) pumpkin

■ Heat 1 tablespoon of the oil in a large soup pot over medium-high heat. Add the beef and cook until just browned, about 5 minutes, turning regularly. Add the onion and garlic and cook for 2 minutes, stirring continuously. Add the broth, tomato sauce, allspice, and salt and pepper and bring to a boil. Reduce the heat to medium low and simmer for 1 hour.

■ Add the carrots and potatoes and bring back to a simmer and cook for an additional 20 to 25 minutes.

■ Preheat the oven to 325°F.

■ Wash the outside of the pumpkin and then cut a circle around the stem. Remove the stem and set aside. Scrape out the fibers and seeds and discard. Place the pumpkin on a cake pan or baking sheet with sides. Pour the stew inside the pumpkin and cover with the top of the pumpkin. Brush the outside of the pumpkin with the remaining oil and bake for 2 hours. Serve the soup right from the pumpkin.

—Jane Durant
Middletown, Maryland

Nigerian-Style Okra Stew

We learned to eat okra in Nigeria. The spice of the peppers and *the green okra gave us a nice vegetarian alternative to the same old marinara sauce. We learned to eat this over pounded yam and corn pudding. We now grow okra just so that we can have it fresh and frozen.*

Serves 4

 2 tablespoons vegetable oil
 2 cups sliced okra (fresh or frozen)
 1 medium onion, chopped
 2 garlic cloves, chopped
 1 jalapeño pepper, chopped
 6 tomatoes (fresh or canned), chopped
 2 bouillon cubes (chicken, beef, or vegetable)
 Salt and pepper to taste
 2 cups cooked white rice

■ Heat the oil in a soup pot over medium-high heat. Fry the okra.

■ Reduce the heat to medium, add the onion, and sauté for 5 minutes. Add the garlic and jalapeño pepper and sauté until the onions are translucent.

■ Add the tomatoes and cook for 10 to 15 minutes. Some water ($1/4$ to $1/2$ cup) may need to be added to keep the mixture moist.

■ Add the bouillon and salt and pepper. Cook until the bouillon is completely dissolved. Serve over rice.

Notes: This stew is also good with meat. You can add seared chicken or steak cubes before the tomatoes. Use chicken bouillon with chicken and beef bouillon with steak. Use vegetable bouillon if you want a vegan or vegetarian option.

—Bonnie Jean Rager Bohrer
South Bend, Indiana

SWEET POTATO CHILI

This chili was shared with the women at the women's prison where I volunteer. They are always looking for new recipes. This one works well in a slow cooker too. And the taste improves the next day. It freezes well.

Serves 6 to 8

1 tablespoon olive oil
¾ cup chopped onion
¾ cup chopped celery
2 garlic cloves, crushed or finely chopped
3 to 4 cups cubed, peeled sweet potatoes
1½ teaspoons ground cinnamon
2 teaspoons ground cumin
½ teaspoon cayenne pepper
1 teaspoon paprika
1 teaspoon ground nutmeg
2 bay leaves
2 cups vegetable broth
1 cup dry red lentils
1 (15-ounce) can navy beans
1 (15-ounce) can kidney beans
1 cup tomato sauce
3 cups diced tomatoes (canned or fresh)

■ Heat the oil in a soup pot over medium heat. Add the onion and celery and sauté for 5 minutes. Add the garlic and sauté for 2 to 3 minutes more.

■ Add the sweet potatoes, cinnamon, cumin, cayenne pepper, paprika, nutmeg, bay leaves, vegetable broth, lentils, navy beans, kidney beans, tomato sauce, and tomatoes. Bring to a boil over high heat.

■ Reduce the heat to medium low and simmer until the sweet potatoes are tender and the seasonings are well dispersed. You may add some water if it's too thick.

—Marg (Hess) Strom
Guelph, Ontario

CREAMY CHICKEN CHILI

This is a favorite of my husband, Rich. It is good enough to serve to company as well.

Serves 7

1 tablespoon vegetable oil
1 pound skinless, boneless chicken breast, cut into ½-inch cubes
1 medium onion, chopped
1½ teaspoons garlic powder
2 (15-ounce) cans Great Northern beans, drained and rinsed
1 (14½-ounce) can chicken broth
2 (4-ounce) cans chopped green chilies (optional)
1 teaspoon salt
1 teaspoon cumin
1 teaspoon dried oregano
½ teaspoon black pepper
¼ teaspoon cayenne pepper
1 cup sour cream
½ cup whipping cream

■ Heat the oil in a large saucepan over medium heat. Add the chicken, onion, and garlic powder and sauté until the chicken is no longer pink, about 6 minutes.

■ Add the beans, broth, chilies, if using, salt, cumin, oregano, black pepper, and cayenne pepper. Bring to a boil over high heat. Reduce the heat to medium low and simmer, uncovered, for 30 minutes.

■ Remove from the heat and stir in the sour cream and whipping cream. Serve immediately.

—Annette Eileen Sommer
Brookville, Ohio

THE MODEL PRAYER

Our Father in heaven, hallowed be your name, your kingdom come, your will be done, on earth as it is in heaven. Give us today our daily bread. And forgive us our debts, as we also have forgiven our debtors. And lead us not into temptation, but deliver us from the evil one, for yours is the kingdom and the power and the glory forever. Amen.

—Matthew 6:9-13
New International Version

AWARD-WINNING CHESAPEAKE CHILI

One year I decided to add crabmeat to the chili I made for a
company potluck Christmas party. They ended up putting the
recipe in the company newsletter. Later, our congregation had a chili
cook-off, and my Chesapeake Chili came in first place. A few years
after that I sold my Chesapeake Chili to raise money for the Epilepsy
Foundation of Washington, D.C. It was right before the Super Bowl,
and I spent many evenings and weekends canning jars of chili.
We ended up raising about a thousand dollars.

Serves 6

½ pound ground beef
3 slices bacon
1 (29-ounce) can tomato sauce
1 (15-ounce) can kidney beans
½ pound crabmeat
¼ cup sugar
½ teaspoon onion powder
½ teaspoon garlic powder
½ teaspoon black pepper
1 teaspoon seafood seasoning (like Old Bay)

■ Brown ground beef in a skillet over medium heat. Drain and set
aside.

■ Fry the bacon in the same skillet over medium heat until well done
and crispy, about 4 minutes per side. Crumble into small pieces
and set aside.

■ Pour the tomato sauce into a large soup pot. Fill the empty tomato
sauce can half full of water and add to sauce. (For thicker chili omit
the water.) Add the ground beef, bacon, kidney beans, crabmeat,
sugar, onion powder, garlic powder, black pepper, and seafood
seasoning. Bring to a boil over high heat, stirring often. Then
reduce the heat to low and simmer for at least 10 minutes.

—James L. Showalter
Laurel, Maryland

SALADS

O thou greenest green chlorophyll-filled
Vegetable
How wrinkly crinkly is thy leaf
How rich in vitamins and
Minerals is thine essence.
Arrange thyself invitingly
In my salad bowl.
Caress my waiting
Palate with thy garden freshness
And I
Like the sailor man
Of cartoon yore
Shall be strong to the
Finish.

—Ken Gibble
Camp Hill, Pennsylvania

QUICK
& EASY

SPECIAL
OCCASION

GLUTEN
FREE

VEGETARIAN

VEGAN

24-Hour Coleslaw

This is a great staple to have on hand. It keeps well in the refrigerator for an extended time.

Serves 8 to 10

1 medium cabbage, shredded	⅔ cup white vinegar
1 green bell pepper, chopped	½ teaspoon salt
½ cup chopped celery	½ teaspoon celery seed
1½ cups sugar	½ teaspoon mustard seed

■ Mix the cabbage, bell pepper, celery, sugar, vinegar, salt, celery seed, and mustard seed in a large bowl. Transfer to a container with a tight-fitting lid and refrigerate for 24 hours before serving.

—Shirley Danner
Bloomington, Illinois

Creamy Coleslaw

Serves 10 to 12

1 (16-ounce) container sour cream	1¼ cups mayonnaise
⅔ cup sugar	1 large cabbage, shredded
½ teaspoon salt	¼ teaspoon nutmeg
¼ cup vinegar	

■ For the dressing, mix the sour cream, sugar, and salt in a large bowl. Add the vinegar and stir until well mixed. Add the mayonnaise and stir until well mixed.

■ Put the cabbage in a large bowl, add the nutmeg, and gently toss to coat. Pour on as much dressing as you like and stir well.

■ Keep any leftover dressing in the refrigerator.

Note: This dressing works well for a lettuce salad too.

—Mary Good
Harrisonburg, Virginia

Fresh Summer Cucumber Salad

Serves 4

1 cucumber, sliced
1 red bell pepper, chopped
½ red onion, chopped
1 avocado, chopped
1 pint of cherry tomatoes
3 tablespoons chopped fresh cilantro
⅛ teaspoon salt
⅛ teaspoon pepper
Juice of 1 lime

- Toss together the cucumber, bell pepper, onion, and avocado in a bowl. Add the tomatoes, cilantro, salt, and pepper and gently stir to mix. Sprinkle the lime juice over the salad and toss. Serve immediately.

—Nancy Shifflett Bowman
Fishersville, Virginia

Cauliflower-Pea Salad

Serves 6

2 cups chopped cauliflower
1 (16-ounce) bag frozen peas, thawed
1 cup diced celery
½ cup chopped red onion
¼ cup shredded carrots

1 cup mayonnaise
1½ teaspoons dried dill weed
¼ teaspoon salt
2 tablespoons sugar
½ cup shredded sharp Cheddar cheese

- Combine the cauliflower, peas, celery, onion, and carrots in a bowl.
- In a second bowl, combine the mayonnaise, dill weed, salt, and sugar. Mix well and spoon over the vegetables. Add the cheese and toss to coat well. Cover and refrigerate several hours or overnight.

—Katy Stump
Leeton, Missouri

Marinated Vegetable-Bean Salad

From church suppers to holiday gift giving, my mother and I *have made this colorful salad on many occasions. You don't have to be exact, and if you don't like a particular vegetable, leave it out and add more of another.*

Serves 16

SALAD
1 (15-ounce) can cut green beans, drained
1 (15-ounce) can yellow wax beans, drained
1 (15-ounce) can light kidney beans, drained
1 (15-ounce) can dark red kidney beans, drained
1 (15-ounce) can garbanzo beans (chickpeas), drained
1 cup chopped broccoli florets
1 cup chopped cauliflower
1 cup sliced carrots
1 cup sliced red onion
1 cup sliced zucchini
1 cup sliced yellow squash
1 cup sliced bell pepper (any color)

DRESSING
1 cup vegetable or canola oil	2 teaspoons salt
1 cup vinegar	1 cup sugar
1 teaspoon pepper	½ teaspoon dried mustard

■ For the salad, combine all the beans into a large bowl. Add the broccoli, cauliflower, carrots, onion, zucchini, squash, and bell pepper and set aside.

■ For the dressing, combine the oil, vinegar, pepper, salt, sugar, and mustard in a large saucepan over medium-high heat. Bring to a boil, stirring constantly, and cook until the sugar and salt are dissolved. Pour over the salad mixture while still hot.

■ Stir to mix dressing with beans and vegetables. Cover and refrigerate at least overnight. The longer it sits, the better it tastes!

—Elizabeth Flora Cooper
Boones Mill, Virginia

THE BELOVED GELATIN SALAD

During my college years I lived off gelatin salads served in the cafeteria. My stressed-out stomach could digest them, and they provided some semblance of nutrition with the fruit, nuts, or cream blended inside. Now I rarely make or see a gelatin salad, and the few I encounter—mostly at holiday dinners—are special family recipes loaded with tradition. Unlike Grandma's made-from-scratch rolls, Grandma's famous gelatin recipe can be easily replicated today and brings her memory and love back to the table.

Gelatin salads qualify as comfort food, but many people today are choosing other foods based on health or simplicity. Many seek fresh salads made from foods closer to their natural form, avoiding processed and refined products as well as artificial dyes and flavorings. Vegetarians avoid salads with animal products, and other conscious eaters avoid salads full of sugar or sugar substitutes. And although gelatin salads are easy to make, the necessary chilling time makes preparing one at the last minute a challenge.

But gelatin salads graced our tables frequently in another era. They provided an easy, colorful dish and made use of new technologies such as processed foods and refrigeration. One-third of the salad recipes in the 1942 *Granddaughter's Inglenook Cookbook* contain gelatin. Half of these gelatin salads include vegetables such as asparagus, beets, celery, and green peppers.

A few even contain meat. Filled with perplexing ingredients by today's standards, perhaps these recipes originated from the same sensibility: "Salads offer opportunity for introducing into the diet many valuable foods that would otherwise be neglected" (p. 236). Or perhaps these salads simply hark back to the savory aspic dishes of an earlier time when meat and vegetables were preserved in a gelatin made from meat stock.

However the dishes were conceived or popularized, the "Avocado Salad" from the 1942 cookbook is typical of a vegetable gelatin salad from the mid-twentieth century (p. 238). Loaded with green vegetables within a green gel, the salad looks attractive when molded. In the contributor's locality of California, the salad would have provided a novel way to present common, easy-to-find ingredients. My family actually liked the taste of the salad before they knew what it contained. My teenage daughter said, "Once I knew there were vegetables in there, it wasn't so appealing to my mind even though it tasted good in my mouth. Vegetables do not belong in gelatin." This may be why these salads have fallen out of fashion today.

LaVerne R. Yeager's "Fresh Salsa Salad" is a more typical vegetable salad prepared in the early part of the twenty-first century. When made with local produce at the peak of flavor, this salad represents the best of what we can bring to the table. Although it could be prepared in advance, it is easy to assemble at the last minute. While simple, it is elegant and appealing enough to share with guests. Full of vegetables, the recipe is colorful without highly processed ingredients and can be varied according to personal taste or the ingredients on hand.

Even though vegetable gelatin salads are no longer popular, gelatin salads made with fruit are still a part of our food culture. They comfort us and connect us with the past. Embrace these memories, but also look to simple and wholesome recipes like "Fresh Salsa Salad" to create new traditions for the future.

—Lori Steiner Jans
Tipp City, Ohio

AVOCADO SALAD

1 pkg. lime jello	1 c. celery
1½ c. boiling water	1 green pepper
1 tb. lemon juice	½ c. mayonnaise
1 tb. onion juice	½ c. thick cream
1 large avocado	

Dissolve jello in boiling water, add lemon and onion juice. When jello begins to thicken add diced avocado, celery and pepper. Fold in mayonnaise and whipped cream. Chill.

—Hazel E. Frantz, La Verne, California

FRESH SALSA SALAD

Using different colored bell peppers gives this salad a nice summery look. This is a beautiful side dish.

Serves 4 to 6

3 cups diced tomatoes (4 to 5 tomatoes)
2 cups diced bell peppers (2 large peppers)
½ cup diced onion
½ cup sugar
½ cup apple cider vinegar

■ Lightly toss the tomatoes, bell peppers, and onion in a large bowl. Set aside.

■ Mix the sugar, vinegar, and ¼ cup water in a separate bowl. Stir until the sugar is dissolved.

■ Pour the vinegar dressing over the vegetables just before serving.

Note: If you pour the dressing on too soon, the vinegar will draw the water out of the vegetables, making the salad too soupy.

—LaVerne R. Yeager
Saint Thomas, Pennsylvania

MORE ON GELATIN

Before the advent of packaged gelatin powder, cooks labored to create a gelatin from the bones and connective tissues of animals. With the mass production of granulated gelatin around 1900, jellied dishes could be made cheaply and easily. The 1901 cookbook contained two fruit salad recipes made with packages of "good gelatin" (p. 124). One recipe directed the cook to "set [the salad] in a cool place to harden; or if it is warm, put [it] on ice." The 1911 edition added one more recipe, which called for "a ten-cent package of Advo Jell" (p. 173).

—Lori Steiner Jans
Tipp City, Ohio

Gin Dolan's Vegetable Salad

Our dear friend Virginia Dolan made this for us when we visited her many years ago. She claimed to be not much of a cook, but this is such a good salad I have shared the recipe time after time! I think of her so fondly every time I make this colorful salad.

Serves 8 to 10

1 (15-ounce) can baby peas, drained
1 (15-ounce) can shoepeg corn, drained
1 (15-ounce) can French cut green beans, drained
1 (2-ounce) jar chopped pimento, drained
½ small sweet onion, chopped
½ green bell pepper, chopped
½ cup finely chopped celery
¼ cup vinegar
¼ cup canola or vegetable oil
¾ cup sugar

■ Combine the peas, corn, beans, pimento, onion, bell pepper, and celery in a large bowl. Set aside.

■ Briskly whisk together the vinegar, oil, and sugar in a separate bowl. Pour the dressing over the salad in the large bowl.

■ Stir to mix well and chill for 8 to 10 hours, stirring occasionally. This salad keeps up to two weeks in the refrigerator.

Notes: You can substitute honey or artificial sweetener for the sugar, but you don't get as much juice. The best corn is the tiny white variety, but other kinds will work.

—Libby Polzin Kinsey
Lake Odessa, Michigan

ENDIVE SALAD WITH HOT BACON DRESSING

My mother made hot bacon dressing in a cast-iron skillet and served **GF** *it on spring dandelion greens. In this updated version I serve it on roughly chopped endive.*

Serves 4

6 to 8 strips bacon
1 tablespoon cornstarch
2 whole eggs, beaten
2 tablespoons sugar
⅛ teaspoon salt
6 cups roughly chopped endive

■ Fry the bacon in a skillet or saucepan over medium heat until crisp, reserving 2 tablespoons of the bacon drippings.

■ Combine the cornstarch, sugar, salt with 1 cup of water in a large saucepan. Add the reserved bacon drippings and the beaten eggs, and whisk together to blend. Cook over low heat until thickened, about 10 minutes. Keeping the heat low and stirring continually will help temper the eggs and make a smooth dressing.

■ Add the endive and sauté just until it begins to wilt. Transfer the endive to bowls and top each bowl with crumbled bacon.

—Ruth Rishel Gleim
York, Pennsylvania

POPPY SEED SALAD

Serves 8 to 10

⅔ cup canola oil
½ cup sugar
⅓ cup lemon juice
1 tablespoon poppy seeds
1 teaspoon Dijon mustard
1 tablespoon diced onion

4 cups torn Romaine lettuce
½ cup small cubed Swiss cheese
½ cup dried cranberries
1 apple, cubed
1 pear, cubed
½ cup cashews

- Mix the canola oil, sugar, lemon juice, poppy seeds, mustard, and onion together in a bowl.

- Pour the dressing over the Romaine lettuce and sprinkle the cheese, cranberries, apple, pear, and cashews on top. Gently toss the salad before serving.

—Bonnie Harmon
Westminster, Maryland

MEDITERRANEAN SALAD

You need to prepare this salad at least one hour before eating. It is best if made the day before and stored overnight in the refrigerator. It's a wonderful way to celebrate the plentiful bounty of the garden.

Serves 6

1 large cucumber, sliced
3 medium tomatoes, sliced
1 large onion, sliced
6 kalamata olives,
   pitted and halved

2 ounces feta cheese, crumbled
2 tablespoons extra virgin olive oil
½ teaspoon sea salt
½ teaspoon dried oregano
⅛ teaspoon ground red pepper

- Arrange the cucumber and tomatoes on a large platter. Alternate the slices and make them spiral inward. Scatter the onion and olives on top and then sprinkle the feta cheese over the salad.

- Drizzle the oil on top and season with the salt, oregano, and red pepper.

—Carol A. Jackson
Troy, Ohio

SPINACH SALAD

This recipe came to my mother, Mabel (Susie) Myers, while Dad, *Cletus Myers, was pastor at the Cleveland First Church of the Brethren. It was originally from Lee Stewart, who attended the same church.*

Serves 6 to 8

½ pound bacon
1 cup canola oil
¾ cup sugar
⅓ cup ketchup
¼ cup apple cider vinegar
1 tablespoon Worcestershire sauce
1 medium onion
Salt and pepper to taste
1 (12-ounce) bag spinach, shredded
6 hard-cooked eggs, chopped

■ Fry the bacon in a skillet over medium heat until crisp, about 8 minutes. Drain on paper towels and crumble when cool.

■ Make the dressing by combining the oil, sugar, ketchup, vinegar, Worcestershire sauce, onion, and salt and pepper in a blender. Process until well blended and the onions are finely chopped.

■ To assemble the salad, combine the spinach, eggs, and bacon in a large bowl. Pour the dressing over the salad and toss to coat.

—Karen Sue Tuck
Asheboro, North Carolina

Roasted Beet and Blue Cheese Salad with Shallot Vinaigrette.

This salad may require some effort but is delicious, attractive, and worth the time.

Serves 2

> 10 baby beets, scrubbed clean
> 2 tablespoons vegetable oil
> 1 tablespoon coarsely chopped toasted pistachios (see note)
> 1 small shallot, finely chopped
> 2 teaspoons sherry vinegar
> ¼ teaspoon salt
> ¼ teaspoon pepper
> 12 Bibb lettuce leaves
> 2 tablespoons sliced red onion
> 2 ounces blue cheese

■ Preheat oven to 400°F. Remove the stem and root from each beet, wrap them in heavy aluminum foil, and place them on a baking sheet. Roast the beets for 1 hour or until they are tender when pierced with a knife. Allow to cool in the pouch. (This can be done a day or two ahead.) Remove the beets from the foil, rub off the skins, and set aside.

■ For the vinaigrette, combine the oil, pistachios, shallot, vinegar, salt, and pepper in a bowl. Whisk briskly until emulsified or the vinegar and oil are well mixed.

■ Line 2 salad plates with 6 leaves of Bibb lettuce each. Top each salad with 5 of the roasted beets, 1 tablespoon of sliced red onion, and 1 ounce of blue cheese. Drizzle the vinaigrette over each salad.

Note: To toast the pistachios, preheat the oven or toaster oven to 350°F. Put them on a baking sheet or some foil in a toaster oven and toast. Remove them when they are fragrant, about 3 minutes.

—Darlene R. Creighton
Lancaster, Pennsylvania

DIETER'S DELIGHT SALAD

Cooking for one person is sometimes a challenge. This salad can be quickly put together and can be a whole meal.

Serves 1

¼ cup sliced carrots
¼ cup chopped red cabbage
2 cups chopped Romaine lettuce
½ Roma tomato, cubed
1 tablespoon olive oil and vinegar dressing (see note)
1 tablespoon grated Parmesan cheese

■ Put the carrots in a steamer basket over a small amount of water. Cover and bring to a boil over high heat. Reduce the heat to medium low and steam the carrot for 5 minutes. Add the cabbage and continue to steam for another 7 or 8 minutes. (The vegetables can also be steamed in a microwave for 4 to 6 minutes.) Cool them in the refrigerator before making the salad.

■ In a serving bowl, toss together the steamed vegetables, lettuce, tomato, and dressing. Sprinkle cheese on top and serve.

Note: To make the dressing, combine equal amounts of good quality olive oil and vinegar in a dressing shaker and shake vigorously to mix well.

—Virginia Crim
Greenville, Ohio

GARDEN CONVICTION

I know God—standing in the bright sunshine, sinking my teeth into a warm, ripe tomato, feeling the juices tickle my chin as my tongue dances in my mouth. This moment is not about beliefs or creeds. In the garden I know God.

—Lori Steiner Jans
Tipp City, Ohio

CRUNCHY BROCCOLI TOSS

Serves 4 to 6

4 cups broccoli florets
1 cup shredded carrots
1 medium onion, sliced
2 garlic cloves, minced
1 teaspoon cornstarch
¼ cup vegetable broth
3 tablespoons teriyaki sauce
1 (6-ounce) package trail mix (nuts, seeds, and raisins)

■ Combine the broccoli, carrots, onion, garlic, and 2 tablespoons water in medium saucepan and cover. Bring to a boil over medium-high heat. Reduce the heat to medium low and cook for 3 to 5 minutes, or until the broccoli is crisp-tender.

■ Combine the cornstarch, broth, and teriyaki sauce in a bowl. Stir until the cornstarch is dissolved and well mixed. Add to the vegetable mixture, cover, and continue to cook over medium heat until the broccoli is tender.

■ When the broccoli is tender, transfer the vegetables to a serving bowl. Add the trail mix and lightly toss. Serve warm.

—Mary (Kitty) V. Reish
Dayton, Virginia

Autumn Apple Salad

Serves 8 to 10

1 (20-ounce) can crushed pineapple, undrained
4 teaspoons sugar
1 (3-ounce) package lemon gelatin
8 ounces cream cheese, softened
1 cup chopped unpeeled apples
½ to 1 cup chopped nuts
1 cup chopped celery
1 cup frozen whipped topping, thawed

■ Combine the pineapple and sugar in a saucepan over high heat. Bring to a boil, reduce the heat to medium and cook for 3 minutes.

■ Add the gelatin and stir until dissolved. Add the cream cheese and stir until thoroughly combined. Remove from the heat and let cool for 10 minutes.

■ Fold in the apples, nuts, celery, and whipped topping. Pour into a 9-inch square dish and chill until firm.

—Carolyn G. Cline
Harrisonburg, Virginia

STRAWBERRY YOGURT GELATIN

This is a favorite at potlucks. Different types of gelatin and fruit can be substituted for the strawberries. Orange gelatin with Mandarin orange slices works very well too. This can also be used as a dessert.

Serves 12 to 14

> 2 (3-ounce) packages strawberry gelatin
> 2 cups sliced strawberries, frozen or fresh
> ¾ cup crushed pineapple
> 1 banana
> 2 cups low-fat vanilla yogurt
> 1 cup chopped nuts (optional)

■ Dissolve the gelatin in 2 cups boiling water. Drain the strawberries and pineapple, reserving the liquid. Add enough water to make 1 cup and add to gelatin. Mash the banana and add to gelatin. Add the strawberries and pineapple. Pour half the gelatin mixture into a 2-quart baking dish and chill until firm, about 1½ hours.

■ When gelatin is firm, spread the yogurt over the top.

■ Gently spoon the remaining gelatin over the yogurt layer and chill for another hour. Garnish with chopped nuts, if desired.

—Anna Leiter Lease
Walkersville, Maryland

CRANBERRY SALAD

This is a decorative and tasty side dish for holiday meals. My
mother, Eula Brumbaugh, has made this cranberry salad for
nearly every holiday meal I can remember. She makes it without
nuts for me because I don't like nuts. Her friend Doris Walbridge
makes it with nuts, which I'm told gives the salad a richer flavor.

Serves 8 to 10

1 (6-ounce) package red gelatin (strawberry, raspberry, or cherry)
1 (15-ounce) can cranberry sauce
1 (8-ounce) can crushed pineapple
1 cored apple
1 seeded orange
½ cup finely chopped nuts (optional)

■ Combine the gelatin with 2 cups boiling water in a large bowl. Stir until all the gelatin is dissolved. Add the cranberry sauce to the gelatin mix and stir until it is well blended. Reserve the juice of the crushed pineapple and stir the pineapple into the gelatin mix.

■ Wash the apple and orange well, and do not peel. Cut the fruit into large pieces, including the peels, and then chop finely in a blender. Add some of the reserved pineapple juice to help the blending process.

■ Stir the fruit into the gelatin mixture. Add the chopped nuts, if using. Pour into a large serving bowl and refrigerate overnight.

Note: We deliberately choose not to make it with cranberry-flavored gelatin because the mix of flavors is better using a strawberry, raspberry, or cherry gelatin with the cranberry sauce.

—Joel Brumbaugh-Cayford
Elgin, Illinois

PEAR SALAD

Serves 6

1 (10-ounce) bag Romaine lettuce
½ cup cashews or slivered almonds
½ cup dried cranberries
1½ cup sliced unpeeled pears
1 cup grated Swiss cheese
½ cup sugar
⅓ cup lemon juice
⅔ cup olive oil
½ teaspoon salt
1½ teaspoons yellow mustard
2 teaspoons finely chopped onions

- Toss the lettuce, cashews or almonds, cranberries, pears, and cheese in a large bowl and set aside.

- Combine the sugar, lemon juice, oil, salt, mustard, and onion in a separate bowl and mix well. Pour the dressing over the salad when ready to serve.

Note: To keep the pears from turning brown, keep them in the same container as the dressing until ready to serve.

—Rosene M. Brubaker
Columbia, Pennsylvania

ISLAND FRUIT RELISH

Here is a versatile dish that can be used as a salad, a side dish, a topping for chicken or fish, or a salsa served with corn or pita chips.

Serves 8 to 10

¾ cup diced cucumber
¾ cup diced mango
¾ cup diced papaya
¾ cup diced pineapple
2 cups finely diced tomatoes
1 jalapeño pepper, diced
¼ cup finely chopped cilantro
¾ cup diced red onions
1 tablespoon salt
2 tablespoons hot sauce
2 tablespoons honey
¼ cup lemon juice
4 tablespoons lime juice

■ Combine all the ingredients—the cucumber, mango, papaya, pineapple, tomatoes, jalapeño pepper, cilantro, onions, salt, hot sauce, honey, lemon juice, and lime juice—in a bowl, cover, and chill at least 30 minutes before serving.

—Chris Fogerty and JoAnn Myers
North Manchester, Indiana

RICH RELATIONSHIPS

Cookbook collections are seldom the result of deliberate searches for sought-after recipes or culinary trends. More often than not, cookbooks serve as reminders of a rich variety of relationships with congregations, civic organizations, our children's teams and clubs. Opening a book compiled by the Pentecostal cooks next door, I roll out homemade noodles while fondly remembering the World Communion Sunday when we jointly closed the two hundred-yard gap between our congregations. Brethren brought a plate of Inglenook-endorsed communion bread to the open door where grape juice and a new feast at Christ's table awaited us.

—Sandy Bosserman
Peace Valley, Missouri

CRAISIN SALAD

My mother gave me this beautiful salad recipe. We have enjoyed it at many family gatherings. It makes a great side salad as it is or can be a main dish if you add six ounces of chopped cooked chicken. The dressing is a very good all-purpose dressing.

Serves 8 to 10

SALAD
1 bunch red leaf lettuce
1 bunch green leaf lettuce
1 head iceberg lettuce
8 ounces mozzarella cheese, shredded
6 ounces Parmesan cheese, shredded
1 cup craisins
1 pound bacon, cooked crisp and crumbled
½ cup sliced almonds

DRESSING
½ cup chopped sweet onion
1 cup sugar
2 teaspoons dry mustard
½ cup red wine vinegar
1 cup olive oil

■ To make the salad, wash and drain the lettuces. Break or tear them into bite-size pieces in a large bowl. Add the cheeses, craisins, bacon, and almonds and mix.

■ To make the dressing, in a blender or food processor, combine the onion, sugar, mustard, vinegar, and oil. Blend completely till smooth. Either pour the dressing over the salad and toss or serve it on the side.

—Bev Anspaugh
Rocky Mount, Virginia

Spicy Pasta Salad

For a different flavor, try Spanish olives instead of the black olives. Cherry tomatoes may be added, if desired.

Serves 10

1 pound pasta twists (fusilli)
¼ pound provolone cheese
¼ pound pepperoni
¼ pound hard salami
1 green bell pepper
2 celery ribs
1 medium onion

Black olives to taste
1½ tablespoons garlic salt
1 tablespoon oregano
1 teaspoon black pepper
1 cup canola oil
½ cup vinegar
1 tablespoon sugar (optional)

■ Cook the pasta according to the package directions, drain, and put in a large serving bowl. Chop the cheese, pepperoni, salami, bell pepper, celery, onion, and olives, and toss with the pasta. Add the seasonings, oil, vinegar, and sugar, if using, to the pasta, and gently mix to combine.

—Christine Bantz Johns
Elizabethtown, Pennsylvania

Baked Sauerkraut-Tomato Salad

Serves 8 to 10

1 pound bag sauerkraut, drained
1 (28-ounce) can diced tomatoes, not drained
½ pound bacon, cooked and diced
¾ cup diced onion
¾ cup sugar

■ Preheat the oven to 350°F. Grease a 13 x 9-inch glass baking dish with butter.

■ Combine the sauerkraut, tomatoes, bacon, onion, and sugar in a bowl and stir to mix. Pour the mixture into the prepared dish and bake for 1½ hours or until all the liquid is absorbed. Refrigerate and serve cold.

—Mary Lou Van Dyke
Lincoln, Nebraska

GREEK PASTA SALAD

Add leftover chicken or fish or a can of tuna to make this a main dish meal.

Serves 6 to 8

- 1 pound bowtie or rotini pasta
- ½ cup plus 2 tablespoons olive oil, divided
- ¼ cup balsamic vinegar
- 1 tablespoon Dijon mustard
- 1 tablespoon freshly ground black pepper
- 1 teaspoon salt
- 2 tablespoons fresh parsley or 1 tablespoon dried
- ¼ cup sliced kalamata olives
- 1 cup chopped fresh tomatoes
- 2 tablespoons capers or chopped sour pickles

■ Cook the pasta according to the package directions. Drain, rinse with cold water, and drain well again. Coat the pasta with 2 tablespoons of the olive oil and set aside.

■ Combine the remaining ½ cup oil, vinegar, mustard, pepper, salt, and parsley in a small jar and shake well. Pour over the pasta and toss gently. Add the olives, tomatoes, and capers and toss again. Chill for 20 minutes before serving.

—Sondra Eisenbise Simmons
Hershey, Pennsylvania

QUINOA SALAD

This salad improves over time, so I usually make it a day ahead.

Serves 8 to 10

1 cup quinoa, rinsed in cold water and drained
¼ cup olive oil
¼ cup balsamic or red wine vinegar
¼ cup soy sauce
1 teaspoon dried basil
2 teaspoons minced garlic
½ teaspoon sea salt (optional)
⅛ teaspoon black pepper
1 cup cooked or canned black beans, drained
1 cup whole kernel corn
1 large tomato, peeled, seeded, and diced (about ¾ cup)
1 small red bell pepper, chopped (½ cup)
2 green onions, finely chopped (about ¼ cup)
2 tablespoons chopped fresh parsley (optional)

■ Bring 2 cups of water to a boil over high heat. Add the quinoa. Reduce the heat to low, cover, and simmer until the liquid is absorbed, about 10 minutes. Remove the pan from the heat and let it cool completely.

■ In a large bowl, whisk together the oil, vinegar, soy sauce, basil, garlic, sea salt, if using, black pepper, beans, corn, tomato, bell pepper, green onions, and parsley, if using. When cool, add the cooked quinoa and stir, mixing well.

■ Serve at room temperature or refrigerate for 30 minutes before serving.

—Pearl Fruth Miller
Warrensburg, Missouri

Tuna and White Bean Salad

This salad can be served over lettuce or used to stuff a tomato.

Serves 6

½ cup olive oil
2 tablespoons fresh lemon juice
1 teaspoon Italian seasoning
¾ teaspoon salt
½ teaspoon pepper
1 large cucumber, peeled, deseeded, and chopped
4 plum tomatoes, chopped
½ cup chopped red onion
2 tablespoons chopped fresh parsley
1 (15-ounce) can Great Northern beans, rinsed and drained
1 (12-ounce) can solid white tuna, drained

■ In a large bowl, whisk together the olive oil, lemon juice, Italian seasoning, salt, and pepper. Stir in the cucumber, tomatoes, onion, parsley, and beans. Add the tuna and toss gently until evenly coated. Serve immediately or refrigerate until ready to use.

—Margaret A. Wolfe
Waterloo, Iowa

TACO SALAD

1 (29-ounce) can refried beans
1 (10-ounce) can green chilies
1 (8-ounce) container sour cream with chives
2 cups shredded Cheddar cheese, divided
1 (8-ounce) container guacamole
2 cups finely chopped lettuce
1 cup diced tomato (optional)
2 green onions, chopped (optional)
Tortilla chips, pita chips, or flatbread (optional)

■ Layer the ingredients in a 9 x 9-inch baking dish. Spread the refried beans on the bottom. Add the green chilies, sour cream, 1 cup of the cheese, guacamole, lettuce, remaining cup of cheese, tomato, and green onions, if using. Serve with tortilla chips, pita chips, or flatbread, if using.

—Carolyn Dooley
Hutchinson, Kansas

WARM GERMAN POTATO SALAD

This recipe calls for dried herbs, but if you want to use fresh herbs use two tablespoons. Some people I know enjoy this potato salad just as much cold from the refrigerator.

Serves 18 to 20

    5 pounds potatoes, scrubbed and skins on
    ½ pound bacon
    2 tablespoons flour
    ¾ cup vinegar
    1 cup sugar
    Salt to taste
    1 medium onion, thinly sliced
    1 tablespoon dried parsley, or 2 tablespoons chopped fresh
        parsley
    1 tablespoon dried chives, or 2 tablespoons chopped fresh chives

■ Boil the potatoes over high heat in a large pot with enough water to cover until they can be easily pierced with a fork, about 30 minutes. When done, drain and set aside.

■ Fry the bacon strips in a skillet over medium heat until done, about 8 minutes. Reduce the heat to low and transfer the bacon to a paper towel-lined plate.

■ Add the flour to the bacon drippings in the skillet and stir to combine. Add the vinegar, ¾ cup water, sugar, and salt and increase the heat to medium high. Bring to a simmer, reduce the heat to medium, and cook, stirring regularly, until reduced to a pourable sauce, about 20 minutes.

■ Meanwhile, peel and slice the potatoes and put them in a large serving bowl. Add the onion, parsley, chives, and crumbled bacon. Gently toss the mixture.

■ When ready, pour the sauce over the potato mixture and stir to combine. Serve warm.

—Joan H. Wray
Kokomo, Indiana

CREAMY POTATO SALAD

Serves 10

3 pounds potatoes, scrubbed and skins on
3 eggs, beaten
1 cup sugar
2 tablespoons flour
1 cup vinegar
1 teaspoon salt
½ teaspoon dry mustard
1 cup mayonnaise

■ Boil the potatoes over high heat in a large pot with enough water to cover until they can be easily pierced with a fork, about 30 minutes. When done, drain and set aside.

■ Combine the eggs, sugar, flour, vinegar, salt, and dry mustard in a saucepan, and whisk vigorously to mix well. Place over medium heat and continue stirring. When it starts to simmer, cook for 2 minutes more. Remove from the heat and let cool for 10 minutes. Then add the mayonnaise and mix well.

■ Meanwhile, peel and slice the potatoes and put them in a large serving bowl. Pour the dressing over the potatoes and gently toss to mix.

—Mary L. Jenkins
North Manchester, Indiana

A PERSONAL AFFAIR

Potato salad:
A personal affair.
Not like mine—
Too mustardy.
Not enough vinegar.
A tad too much salt.
Onions too finely
    chopped.
Too creamy.
Needs more celery
    seed.
More paprika.
Why so many eggs?
Too dry.
Not like mine—
A personal affair:
Potato salad.

—Phyllis (Angeny)
    Hochstetler
Colorado City, Colorado

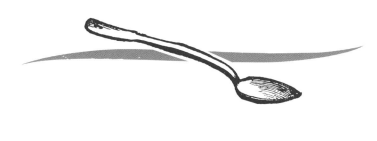

Flying Farmer Chicken Salad

This salad is best when made the day before serving.

Serves 8 to 10

  5 cups cooked diced chicken
  2 tablespoons olive oil
  2 tablespoons orange juice
  2 tablespoons vinegar
  1 teaspoon salt
  3 cups cooked rice
  1½ cups white grapes
  3 celery ribs, chopped
  1 (15-ounce) can pineapple tidbits, drained
  1 (10-ounce) can Mandarin oranges, drained
  1 cup toasted almonds
  1½ cup mayonnaise

■ Combine the chicken, oil, orange juice, vinegar, and salt in a mixing bowl. Stir and set aside.

■ In a separate bowl, combine the rice, grapes, celery, pineapple, Mandarin oranges, almonds, and mayonnaise and stir to mix well. Add to the chicken mixture and gently toss everything together.

—Eullillian Bell
Mooreland, Indiana

CALIFORNIA CHICKEN SALAD

Serves 4 to 6

3 cups diced cooked chicken breast
¼ teaspoon minced garlic
¼ teaspoon sweet chili powder
¾ teaspoon salt, divided
¼ teaspoon freshly ground black pepper
3 teaspoon olive oil, divided
10 blanched asparagus spears, cut in thirds
3 plum tomatoes, diced
½ cup diced red onion
2 tablespoons pine nuts
3 slices turkey bacon, cooked and roughly chopped
6 tablespoons honey
2 tablespoons Dijon mustard
1 teaspoon cider vinegar

- Toss together the chicken breast, garlic, chili powder, ¼ teaspoon of the salt, and pepper in a large bowl. Add 1 teaspoon of the oil, the asparagus spears, tomatoes, onion, pine nuts, and turkey bacon. Toss to mix.

- Combine the honey, Dijon mustard, remaining 2 teaspoons olive oil, cider vinegar, and remaining ½ teaspoon salt in a small bowl. Whisk well and then drizzle over the salad just before serving.

—Chris Fogerty and JoAnn Myers
North Manchester, Indiana

HONEY CHICKEN SALAD

Whether served on a bed of lettuce or in a toasted sandwich, this recipe is delicious. It could be made from leftover rotisserie chicken or leftover grilled chicken.

Serves 6

4 cups cubed cooked chicken (about 4 boneless, skinless breasts)
1½ cups diced celery
1 cup dried cranberries
½ cup plus 3 tablespoons chopped nuts (pecans or walnuts), divided
1½ cups mayonnaise
⅓ cup honey
¼ teaspoon salt
¼ teaspoon pepper

- Combine the chicken, celery, cranberries, and ½ cup of the nuts in a bowl.

- Mix the mayonnaise, honey, salt, and pepper in a separate bowl.

- Spoon the dressing over the chicken mixture and stir to combine. Add the remaining 3 tablespoons of nuts as a garnish.

- Chill for at least 20 minutes before serving.

—Dianne Gleim Bowders
York, Pennsylvania

Balsamic Chicken Pasta Salad

This is an excellent cold salad.

Serves 8

3 cups uncooked bowtie pasta
4 cooked boneless, skinless chicken breasts
2 cups chopped tomatoes (about 2 large tomatoes)
½ cup chopped red onion
4 bacon strips, cooked and crumbled
½ cup olive oil
¼ cup minced fresh basil
¼ cup balsamic vinegar
2 tablespoons brown sugar
1 teaspoon minced garlic
¼ teaspoon salt
¼ teaspoon pepper

■ Cook the pasta for 10 to 12 minutes or until just tender to bite. Drain and rinse under cold water. Chop the chicken and combine in a bowl with the tomatoes, onion, and bacon. Add the pasta and toss to mix.

■ In a small bowl, whisk the oil, basil, vinegar, brown sugar, garlic, salt, and pepper. Drizzle over the salad and toss.

—Donna McKee Rhodes
Huntingdon, Pennsylvania

Terrific Teachers

My mother was a school teacher, a farmer's wife, and the mother of six children. She was masterful at creating thirty-minute meals long before television shows made them popular. Our menus did not vary a great deal, because Mom always used what she had canned or frozen from the garden combined with beef, chicken, or pork that we raised on the farm. Cooking from basic ingredients, rather than using processed foods, is something that I attribute to learning from her. When I became a nurse, a wife, and a mother, being able to create thirty-minute meals seemed easy to do. I learned from a terrific teacher.

—Valda Garber-Weider
Harrisonburg, Virginia

SAUCES AND DRESSINGS

Sauces and dressings are not
the body of the meal;
they are the heart
and passion of the preparer.
Spices and aroma that
lace every bite
reflect a sincere desire
that the meal be a contiguous
delight.

Spice ushers us to
a threshold that houses the meal.
Sauces lead us delicately
to the next taste.
Dressings crown our adventure
with a promise that
what lies beneath is nourishment,
is healthful,
is food.

—Dena Lee
Churchill, Ontario

QUICK
& EASY

SPECIAL
OCCASION

GLUTEN
FREE

VEGETARIAN

VEGAN

Perfect Barbecue Sauce

I don't like the commercial-brand barbecue sauces, so I created this one for my grilled chicken. I like to use home-made apricot jam. It adds a touch of sweetness that is a perfect combination with the other slightly spicy ingredients. If you like it spicier, just add more chili powder. This makes plenty of sauce for several chickens.

Makes 4 cups

1½ cups sugar
¾ cup ketchup
¾ cup tomato paste
¼ cup lemon juice
¼ cup cider vinegar
¼ cup Worcestershire sauce
2 teaspoons chili powder (more if you like it hot)
3 tablespoons prepared mustard
1 teaspoon salt
2 tablespoons molasses
2 tablespoons apricot jam

■ Combine the sugar, ketchup, tomato paste, ½ cup water, lemon juice, vinegar, Worcestershire sauce, chili powder, mustard, salt, molasses, and jam in a saucepan and bring to a boil over high heat. Reduce the heat to low and simmer uncovered until thickened, about 15 minutes.

■ Use to baste grilled chicken during the last 10 minutes of cooking.

—Mark L. Ullery
Olympia, Washington

MEXICAN HOT SAUCE

This hot sauce is great with just about everything. I like to eat it with chips, served over scrambled eggs, or drizzled on burritos. (GF)(✱)(V)

Makes 6 cups

2 medium jalapeño peppers, seeded
1 (29-ounce) can whole tomatoes
1 (15-ounce) can stewed tomatoes
⅛ teaspoon salt

½ teaspoon sugar
¼ teaspoon garlic powder
5 green onions

■ Place the peppers in a food processor or blender and blend for 5 seconds. Drain both cans of tomatoes and add to the peppers and blend for 5 to 8 seconds. Pour into a glass mixing bowl. Add the salt, sugar, and garlic powder. Cut the green onions very thin and add to the sauce. Do not blend. Cover and store in the refrigerator until ready to use. It keeps for several weeks.

—Arlene Werking Barney
North Manchester, Indiana

FRESH TOMATO SAUCE

It is wonderful to use this tomato sauce when the garden blesses us with lots of tomatoes. As it is, this sauce is vegan, but you can use it as a base for other sauces. For a hearty meaty sauce, add half a pound of cooked ground beef or turkey. For a Mexican-flavored sauce, use tomatillos and cilantro instead of tomatoes and basil. Use your imagination to make it many different ways. (GF)(✱)(V)

Makes about 3 cups

2 teaspoons olive oil
1 large onion, finely chopped
2 teaspoons chopped garlic

6 large tomatoes, chopped
½ cup chopped fresh basil
Salt and pepper to taste

■ Heat the olive oil in a large saucepan or skillet over medium heat. Sauté the onions and garlic for 5 minutes, or until soft. Stir in the tomatoes and basil. Increase the temperature to medium high, add the salt and pepper, and cook, stirring often, for about 10 minutes, or until the tomatoes have softened.

—Mary Kay Snider Turner
Gettysburg, Pennsylvania

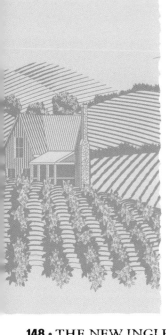

PASTA SAUCE

Makes about 4 cups, enough for 8 servings

3 tablespoons extra virgin olive oil
1 large onion, finely chopped
2 garlic cloves, crushed
2 (14½-ounce) cans tomatoes, chopped
¼ teaspoon red pepper flakes, or to taste
2 teaspoons balsamic vinegar
1 to 2 teaspoons sugar
¾ cup basil leaves, torn into pieces or chopped
Salt and ground black pepper to taste

■ Heat the olive oil in a skillet over medium heat. Add the onion and cook for 3 minutes. Add the garlic and sauté until the onions are tender, about 2 minutes more.

■ Add the tomatoes, red pepper, vinegar, and sugar to the onion mixture and bring to a boil. Reduce the heat to low and simmer until the flavors blend to your liking, 45 to 60 minutes.

■ Stir in the basil, season with salt and pepper, and cook for 2 to 3 minutes longer.

—Ed Lentz
Columbia, Pennsylvania

Sandy's Spaghetti Sauce

This sauce can be frozen up to six months for later use.

Serves 6

1 pound ground beef
1 to 2 medium onions, chopped (about 1½ cups)
¼ cup (½ stick) butter
2 (10-ounce) cans tomato soup
2 (6-ounce) cans tomato paste
1 (10-ounce) can beef consommé (or beef broth)
1 to 2 (4-ounce) cans sliced mushrooms (or fresh mushrooms)

½ teaspoon salt
¼ teaspoon pepper
1 teaspoon garlic powder

■ Combine the beef and onions in a large skillet over medium heat. Cook until the beef is browned throughout. Add the butter, soup, tomato paste, beef consommé, mushrooms, salt, pepper, and garlic powder and cook for ½ hour or longer.

—Sandra S. Bowman
Covington, Ohio

Fred's Dry Rub

Makes ¾ cup   GF · V

1 teaspoon onion powder
1 teaspoon paprika
3 teaspoons black pepper
1 tablespoon kosher salt
2 tablespoons raw sugar
2 tablespoons brown sugar

1 teaspoon dried thyme
1 teaspoon cumin
½ teaspoon ground nutmeg
1 tablespoon cayenne pepper
2 tablespoons chili powder
2 tablespoons garlic powder

■ Combine the onion powder, paprika, black pepper, salt, raw sugar, brown sugar, thyme, cumin, nutmeg, cayenne pepper, chili powder, and garlic powder in a container with a tight-fitting lid. Shake the mix and store at room temperature. This is a great rub for beef, pork, or chicken. Coat the meat at least 30 minutes prior to grilling.

—Fred V. Wilhelm
Baltimore, Maryland

Sweet and Sour Sauce

This recipe is submitted in memory of Mary Naff Layman, who shared this recipe with me. It's very good served over pork loin roast and other meats, and, if you like onions, try adding one cup chopped onions with the peppers.

Makes about 4 cups

1 (15-ounce) can pineapple chunks
2 tablespoons cornstarch
½ cup vinegar
½ cup brown sugar
2 tablespoons soy sauce
2 tablespoons lemon juice
1 cup coarsely chopped green bell peppers
1 tablespoon chopped pimento

■ Drain the pineapple chunks, reserving the juice. Add water to the juice to make 1 cup. Combine the pineapple juice and cornstarch in a saucepan over medium heat and stir until smooth. Stir in the vinegar, brown sugar, soy sauce, and lemon juice.

■ When beginning to bubble, reduce the heat to medium low and cook until the mixture is thickened and clear, about 10 minutes. Add the pineapple, green pepper, and pimento. Mix well. Cover and simmer for 15 minutes. Serve warm.

—Lois L. Willis
Rocky Mount, Virginia

RECIPES AS SHARED WISDOM

I grew up in the Shenandoah Valley, in the apple capital of Virginia, and my family ate apple butter on homemade rolls for breakfast, lunch, and dinner. Now as an adult with a family of my own, I have attempted to re-create the magical experience of homemade apple butter with mixed results.

Traditionally, apple butter was made outdoors in a copper kettle over an open fire. Making apple butter this way took a large group two days—one day to cut enough apples to fill a twenty-gallon pot and a second day to boil the apples, sugar, and spices down into a thick, dark concoction. Although it is still possible to find apple butter made the traditional way (especially in rural areas), it's not easy to re-create that recipe in a small batch suitable for a family of five.

My research on apple butter for *The New Inglenook Cookbook* has been a lifesaver in my attempt to scale down my family's recipe. There were quite a few tips I gleaned from reading all the recipes and memories that were submitted. The most revolutionary technique I learned was how to reduce the apple butter in a conventional oven. Not only does it save you time by not having to stir constantly, it allows you to make small batches you don't even have to can. Just pour the apple butter into airtight containers and keep in the refrigerator for a few weeks. Share some with friends and family if you don't think you'll eat it fast enough.

The women who submitted recipes and memories had so much wisdom to share. Susan B. Hertzog, of Lebanon, Pennsylvania, advised me to use good baking apples such as McIntosh, Jonathan, or Winesaps. Susan K. Morris, of Buckley, Michigan, reminded me not to add too much liquid to the pan when I first soften the apples on the stove. Alice Rohrer, of North Manchester, Indiana, suggested an alternative to the oven—an electric turkey roaster—for boiling down the apple butter.

This was only the beginning of Mrs. Rohrer's apple butter innovations. She gave me so many new ideas for making old-fashioned apple butter, and I must say there is nothing more humbling than talking to an 89-year-old woman who could cook you under the table. I've already asked my dad to make me a new stirring spoon based on her design specifications. I have my eye on a new Victorio food strainer, and I'm on the hunt for modified food starch, which I will add to the final product to keep it from weeping.

The Inglenook community has always been a vast resource of collective skills and wisdom. Today I still use my grandmother's tattered 1911 edition, which comes in handy in unexpected ways. When I first moved to a house with a loquat tree in Southern California, I had no idea what to do with this unfamiliar fruit. I'd never seen a loquat tree, much less eaten its fruit, and loquat recipes are few and far between. So I consulted my grandmother's *Inglenook Cook Book* and was delighted to find a recipe for "Loquat Jelly" by Sister Barbara Kindig, of Inglewood, California (p. 326). This woman lived not too far from me, although separated by a hundred years, and she gave me hope. She also gave me the beginning of a recipe that has turned into my own version of loquat butter, which we enjoy making each spring.

The recipes, memories, and helpful tips found in this cookbook stand in the grand culinary tradition of the Brethren community. I fully expect that some reader one hundred years from now will gratefully discover and use one of these recipes. As for me, I can't wait until apple season.

—Susan Lutz
Los Angeles, California

LOQUAT JELLY

Pit the loquats and cover the pulp with water, cook until soft, and strain in a close sack. To 1 pint of juice take 1 pint of sugar. It is best to make it in small quantities, as it gets clearer. Always cook in a granite saucepan, never use tin. Cook until a little tried in a saucer will jell.

—Sister Barbara Kindig, Inglewood, California

OVEN APPLE BUTTER

For years our mother made apple butter this way, which allows you to make smaller batches using an oven. It's important to note that this recipe begins with you making applesauce.

Makes approximately 4 pints

> 10 pounds cooking apples (such as Jonathan or Winesap)
> 1 cup sugar per pint applesauce
> 2 teaspoons apple cider vinegar per pint applesauce
> ¼ teaspoon cinnamon per pint applesauce (see note)

- Begin by making applesauce. First, core and chop the apples, but do not peel. Stew the apples in 1 to 1½ cups water in a large non-reactive saucepan over medium heat. Stir frequently to prevent burning. When the apples are very soft, remove from the heat.

- Preheat the oven to 350°F.

- Press the cooked apples through a sieve or a food mill in batches. Measure the total amount of applesauce (should be about 4 to 5 pints). Pour the applesauce into a large non-reactive pan such as an enameled or stainless steel roasting pan.

- For each pint of applesauce, add 1 cup sugar, 2 teaspoons apple cider vinegar, and ¼ teaspoon ground cinnamon. Stir to incorporate.

- Bake uncovered, stirring once an hour for two hours. Be sure to scrape the sides and bottom of the pan to blend in the browned edges, which will enhance the flavor and prevent burning.

- After two hours, reduce the oven temperature to 300°F and continue baking for about one more hour until the apple butter reaches the desired color and consistency.

- To test for proper consistency, drop a teaspoonful of apple butter on a saucer that has been cooled in the freezer. It is done if it stays slightly mounded on the plate.

- Store apple butter in the refrigerator for several weeks. (Apple butter may be canned, but it is recommended that you consult U.S.D.A.-approved home canning guidelines.)

Note: For spicier apple butter, place 1 tablespoon whole cloves in a cheesecloth bag and tie tightly with clean kitchen string. Add the bag of cloves to the applesauce and sugar mixture before baking. Remove the bag of cloves after about an hour of baking, or until the desired taste is reached.

—Annabel J. Rupel and Alice Rohrer
North Manchester, Indiana

APPLE BUTTER DAYS

Each fall our congregation, Prince of Peace, hosted an event known as Apple Butter Days. Apple butter was made on one fire pit, ham and bean soup in a 28-gallon cast-iron kettle on another. Everyone—young and old alike—had an opportunity to stir the apple butter. It was a wonderful all-day, all-church activity. At the conclusion of the jarring of the apple butter, we enjoyed a ham and bean soup dinner. I remember the fellowship hall smelling like onions and everyone smelling like campfire smoke for days afterward.

—Vicki Yoder Ferguson
Dayton, Ohio

CREAMY SALAD DRESSING

This was my mother's favorite salad dressing. It's very good with salad consisting of several varieties of lettuce, hard-cooked eggs, and bacon. For color, add cherry or grape tomatoes.

Makes 4 cups

3 eggs
1 tablespoon butter,
   at room temperature
3 tablespoons flour

2 cups sugar
1 cup white vinegar
1 cup milk

■ Combine the eggs and butter in a bowl and beat well. Add the flour and sugar and mix until creamy. Pour the egg mixture into a saucepan over medium low heat. Add the vinegar and milk. Stirring constantly, cook until thickened, about 10 minutes. Remove from the heat and cool to room temperature, and then refrigerate.

■ This will keep for several weeks stored in a container with a tight-fitting lid in the refrigerator. If it's too thick, add a little water.

—Bernice E. Petticoffer
Ephrata, Pennsylvania

BUTTERMILK BACON SALAD DRESSING

This special dressing was always served at our family reunions. It is especially good on spinach salad.

Makes 2 cups

¼ cup sour cream
1 cup mayonnaise
¾ cup buttermilk, divided
¼ cup bacon bits

1 tablespoon chopped
   fresh green onion
1½ teaspoons chopped fresh dill

■ Combine the sour cream, mayonnaise, ½ cup of the buttermilk, bacon, green onion, and dill. Stir to mix. If the dressing is too thick, add the remaining buttermilk and stir.

—Marilyn D. Gryder
Tallmadge, Ohio

CELERY SEED
SALAD DRESSING

When I was working, a restaurant that I frequented for lunch served this dressing over potato or macaroni salad. It is delicious. I use it on all kinds of salad, even on a side or chef salad.

Makes about 5 cups

  2 cups sugar
  2 teaspoons salt
  2 teaspoons garlic salt
  2 tablespoons celery seed
  ⅔ cup apple cider vinegar
  1 cup mayonnaise-type salad dressing (like Miracle Whip)
  2 cups olive oil

■ Combine the sugar, salt, garlic salt, celery seed, and vinegar in a bowl. Beat for 2 minutes with a handheld electric mixer. Add the mayonnaise dressing and oil and beat until clear and shiny, 10 to 15 minutes.

—Bickey Myers Garber
North Manchester, Indiana

RANCH SALAD DRESSING

The salt can be omitted if you need a salt-free diet.

Makes 2 cups

1 tablespoon dried parsley flakes
2½ teaspoons paprika
2 teaspoons sugar
2 teaspoons salt
2 teaspoons garlic powder
2 tablespoons plus 2 teaspoons dried minced onion
1 cup mayonnaise
1 cup buttermilk

■ Combine the parsley, paprika, sugar, salt, and garlic powder in a small bowl. (This basic seasoning blend can be stored in an airtight container in a cool dry place for up to 1 year.)

■ Combine 1 tablespoon of the seasoning blend with the mayonnaise and buttermilk. Whisk to mix. Store in an airtight container in the refrigerator.

Variation: To make a ranch dip, combine 1 tablespoon of the seasoning blend with 1 cup sour cream and stir to mix well; refrigerate at least 1 hour before serving.

—Gloria Faye Craig
Bassett, Virginia

FRENCH SALAD DRESSING

Makes 3 cups

1 cup vegetable or olive oil
½ cup ketchup
1 cup sugar
½ cup vinegar
1 teaspoon salt
1 small onion, minced
1 garlic clove, minced

■ Combine the oil, ketchup, sugar, vinegar, salt, onion, and garlic and mix thoroughly. Pour into an airtight container and refrigerate. It will keep for 2 to 3 months.

—Anne S. Harvey
Easton, Maryland

FRESH LEMON SALAD DRESSING

Makes 1 cup

⅔ cup vegetable oil
⅓ cup olive oil
½ teaspoon salt
½ teaspoon dry mustard
¼ fresh lemon, deseeded but with peel

■ Combine both the oils, salt, mustard, and lemon in a blender or food processor. Blend until the lemon is shredded completely.

—Nancy Shifflett Bowman
Fishersville, Virginia

CREAMY CUCUMBER SAUCE

There are three ways I use this sauce. I love it with pita bread as a spread, on chicken breasts as a sauce, and on a lettuce, tomato, and onion salad as a dressing.

Makes about 4 cups

1 cucumber, minced
1 (16-ounce) container sour cream
5 tablespoons olive oil
3 tablespoons red wine vinegar
1 tablespoon lemon juice
1 teaspoon garlic powder

■ Lay the cucumber between two paper towels on a plate to extract all the moisture. Combine the dried cucumbers with the sour cream, oil, vinegar, lemon juice, and garlic powder. Mix well, pour into an airtight container, and chill for about 1 hour in the refrigerator to let the flavors combine.

—Sharon I. Hausenfluck
Stephens City, Virginia

HOMEMADE DRESSINGS

Grandma made all her salad dressings. For fresh spring lettuce equal parts vinegar and sugar were mixed, and then thick cream was added. The vinegar that she used was kept in barrels down in the cellar. When vinegar was needed in the kitchen, a hose was placed in the barrel's bunghole and then sucked on to siphon out vinegar into a gallon jug. It was then transferred to a small cruet. After all these years I still have Grandma's little antique cruet, a reminder of days gone by.

—Alice Rohrer
North Manchester, Indiana

MAIN
DISHES

There will be no program afterward,
no entertainment, no proposals

needing a vote, not even an announcement.
Just casseroles lined up on long,

paper-covered tables. Take a little
of each one. Don't miss Emma's famous

hamloaf, one slice only, please.
Here are the salads: potato, five-bean, macaroni.

Grab the obligatory celery strip, a carrot
or two; set a good example for the kids.

Pile your plate high. No shame.
It's expected. Bypass the dessert table—

for now. (There will be time enough later.)
Time too for catch-up conversations,

easy laughter, hearing the latest
about the Harpers' grandchildren.

It's why everybody comes. To talk, to listen,
to keep hold of the blest tie that binds.

And for the food. The food.

—Ken Gibble
Camp Hill, Pennsylvania

QUICK
& EASY

SPECIAL
OCCASION

GLUTEN
FREE

VEGETARIAN

VEGAN

BULGOGI

This recipe was handed down to me by my husband's parents who grew up in Korea. It is so simple to prepare, cook, and deliver to the table. It reminds my husband of the Korean meals he enjoyed as a child, and it is now my children's favorite meal too. I usually double the recipe so they can enjoy the leftovers for lunch the next day.

4 to 6 servings

- ¼ cup soy sauce
- 2 green onions, finely chopped
- 2 garlic cloves, minced
- 1 tablespoon sugar
- ⅛ teaspoon black pepper
- ½ tablespoon sesame seed oil or vegetable oil
- 1 pound roast, sliced into ⅛-inch strips
- 4 to 6 cups cooked rice

■ Prepare the marinade by mixing the soy sauce, onions, garlic, sugar, pepper, oil, and 2 tablespoons water in a bowl. Pour the mixture over the slices of beef, cover, and let marinate in the refrigerator 2 to 5 hours, or refrigerate overnight for better results. Stir occasionally.

■ Heat a skillet over medium-high heat. Cook the beef strips for 2 to 3 minutes on each side, until browned. Serve with rice.

Note: The beef is easier to slice thinly when it is slightly frozen.

—Bobbie S. Oh
Centerville, Ohio

SWEET AND SOUR MEATLOAF

Serves 6 to 8

1 (15-ounce) can tomato sauce
½ cup firmly packed brown sugar
½ cup white vinegar
1½ to 2 teaspoons yellow mustard
2 pounds ground chuck
½ to 1 pound ground pork
1 cup chopped onion
½ cup dry bread crumbs or cracker crumbs
2 eggs, beaten
1½ teaspoons salt
¼ teaspoon pepper

■ Preheat the oven to 350°F.

■ Mix the tomato sauce, brown sugar, vinegar, and mustard in a bowl and stir until the sugar is dissolved.

■ Combine the beef and pork in a bowl. Add the onion, bread or cracker crumbs, eggs, salt, and pepper, and ½ cup of the tomato sauce mixture. Mix together with your hands and shape into a loaf, making one large (9 x 5-inch) or two smaller (5 x 2-inch) loaves. Place into a pan at least 1½ to 2 inches deep.

■ Pour the remaining tomato sauce over the top and bake for about 1 hour. Baste occasionally with the sauce.

■ When done, remove the meatloaf from the pan. Skim the fat off the sauce. Serve the sauce on the side.

—Margaret Drafall
Elgin, Illinois

LITTLE CRANBERRY MEATLOAVES

Leftovers are great for sandwiches.

Serves 6 to 8

  1 pound lean ground beef
  1 cup cooked rice
  ½ cup tomato juice
  1 egg, lightly beaten
  ¼ cup minced onion
  ½ teaspoon salt
  1 (16-ounce) can whole cranberry sauce
  ⅓ cup packed brown sugar
  1 tablespoon lemon juice

■ Preheat the oven to 350°F. Lightly coat a 13 x 9-inch baking dish with oil and set aside.

■ For the meatloaves, combine the beef, rice, tomato juice, egg, onion, and salt in a large bowl. Mix thoroughly.

■ Shape the mixture into two individual loaves and arrange them side by side in the prepared baking dish.

■ Combine the cranberry sauce, brown sugar, and lemon juice in a bowl and stir to mix well. Spoon the sauce over the loaves.

■ Bake for 40 minutes. Transfer the meatloaves to a warm platter. Pour the cranberry sauce gravy from the baking dish into a gravy boat and serve with the meatloaves.

—Mary Lou Van Dyke
Lincoln, Nebraska

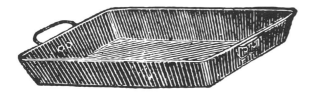

BEEF GOOLOP

This was a special company meal in my husband's childhood. He couldn't remember the name and renamed it for the sound it made dropping from the spoon.

Serves 6

3 tablespoons vegetable oil, divided
2 pounds beef, cut into 1-inch pieces
1 large onion, chopped
½ cup chopped celery
1 garlic clove, minced
2 tablespoons flour
1 (4-ounce) can mushrooms
1 cup sour cream or yogurt
1 (8-ounce) can tomato sauce
1 tablespoon Worcestershire sauce
1 teaspoon salt
¼ teaspoon pepper
4 to 6 cups cooked rice or mashed potatoes

■ Preheat the oven to 325°F. Grease a 13 x 9-inch baking dish with 1 tablespoon of the oil and set aside.

■ Add the remaining 2 tablespoons of oil to a skillet over medium-high heat. When shimmering hot, add the beef and cook for 2 to 3 minutes, stirring to brown on all sides. Add the onion and celery and cook for 2 more minutes. Add the garlic and sauté until golden. Stir in the flour. Add the mushrooms, sour cream or yogurt, tomato sauce, Worcestershire sauce, salt, and pepper.

■ Transfer to the prepared baking dish. Bake for 45 minutes uncovered. Cover to prevent all the liquid from evaporating and the food from getting too dry. Bake for 45 minutes more.

■ Serve over rice or mashed potatoes.

—Sharon Bunch Helbert
Broadway, Virginia

SLOPPY JOES

This recipe was a favorite at our small mom and pop store when it was still in existence. I'd make them on the same day once a week, and they sold out every time.

Serves 6

    1 tablespoon oil
    1 pound lean ground beef
    1 small or medium yellow onion, finely chopped
    ½ cup chili sauce
    ½ cup ketchup
    2 tablespoons yellow mustard
    2 tablespoons sugar
    ¼ cup white vinegar
    1 tablespoon Worcestershire sauce
    1 teaspoon salt
    Dash of pepper
    6 hamburger buns (warmed if preferred)

- Add the oil to a skillet over medium heat. Add the ground beef and onion. Sauté for 10 minutes, stirring often.

- Slowly add the chili sauce, ketchup, mustard, sugar, vinegar, Worcestershire sauce, salt, pepper and ⅓ cup water. Simmer for 20 minutes, uncovered.

- Fill split hamburger buns and serve.

Note: To make these a little less sloppy, add a ⅓ cup finely crushed cereal like corn flakes or crisp rice during the last 10 minutes of simmering.

Variation: For Zucchini Sloppy Joes, add 4 cups diced zucchini to the beef and instead of the chili sauce, mustard, sugar, vinegar, and Worcestershire sauce use 2 teaspoons brown sugar, an extra ½ cup ketchup, and 1 tablespoon grated Parmesan cheese. Thanks to Miriam Wagner of Elkhart, Indiana.

—J. Suzann Rhoades
Shippensburg, Pennsylvania

SLOW COOKING
THROUGH THE YEARS

Times may change, but the demand for time-saving cooking methods and appliances does not.

Even in the early days of the *Inglenook Cook Book*, sisters across the denomination were eager for recipes that would minimize the amount of time spent in the kitchen. As evidenced in the 1911 edition, they found slight relief in the form of the "fireless cooker," a simple, insulated container into which one or two preheated vessels of food could be placed for slow cooking.

After initial preparation on a stovetop, rice could be coaxed to tenderness in one to two hours. Dried lima beans required three hours of fireless cooking, while cornmeal mush took five or more. Hulled wheat was an overnight affair.

"It is supposed that most cereals can be cooked sufficiently within a few minutes, but they really require considerably more time in the cooking to make them thoroughly digestible," said the 1911 cookbook in support of fireless cooking (p. 160). "These can be cooked in the fireless cooker for several hours with the least amount of gas or other fuel, to say nothing of the need of watching to prevent burning or boiling over."

The cookbook devoted four pages of its vegetable section to fireless cooking. The May 30, 1911, issue of *The Inglenook* magazine also took up the cause of fireless cooking by publishing specific instructions for assemblage of a fireless cooker. Among the components were hay, old newspapers, buckets, and lard cans. Not surprisingly, these items were commonplace in Brethren households of the early 1900s.

A quick study of those quaint, although somewhat scholarly, instructions brings to mind a more modern kitchen appliance, the electric slow cooker, which now may be purchased—thankfully—for not much more than the price of the ingredients in a good, meaty stew.

Whereas foods cooked in a fireless cooker required a specific amount of stovetop heating, most foods prepared in a modern slow cooker require no preheating or precooking, unless, of course, the cook wishes to brown or sear meat to enhance flavor and texture. With a slow cooker, a few minutes of morning preparation result in a perfectly cooked evening entrée.

By 1942, the year the *Granddaughter's Inglenook Cookbook* was published, the fireless cooker craze apparently had run its course, because fireless cooker recipes disappeared from the book. The concept of slow cooking has returned, however, in *The New Inglenook Cookbook* with the inclusion of modern slow cooker recipes. Clearly, contemporary cooks also demand recipes for foods that don't need to be micromanaged to be delicious.

Electric slow cookers made their debut in the appliance aisles of local hardware stores in the 1970s. Nearly every modern kitchen now has one, or possibly two, tucked away in an easily accessible cupboard. Many slow cookers have dials with only two heat settings—low and high. Other more expensive models feature digital displays, timers, and adjustable heat. But the transformative power of low, moist heat is accessible through every model. As was the case with fireless cookers, electric slow cookers are maximally efficient when no heat is allowed to escape during cooking. In other words, no peeking once the lid has been lowered!

Most importantly, slow cookers have revolutionized carry-in dinners. Casseroles and stews transported to church in slow cookers are hot and ready whenever the lines begin to form. Amen.

—Janette Hess
McPherson, Kansas

A FIRELESS COOKER

The principle of the [fireless] cooker is quite simple. All that is necessary is to heat the food to the cooking point and then surround it with some material that is a good nonconductor [such as newspaper], and by keeping the heat from escaping the cooking will be completed without more heating.

—M. F. Hale, *The Inglenook* magazine, May 30, 1911

Savory Slow Cooker Beef Sandwiches

Gluten-free rolls can be easily substituted for the wheat sandwich rolls, making this a great gluten-free treat. This is a wonderful alternative to barbecue beef sandwiches.

Serves 8 to 10

- 1 tablespoon dried minced onion
- 2 teaspoons salt
- 2 teaspoons garlic powder
- 2 teaspoons dried oregano
- 1 teaspoon dried rosemary
- 1 teaspoon dried marjoram
- 1 teaspoon caraway seeds
- 1 teaspoon celery seeds
- ¼ teaspoon cayenne pepper
- 1 (3- to 4-pound) boneless chuck roast
- 8 to 10 sandwich rolls, split

■ Combine the onion, salt, garlic powder, oregano, rosemary, marjoram, caraway seeds, celery seeds, and cayenne pepper; rub over the chuck roast completely. Place in a slow cooker. Cover and cook on low for 6 to 8 hours or until the meat is tender.

■ Shred with a fork and serve on the rolls.

—Catherine A. Patrick
Lindsborg, Kansas

SLOW COOKER APPRECIATION

I love my slow cooker! It is a must for our church soup-suppers and carry-in dinners. Slow cookers are the foundation for preparing our large family Thanksgiving dinners. Most of the side dishes (potatoes, veggies, gravy, etc.) are heated in slow cookers, saving stove and oven space for other menu items. I'm glad they now come in several different sizes.

—Karen Hoch
McPherson, Kansas

Barbecued Beef Sandwiches

Serves 12

3 pounds boneless chuck roast
1½ cups ketchup
¼ cup packed brown sugar
¼ cup red wine vinegar
2 tablespoons Dijon mustard
2 tablespoons Worcestershire sauce

1 teaspoon liquid
  smoke flavoring
½ teaspoon salt
¼ teaspoon pepper
¼ teaspoon garlic powder
12 hamburger buns

■ Place the roast in a slow cooker. Combine the ketchup, brown sugar, vinegar, mustard, Worcestershire sauce, liquid smoke, salt, pepper, and garlic powder. Stir to mix well and pour over the roast.

■ Cover and cook for 8 to 10 hours on low or for 4 to 5 hours on high. Remove the meat and shred with a fork.

■ Place the shredded beef back in the slow cooker, stir to coat evenly with the sauce. Spoon onto the buns and top with more sauce.

—Al Zebrowski
Oakton, Virginia

Spicy Beef Burgers

Serves 6

1½ pounds lean ground beef
1 medium onion, chopped fine
¾ cup soft bread crumbs
¼ cup milk
½ cup ketchup

2 teaspoons horseradish
2 teaspoons Worcestershire
  sauce
1 tablespoon prepared mustard
1½ teaspoons salt

■ Combine the beef, onion, bread crumbs, milk, ketchup, horseradish, Worcestershire sauce, mustard, and salt and mix well. Shape into patties and grill on a hot grill until cooked to your desired degree of doneness.

—Helen May Rocha
Northwood, Ohio

CABBAGE ROLLS

Makes 20 to 25 rolls

1 cup uncooked rice
1 large head of cabbage
2½ pounds lean cooked ground beef
1½ teaspoons salt
¼ teaspoon pepper
2¼ tablespoons minced onion
1 (10¾-ounce) can tomato soup, divided

- Prepare the rice according to the package directions. It should make about 4 cups cooked rice.

- Remove the core and steam the cabbage in a steamer. Remove the outer leaves that separate easily (about 20 leaves) from the head and reserve or cook the remaining cabbage for another use. Continue steaming the outer leaves for 3 to 5 minutes. Drain; cool slightly.

- Combine the rice, beef, salt, pepper, and onion with ½ can of the tomato soup in a bowl and stir until well mixed.

- Preheat the oven to 350°F. Coat a 13 x 9-inch baking dish with oil or butter and set aside.

- Place about ½ cup of the beef and rice mixture on each cabbage leaf, roll up tightly, and place side by side in the prepared baking dish. Pour the remaining ½ can of soup diluted with an equal amount of water over the rolls.

- Bake for 1½ hours, covered to prevent the tops of the rolls from drying out.

—Darlene Uhrich
Wenatchee, Washington

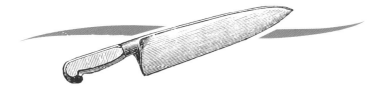

PASTITSIO

This is a Greek recipe. It has become a family favorite over the years and is often requested by my grandchildren.

Serves 6

1 cup dry elbow macaroni
1 pound ground beef
½ cup chopped onion
1 (8-ounce) can tomato sauce
¼ cup grated Parmesan cheese, divided
½ teaspoon salt
½ teaspoon dried thyme, crushed
¼ teaspoon ground cinnamon plus some for garnish
1½ cups milk
½ teaspoon salt
3 tablespoons flour
2 eggs, beaten

■ Lightly coat a 13 x 9-inch baking dish with oil and set aside. Cook the macaroni according to package instructions. Drain.

■ Brown the beef and onion in a skillet over medium-high heat until the beef is cooked through; drain. Stir in the cooked macaroni, tomato sauce, 2 tablespoons of the Parmesan cheese, salt, thyme, and cinnamon and cook until heated through. Spread the beef mixture into the prepared baking dish.

■ Preheat the oven to 375°F.

■ In a blender, mix the milk, salt, and flour. Blend thoroughly and then pour into a saucepan over low heat. Add the eggs and stir until just thickened. Stir in the remaining Parmesan cheese. Pour the sauce over the top of the beef mixture. Sprinkle with cinnamon.

■ Bake for 30 minutes, or until a knife inserted into the center comes out clean. Let stand for 10 minutes before serving.

—Elaine R. Smith
Bridgewater, Virginia

STROMBOLI

This is a favorite of campers at Camp Colorado.

Serves 6

- 1 pound frozen bread dough, thawed
- 2 tablespoons butter
- 1 tablespoon mustard
- 1 pound ground beef, browned and drained
- 8 ounces American cheese, shredded
- 8 ounces mozzarella cheese, shredded
- 3 ounces pepperoni slices
- 4 ounces (¼ pound) ham, thinly sliced
- 1 (14-ounce) jar pizza sauce (optional)

- Preheat the oven to 350°F. Line a baking sheet with parchment paper and set aside.

- Roll the dough into a rectangle. Spread with butter and mustard. Layer the ground beef, American cheese, mozzarella, pepperoni, and ham on half the dough. Fold the dough over and seal. Transfer to the prepared baking sheet, seam side down, and bake for 20 minutes.

- Slice into serving sizes and serve with pizza sauce, if desired.

Variation: For a Spicy Mushroom Stromboli, add 1 (4-ounce) can sliced mushrooms, use salami instead of the pepperoni, and add ½ grilled onion. Thanks to Sharon L. Barr of Ashland, Ohio.

—Anna Marie Achilles
Quinter, Kansas

HOBGOBLIN GOULASH

We made this recipe after Halloween, cutting up the jack-o-lanterns
or using pumpkins from the garden. It has a special place in the hearts
of my adult offspring. This recipe calls for chili seasoning mix because
that's easier. But I usually use a mixture of chili powder, ground cumin,
and garlic powder, adjusting for my family's taste.

6 servings

2 slices bacon, diced
1 pound ground beef
1 medium onion, chopped
1 green bell pepper, coarsely chopped
1½ cups pumpkin or winter squash, peeled and cubed
1 (15-ounce) can tomatoes
1 (15-ounce) can kidney beans, undrained
1 (1¾-ounce) envelope chili seasoning mix
1 cup uncooked elbow macaroni

■ Cook the bacon in a large saucepan over medium heat until crisp but not brown. Drain on paper towels.

■ Cook the ground beef, onion, and bell pepper in the bacon drippings over medium heat. Pour off the excess fat.

■ Add the pumpkin or squash, tomatoes, beans, chili seasoning, cooked bacon, and 2½ cups water to the beef in the saucepan. Bring to a boil over high heat.

■ Add the macaroni, cover, and reduce the heat to medium low. Simmer, stirring occasionally, for 15 minutes or until the macaroni and vegetables are tender.

—Merry Christina Roy
East Wenatchee, Washington

Lynn's Beef Brisket

Serves 10 to 12

5 pounds beef brisket
⅓ cup lemon juice (2 to 3 lemons)
⅓ cup packed brown sugar
½ cup ketchup
1 tablespoon brown or yellow mustard
3 tablespoons Worcestershire sauce
1 teaspoon salt
2 tablespoons cornstarch

■ Preheat the oven to 275°F.

■ Place the beef brisket in a large Dutch oven. Combine the lemon juice, brown sugar, ketchup, mustard, Worcestershire sauce, and salt in a bowl. Mix well and pour over the brisket. Cover with the lid and bake for 4 hours, until the meat is falling apart.

■ Remove the brisket and let it cool. Skim off the fat from the broth and discard, and then place the Dutch oven over medium heat. Mix the cornstarch with 2 tablespoons water, add to the broth, and cook until thickened, about 8 minutes. Either serve the gravy on the side or pour it back over the brisket, and warm briefly in the oven before serving.

—Carolyn Dooley
Hutchinson, Kansas

Love Feast Sandwiches

When I was a child, my parents were deacons in the First Church of the Brethren, Long Beach, California. At love feast twice a year they served these ground meat sandwiches—white bread slathered with butter, ground meat, and another piece of white bread with butter. I loved those sandwiches! After love feast my parents, being deacons, were able to take some of these sandwiches home. Mom toasted them the next day for breakfast, and they were even better than the night before.

—Jan Dull Eller
Portland, Oregon

ROULADEN

This is a German dish we have all learned to enjoy. It was passed down from an exchange student. It can be made on top of the stove, but I find the slow cooker is an easier way to prepare it. This is wonderful when served with mashed potatoes or noodles. Leftovers make great sandwiches.

Serves 8 to 10

2 pounds round steak
3 teaspoons prepared mustard
Salt and pepper
4 slices bacon, cut in thirds
6 dill pickle spears, halved
2 tablespoons vegetable oil
½ cup flour

■ Trim the fat off the steak and then cut into 2-inch thick strips. Pound the strips to about 1 inch thick to tenderize them. Spread each steak strip with mustard and season with salt and pepper to taste.

■ Wrap a piece of bacon around a pickle spear and place it on the steak. Roll the steak over the pickle and secure with two toothpicks.

■ Heat the oil in a large skillet over medium-high heat. Brown the steak rolls in hot oil. Transfer to a slow cooker.

■ When finished browning all the steak rolls, add the flour to the oil and brown, about 1 minute. Add 1 cup water to make a medium-thick gravy. Pour the gravy over the steaks in the slow cooker.

■ Cook on high for 1 hour, and cook on low for 4 to 5 hours.

—Betty Myers
Harrisonburg, Virginia

BEEF FILETS WITH SPICY CREAM SAUCE

Feel free to substitute your favorite steak seasoning for the salt and pepper. This recipe calls for two tablespoons of hot sauce. Although this sounds like a lot, it mellows some during cooking.

Serves 4

- 4 (4- to 6-ounce) beef tenderloin filets
- Salt and pepper to taste
- 3 tablespoons butter
- 3 tablespoons Worcestershire sauce
- 2 tablespoons Tabasco sauce
- ½ cup half-and-half

- Preheat the oven to 350°F.

- Season both sides of each filet with salt and pepper.

- Preheat a large, well-seasoned iron skillet or an ovensafe non-stick skillet over high heat until hot. Sear the seasoned filets for 1 minute on each side. Turn off the heat. Add the butter, Worcestershire sauce, and hot sauce. Place the uncovered skillet in the oven and cook until the steaks reach a desired degree of doneness. This will take approximately 12 minutes for medium and 15 minutes for well done.

- When done, remove them from the oven and set aside on a platter covered with foil to keep warm.

- Add the half-and-half to the skillet, stirring over a low heat. Scrape up the browned bits from the skillet and stir until the sauce is thickened and the half-and-half is warmed through, about 8 minutes. Do not allow the sauce to boil.

- Pour some of the spicy cream sauce over each steak to serve. Can be served with rice, noodles, or mashed potatoes.

—Julia K. Miller
Charleston, Illinois

Sweet and Sour Beef

The recipe can be served over rice, mashed potatoes, or noodles. *Leftovers can be made into burritos or sandwiches.*

Serves 10 to 12

   2 tablespoons vegetable oil
   2 pounds boneless round or chuck steak, cut into 1-inch cubes
   2 (8-ounce) cans tomato sauce
   2 cups sliced carrots
   2 cups pearl onions
   1 large green bell pepper, cut into 1-inch pieces
   ½ cup molasses
   ⅓ cup cider vinegar
   ¼ cup sugar
   2 teaspoons chili powder
   2 teaspoons paprika
   1 teaspoon salt

■ Heat the oil in a large skillet over medium-high heat. Brown the steak in the hot oil; transfer to a slow cooker. Add the tomato sauce, carrots, onions, bell pepper, molasses, vinegar, sugar, chili powder, paprika, and salt; stir well.

■ Cover and cook on low for 7 to 8 hours, until the meat is tender. When done you can thicken the sauce, if desired, in a saucepan mixed with a cornstarch slurry (1 tablespoon cornstarch mixed with 2 tablespoons cold water) and heated over medium-low heat.

—Catherine A. Patrick
Lindsborg, Kansas

VIETNAMESE BEEF AND VEGETABLES

When we were waiting to adopt our Vietnamese daughter, I took a  *cooking class with a Vietnamese woman in Boston. This recipe became very popular with our whole family, not just with Mai Anh. This recipe can be easily extended with more flank steak and broccoli.*

Serves 3 to 4

½ pound flank steak
1½ tablespoons soy sauce
3 tablespoons wine vinegar diluted with 1 tablespoon water
1 teaspoon cornstarch
1 teaspoon salt
½ teaspoon pepper
1 tablespoon vegetable oil
2 cups chopped broccoli florets
1 onion, cut into thin wedges
Fish sauce (optional)
2 cups cooked rice or Asian noodles

■ Cut the flank steak across the grain in thin slices. Combine the soy sauce, vinegar, cornstarch, salt, and pepper in a shallow bowl. Add the flank steak and set aside.

■ Add the oil to a skillet or wok over medium-high heat. Fry the broccoli in the hot oil, adding 1 tablespoon water after 3 to 4 minutes and frying until the broccoli is tender, about 7 minutes total.

■ Remove the broccoli and add the onion and flank steak to the skillet or wok. Stir with chopsticks or a wooden spoon, adding the broccoli while the meat is still rare. Cook until the meat is cooked through, about 5 minutes. Season with fish sauce to taste. Serve with rice or Asian noodles.

Note: Fish sauce is found in the Asian section of the grocery store.

—Merry Christina Roy
East Wenatchee, Washington

CALLING FOR A CROWD

Pot roast—just the words bring memories of Sunday dinners, cold winter evenings, and family gatherings at the beach.

My husband's mother faithfully made a pot roast every Sunday. She followed the Pennsylvania Dutch tradition that you shouldn't work too much on the sabbath, so this was an easy meal to get ready the night before. When you got home from church, all you had to do was set the table and eat. After we were married, I went to my in-laws for pot roast about once a month. My mother-in-law still cooked one every Sunday. You can imagine why my beloved asked me not to serve him pot roast for a while.

I remember my mom making pot roast a lot in the winter. She could prepare this wonderful meal while we were in school, feed us once school was out, and then still have an incredible meal for my dad when he arrived home hours later. Her standby was the "Pot Roast of Beef with Vegetables" recipe from the *Granddaughter's Inglenook Cookbook*, but she usually added onions and an envelope of onion soup mix (p. 191). We always knew what was for supper as soon as we walked in—the smell of the meat and vegetables cooking would permeate the house and make our tummies rumble. A few days later, Mom would chop up the leftovers, add some Worcestershire sauce, and create an easy, hearty beef stew. Two tasty meals came from one—a great busy cook's time-saver.

For years, my extended family gathered in North Carolina at the beach, for a week-long family reunion. We came from all over—Pennsylvania, Florida, Massachusetts, Montana, and Maine. As the grandkids were being born, Christmas became too hectic for all of us to get together, so summertime was family time. And it may sound funny, but pot roast was the best beach meal ever. We spent the morning at the beach, had lunch, and then during afternoon nap-and-game time we'd start the pot roast. Then it was back to the beach. After a day of fun in the sun, you'd be welcomed back by the smell of savory beef and onions. It was such an easy meal with no last-minute preparation, and there was something to please everyone—even toddlers could pick up the bite-size chunks.

You don't make pot roast for two people. No, a pot roast calls for a crowd—family, friends, a warm gathering of loved ones. It's like an everyday Thanksgiving, cooking for hours and blessing everyone with a wonderful smell and opportunities for conversation and laughter. And although pot roasts make a lot of food, they're economical because you can use low heat to slowly transform a tough, inexpensive cut of beef into a tender, one-pot meal.

There are two pot roast recipes in this Inglenook incarnation. Both make an easy, delicious meal, but Patricia L. DeHook's "California Pot Roast" has a different twist. The tangy, sweet tomato sauce gives it a barbecue-like flavor. Pot roasts are quite versatile, and once you're comfortable with a basic recipe, don't be afraid to be creative. I always add onions and button mushrooms, and sometimes sweet potatoes. I'm working up to turnips—my sister and mother say they're delicious. Tap into your inner cook and have fun! After all, creating good food is a Brethren tradition. And sharing good food with loved ones provides nourishment for body and soul.

—Nancy Brubaker Dotter
Wyomissing, Pennsylvania

POT ROAST OF BEEF WITH VEGETABLES

2 lb. beef	1 tb. salt
6 large carrots	Pepper
6 potatoes	

Select a less tender cut of meat. Arrange all in heavy covered utensil. Heat rapidly to steaming, then reduce heat and cook slowly for several hours. When ready to serve place meat on large platter and arrange vegetables around it. Make gravy by adding 2 tb. flour mixed to paste with a little milk or water to the broth left after vegetables and meat are removed. Cook until thickened.

—Mrs. Wayne L. Goar, Hagerstown, Indiana

California Pot Roast

This has been my son's requested "birthday dinner" for many years. This recipe is tender, tasty, and different. It could be made in a slow cooker.

Serves 6 to 8

    3 tablespoons vegetable oil
    4 to 5 pounds chuck or rump pot roast
    2 teaspoons salt
    ¼ teaspoon pepper
    1 (8-ounce) can tomato sauce
    3 medium onions, thinly sliced
    2 garlic cloves, minced
    2 tablespoons firmly packed brown sugar
    ½ teaspoon dry mustard
    ¼ cup lemon juice
    ¼ cup vinegar
    ¼ cup ketchup
    1 tablespoon Worcestershire sauce
    6 tablespoons flour

■ Heat the vegetable oil in a Dutch oven over medium-high heat. Brown the roast on all sides, about 8 minutes total. Add the salt, pepper, ½ cup water, tomato sauce, onions, and garlic. Bring to a boil, then reduce the heat to medium low and simmer for 1½ hours.

■ Combine the brown sugar, mustard, lemon juice, vinegar, ketchup, and Worcestershire sauce in a bowl and mix well. Pour the sauce over the meat. Cover and simmer for 1½ hours or until tender.

■ When done transfer the meat to a platter. Skim off most of the fat; pour the broth into a large measuring cup. Add enough water to make 3 cups. Return the liquid to the Dutch oven.

■ Mix the flour with ½ cup water to make a smooth paste. Stir into the broth. Cook, stirring constantly, until the mixture comes to a boil. Boil for 1 minute or until desired thickness.

■ Slice the roast and serve with the gravy.

—Patricia L. DeHook
Pemberville, Ohio

Pot Roast Carrots

My middle daughter would not eat carrots— raw, cooked, shredded, or otherwise. No matter how I tried to hide them, the dog always ended up getting them. When my mom came to visit she made a pot roast for dinner, and she heard Sarah's whole carrots-are-icky speech. "Sarah, have you ever tried *pot roast carrots*? They are so yummy, and they're Grandma's favorite." I watched with a smirk as my mom speared a carrot and offered it to Sarah, and then my mouth dropped open. "Oh, Grandma, these are so yummy! I love them." Sarah proceeded to eat more carrots than meat. Grandmas and granddaughters—they have a very special connection.

—Nancy Brubaker Dotter
Wyomissing, Pennsylvania

CLASSIC POT ROAST

Serves 8 to 12

3 to 4 pounds bottom round roast
1 cup black coffee
1 medium onion, sliced
2 tablespoons garlic powder
2 tablespoons rosemary
2 tablespoons thyme
2 tablespoon paprika
1 tablespoon sage
1 tablespoon lemon pepper
1 tablespoon salt

■ Preheat the oven to 350°F.

■ Place the roast in a roasting pan. Combine the coffee, 1 cup hot water, onion, garlic powder, rosemary, thyme, paprika, sage, lemon pepper, and salt in a large bowl. Pour over the roast and bake for 30 minutes. Reduce the oven temperature to 300°F and bake an additional 3 to 4 hours.

—Dorothy Kesner
Ridgeville, West Virginia

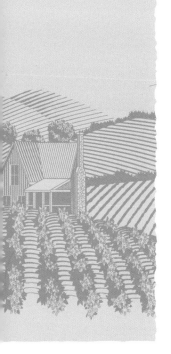

Salisbury Steaks

Ground deer meat can be substituted for part or all of the beef. It will give it a lean and natural flavor.

Serves 12

2½ to 3 pounds ground beef
3 tablespoons vegetable oil, divided
1 cup flour
1 cup chopped onion
1 cup chopped red or green bell pepper
4 tablespoons cornstarch
1 cup ketchup
3 cups tomato juice, divided
¼ teaspoon black pepper
1 teaspoon chili powder

■ Preheat the oven to 350°F.

■ Form the ground beef into 12 hamburger patties. Heat 2 tablespoons of the oil in a large skillet over medium heat. Dredge the hamburgers in flour, shake off any excess, and fry in the hot oil for about 5 minutes per side, until both sides are well browned. Transfer the hamburgers to a 13 x 9-inch baking dish.

■ Using the same skillet with the remaining oil, cook the onion and bell pepper over medium heat until tender, about 7 minutes. Stir often.

■ In a small bowl, stir together the cornstarch, ketchup, and 1 cup of the tomato juice. Add this to the onion and bell pepper in the skillet and stir. Add the remaining tomato juice, black pepper, and chili powder. Stir until it thickens. Pour the sauce over the hamburgers and bake for 30 minutes.

—Jim and Clareen Dunn
Mulberry Grove, Illinois

JACKPOT PIE

This has been my favorite dish as long as I can remember. I've even submitted the recipe to the food service at my university, hoping that someday they'll make it for all of us.

Serves 10 to 12

- 2 pounds ground beef or ground turkey
- ½ cup chopped onion
- 2 (10-ounce) cans condensed tomato soup
- 1 (8-ounce) package medium egg noodles
- 2 tablespoons Worcestershire sauce
- 2 (15-ounce) cans creamed corn
- 1 cup grated Cheddar cheese
- Salt and pepper

■ Preheat oven to 350°F. Lightly coat a 13 x 9-inch baking dish with oil and set aside.

■ Brown the meat in a large saucepan over medium heat. Add the onion and cook till just softened, about 4 minutes.

■ Add the soup, 3 cups water, and uncooked noodles. Bring to a boil, reduce the heat to low, and simmer for 10 minutes. Add the Worcestershire sauce, corn, and cheese. Season to taste with salt and pepper. Pour into the prepared baking dish and bake for 40 minutes.

—Catherine Ullery
Olympia, Washington

CALICO BEANS

Serves 8

½ pound bacon, cut into 1-inch pieces
1 pound ground beef
1 onion, diced
½ to ¾ cup brown sugar
2 (15-ounce) cans pork and beans
1 (15-ounce) can lima beans
1 (15-ounce) can kidney beans
1 tablespoon vinegar
1 cup ketchup
1 to 2 teaspoons mustard

■ Preheat the oven to 350°F. Or you can use a slow cooker on high. Lightly grease a 13 x 9-inch baking dish with oil or cooking spray and set aside.

■ Cook the bacon in a large skillet or saucepan over medium heat for about 7 minutes. Drain the skillet, add the ground beef and onion, and continue to cook until the ground beef is browned. Drain any excess fat.

■ Add the brown sugar, pork and beans, lima beans, kidney beans, vinegar, ketchup, and mustard and stir. Pour into the prepared baking dish and bake for 30 to 45 minutes. Or pour into a slow cooker and cook on high for 1 hour.

—JoAnne C. Bowie
Greenville, Ohio

SPINACH AND CHEESE CASSEROLE

Serves 10

2 (10-ounce) packages frozen spinach, thawed
½ cup (1 stick) butter, melted and divided
1 cup chopped onion
2 garlic cloves, minced
6 eggs, beaten
1 (16-ounce) package ricotta cheese
4 cups (16 ounces) grated Cheddar cheese
2 tablespoons flour
Salt and pepper to taste

- Preheat the oven to 350°F. Lightly grease a 13 x 9-inch baking dish and set aside.

- Drain the spinach well.

- Heat 2 tablespoons of the butter in a large saucepan over medium heat. Sauté the onion and garlic in the butter until the onion is translucent, about 7 minutes.

- Combine the spinach, eggs, ricotta and Cheddar cheeses, flour, and the remaining butter in a bowl and stir to mix. Add to the sautéed onions and garlic. Season with salt and pepper.

- Pour into the prepared dish and bake for 1 hour.

Note: To make this gluten free you can use cornstarch instead of the flour.

—Connie Burk Davis
Westminster, Maryland

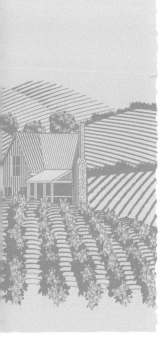

Chicken, Broccoli, and Rice Casserole

When my family went to an Annual Conference in Wichita, Kansas, we stayed with my husband's cousin in Derby, Kansas. She didn't know anything about our tastes, but we loved this casserole, and I have served it many times, even to people who don't like broccoli.

Serves 10 to 12

- 3 (10-ounce) packages frozen broccoli
- 2 cups instant brown rice
- 4 cooked large chicken breasts, cut into bite-size pieces
- 2 (10-ounce) cans condensed cream of chicken soup
- 1 cup chicken broth
- 1 cup mayonnaise
- 2 teaspoons lemon juice
- 1 cup shredded Cheddar cheese
- 1 cup grated Parmesan cheese

- Preheat the oven to 350°F. Lightly grease a 13 x 9-inch baking dish.

- Cook the broccoli in boiling, salted water until barely tender, about 7 minutes. Drain and place in the prepared baking dish.

- Pour the instant brown rice over the broccoli. Cover the rice with chicken pieces.

- Combine the soup, broth, mayonnaise, lemon juice, and Cheddar cheese in a bowl. Spoon this mixture over the chicken layer. Sprinkle the Parmesan cheese on top. This can be made a day ahead and stored in the refrigerator.

- Bake for 25 to 30 minutes.

—Elaine Kessler Yost
Manchester, Kentucky

THE BLESSING OF LEFTOVERS

Our Brethren ancestors living in Penn's Woods in the eighteenth century had limited choices when it came to preparing meals. Very few had stoves for cooking, so most cooked over the fireplace using a collection of tools and utensils we would find foreign today. They relied on what we would call one-dish meals—stews and potpies to make their home-butchered meat or small game stretch to feed a family, or just to save time in meal preparation.

The 1911 *Inglenook Cook Book* contained several of these one-dish meals. One recipe for "Meat Pie" instructed the homemaker to cut up "any left-over meat," whether it is turkey, beef, or pork, and make rich, plentiful gravy to pour over it (p. 65). This meat-and-gravy stew was then covered with a crust and baked. The recipe submitter, Sister Allie Mohler, from Cando, North Dakota, notes that the "pie is best made in the dish it is to be served in," suggesting the efficiency and practicality of one-pot meals.

Our mothers and grandmothers, cooking in the 1930s and 1940s, had an entirely different cooking experience than their grandmothers. Gone were open fireplaces, and for many, even wood stoves. Electric and gas ranges were becoming the mainstay in many kitchens, with temperature-regulated ovens and burners on top that provided quick, even heat.

They also had access to foods that would have astounded (or scandalized) their grandmothers. Conveniences like canned foods—bought at the store, not made at home—were common, and packaged novelties like macaroni, potato chips, and hot dogs were changing how women cooked. But even though the kitchen had a new face, one important principle remained: "Use it up, wear it out, make it do, or do without." In the kitchen, this meant every scrap of food was used.

The 1942 *Granddaughter's Inglenook Cookbook* included an entire chapter on leftovers ("Monday's Meat Pie" is an example, p. 170), as well as a chapter of one-dish meals, "healthful and delectable timesavers" (p. 207). It was around this time that the term casserole was first used, meaning a one-dish meal cooked and served *en casserole*—a French term that originally referred to the baking dish, but in America had come to mean the recipe itself.

We twenty-first-century descendants of our Depression-era grandmothers are faced with a kitchen and cooking styles as different from our grandmothers as theirs were from their immigrant ancestors. We're more likely to live in the city rather than the country. Our milk, eggs, and cheese come from the dairy section of our local supermarket rather than the farm. Our range is only one of several appliances at our disposal—a variety that includes the microwave, slow cooker, and outdoor grill.

Our ingredients are different too, with food fads dictating what the newest diet should be, and a commercial, global food distribution system that causes us to take for granted such miracles as fresh strawberries available for sale in January.

But we are still attached to our roots and cherish our comfort foods and casseroles, such as Lois J. Beckman's "Nina's Zucchini Casserole." We honor our grandmothers in the kitchen by using up leftovers, balancing our meals with a variety of vegetables, and adapting classic recipes to our modern lifestyles. And we find that we still value the same things our grandmothers did when they fixed countless one-dish meals for their families: simple food, simple pleasures, and making time to be together.

—Jan Tomlonson Drexler
Rapid City, South Dakota

MONDAY'S MEAT PIE

½ c. diced celery
½ c. diced onion, if desired
¼ - ½ c. chopped green pepper, if desired
2 c. cubed leftover beef
1 c. cubed leftover potatoes
1 c. cubed leftover carrots
1 c. cooked peas
1 c. gravy
4 slices dried bread cubed

Brown celery, onion and green pepper in hot fat; add combined meat, potatoes, carrots and peas. Add gravy and season to taste. Pour into casserole; top with bread cubes browned in butter. Bake in moderate oven 30 min. Serves 6.

—Mrs. Annie Holsinger, Kensington, Maryland

NINA'S ZUCCHINI CASSEROLE

This recipe belonged to my mother-in-law, who was a wonderful cook as well as a wonderful Christian woman. She taught me a lot about cooking and life. She was ninety-five when she passed away, and I miss her so much.

Serves 6 to 8

4 cups coarsely chopped zucchini

½ cup coarsely chopped onion

1 green bell pepper, chopped

1½ cups crumbled butter crackers (1½ sleeves)

1½ to 2 cups milk

2 cups grated mild Cheddar cheese

3 eggs, beaten

½ teaspoon black pepper

- Preheat the oven to 350°F. Coat a 13 x 9-inch baking dish with oil and set aside.

- Cook the zucchini, onion, and bell pepper in boiling, salted water for 5 minutes. Drain well.

- Combine the crackers, milk, cheese, eggs, and black pepper with the cooked vegetable mixture and pour into the prepared baking dish.

- Bake for 30 to 40 minutes or until a toothpick inserted in the center comes out clean.

—Lois J. Beckman
Eglon, West Virginia

MADE FROM SCRATCH

Family times at Grandma's house were filled with the anticipation of homemade noodles. One of the great-aunts would take Grandma's big wooden bread board to a quiet corner of the kitchen. Sitting on a chair with the bread board on her lap, she would roll out the dough thin as could be, and then roll it up from the edge to make a long log. With a sharp knife, she'd cut the log into thin slices, and then cut 2" lengths of noodle dough. Baked with stewed chicken and broth, these noodles were the highlight of the meal for me!

—Jan Tomlonson Drexler
Rapid City, South Dakota

Chicken Tortilla Casserole

My two sons loved this recipe growing up and still do to this day.
I always make a double recipe when they come over for dinner.

Serves 6 to 8

1 fryer (or 4 chicken breasts), cooked, skinned, and boned
1 (10-ounce) can condensed cream of chicken soup
½ to 1 cup salsa
2 tablespoons quick-cooking tapioca
6 to 8 corn tortillas, broken into large pieces and divided
1 medium onion, chopped or ¼ cup dried onion flakes, divided
2 cups grated Cheddar cheese, divided

- Cut the cooked chicken into bite-size pieces.

- Combine the chicken with the soup, salsa, and tapioca in a bowl.

- Spray the inside of a slow cooker with cooking spray. Line the bottom of the slow cooker with tortillas. Add ⅓ of the chicken and soup mixture, sprinkle ⅓ of the onion and cheese on top. Repeat with 2 more layers of tortillas, chicken-soup mixture, onion, and cheese.

- Cover and cook on high for 3 hours or on low for 6 to 8 hours.

Note: This recipe may easily be doubled, if desired.

—Diana M. Tucker
Glendora, California

Potluck Chicken Casserole

Serves 12 to 14

  8 cups cooked and cubed chicken
  2 (10¾-ounce) cans condensed
    cream of chicken soup, undiluted
  1 cup sour cream
  1 cup butter-flavored cracker crumbs
  2 tablespoons butter, melted

- Preheat the oven to 350°F. Lightly grease a 13 x 9-inch baking dish and set aside.

- Combine the chicken, soup, and sour cream. Spread into the prepared baking dish.

- Combine the cracker crumbs and butter and stir to mix. Sprinkle over the chicken mixture.

- Bake, uncovered, for 30 to 35 minutes or until bubbly.

—Judith F. Stoddard
Bridgewater, Virginia

Ham and Pea Casserole

Serves 6

  2 cups dry shell macaroni
  2 cups cooked and cubed ham
  1 cup frozen peas, thawed
  1 (10½-ounce) can cream of celery,
    chicken, or mushroom soup

  1½ cups milk
  ¼ pound American cheese,
    cubed
  Buttered bread crumbs

- Cook the macaroni in boiling, salted water for about 7 minutes; drain.

- Preheat the oven to 350°F. Lightly grease a 3-quart casserole dish and set aside.

- Combine the ham, peas, soup, milk, and cheese in a large bowl and mix together. Pour the macaroni into the prepared casserole dish.

- Add the ham mixture and top with the buttered bread crumbs. Bake for 30 minutes.

—Marcia S. Myer
Manheim, Pennsylvania

TACO CASSEROLE

This is one of my family's favorite recipes—even the teenagers and their friends love it.

Serves 6

1 pound ground beef
1 (15-ounce) can tomato sauce
1 (15-ounce) can kidney beans
1 (1½-ounce) package chili seasoning mix (about 3 tablespoons)
1½ cup broken corn chips
1 cup shredded Cheddar cheese
2 cups shredded lettuce
1 medium tomato, diced

■ Preheat the oven to 350°F.

■ Brown the ground beef in a large skillet over medium-high heat. Add the tomato sauce, beans, and chili seasoning and cook for 2 minutes. Reduce the heat to medium low and simmer for 5 more minutes. (Or make the chili according to the seasoning mix directions.)

■ Pour the chili mixture into a 2-quart casserole dish. Sprinkle with corn chips and cheese. Bake for 15 minutes till bubbly and the cheese is melted. Just before serving, top with lettuce and tomato.

—Jackie A. Eveland
Plymouth, Iowa

IMPOSSIBLE TACO PIE

This is a complete salad and main course in one. Add a light dessert and you have a whole meal.

Serves 8

1 pound ground beef
½ cup chopped onion
1 (1½-ounce) envelope taco seasoning (about 3 tablespoons)
1 (4-ounce) can green chiles (optional)
1¼ cups milk
¾ cup biscuit mix (see page 24)
3 eggs
1½ cups shredded Cheddar cheese
2½ cups chopped lettuce
2 medium tomatoes, chopped
1 cup sour cream

■ Preheat the oven to 400°F.

■ Brown the ground beef and onions in a large skillet over medium-high heat; drain. Stir in the taco seasoning. Spread the mixture in a 12-inch pie plate or a 10 x 7-inch baking dish. Spread the green chiles over the top, if using.

■ Combine the milk, biscuit mix, and eggs in a large bowl and beat until smooth. Pour over the ground beef and chiles.

■ Bake for 25 minutes. After removing from the oven, immediately spread the cheese on top.

■ Cut into slices or squares and serve hot with tomatoes, lettuce, and sour cream on the side.

—Joann C. Sanbloom
West Lafayette, Indiana

POTLUCKS WITH EXTRA FLAVOR

Many of the West Marva District congregational meetinghouses in the mid-twentieth century were located in areas where some churchgoers still depended on wood-fired stoves for food preparation. One vivid potluck memory includes the unique smoky flavor, however subtle, that added to the delectable taste of homegrown vegetables and meats that had been simmered and baked in the heat of wood-fueled flames. Those contributions to carry-in meals were often the first to disappear.

—Mike Fike
Morgantown, West Virginia

CHEESE AND BEEF CORNBREAD CASSEROLE

Serves 6

1 to 1½ pounds ground beef
1 cup chopped onion
½ teaspoon black pepper
1 (1½-ounce) package taco seasoning, or less, depending on taste
⅔ cup tomato sauce
1¼ cup cubed Cheddar or Longhorn cheese (about 8 ounces)
½ cup sliced green olives stuffed with pimentos
1 (8-ounce) package corn muffin mix
1 egg
1 cup milk

■ Preheat the oven to 350°F. Coat a 13 x 9-inch baking dish with cooking spray or oil and set aside.

■ In a large skillet over medium-high heat, sauté the ground beef, onion, and black pepper until the beef is no longer pink, about 7 minutes. Pour off any excess fat.

■ Mix the taco seasoning mix with 2 tablespoons water and add to the beef mixture. Stir and simmer for 2 to 3 minutes and then add the tomato sauce.

■ When the mixture starts to bubble again, remove it from the heat and stir in the cheese and olives. Spread the mixture evenly over the bottom of the prepared baking dish.

■ Combine the muffin mix with the egg and milk and stir to mix. Spread the batter evenly over the beef mixture.

■ Bake for 30 to 40 minutes until golden brown. Remove from the oven and let stand for 5 minutes. Loosen around the edges and invert onto a serving platter or serve directly from the baking dish.

—Barry L. Deardorff
North Manchester, Indiana

PIZZA CASSEROLE

The best thing about this recipe is that it is so easy to adjust for different tastes. Just add or subtract items you and your family or friends like on your pizza. It's also a great dish to take to carry-ins. You can use any kind of ground meat you like: beef, sausage, turkey, pork, or any combination. It can also be made for vegetarians—just hold the meat and add vegetables like green bell peppers, mushrooms, olives, whatever you like.

Serves 8 to 10

2 cups dry small shell macaroni
1 pound ground beef or pork (or combination)
1 onion, chopped
1 (14-ounce) can tomato sauce
1 cup pizza sauce
¼ teaspoon oregano
1 (8-ounce) package pepperoni
1 cup grated Parmesan cheese
2 cups shredded mozzarella cheese

- Preheat the oven to 350°F. Coat a 13 x 9-inch baking dish with oil and set aside.

- Cook the macaroni in boiling, salted water until just tender, about 7 minutes.

- Brown the ground beef or pork and onion in a large skillet over medium-high heat until the meat is no longer pink, about 10 minutes; drain off any excess fat. Add the macaroni and stir.

- Mix the tomato sauce, pizza sauce, and oregano together in a bowl. Pour over the macaroni mixture and gently stir until everything is evenly coated.

- Transfer the macaroni mixture to the prepared baking dish. Lay the pepperoni slices on top. Then sprinkle on the cheeses. Bake covered for 20 minutes and uncovered for 20 minutes more to brown the top.

—Jeannie Campbell
Beavercreek, Ohio

Pizza Loaf

Serves 8 to 10

DOUGH

1 (.3-ounce) package dry yeast
1 cup warm (100 to 110°F) water
3¾ cup flour
2 tablespoons sugar

⅓ cup dried milk
1 egg, beaten
¼ cup (½ stick) butter,
   melted

FILLING

1 (14- to 16-ounce) jar pizza sauce
1 (6-ounce) can tomato paste
1 (4-ounce) can sliced
   mushrooms (or 1 cup fresh)
¼ cup chopped onion
1 teaspoon salt
¼ teaspoon black pepper
1 teaspoon oregano

½ teaspoon garlic powder
1 pound ground sausage
   or beef (or a combination),
   cooked and drained
1 (16-ounce) bag shredded
   mozzarella or pizza blend
   cheese

■ To make the dough, combine the yeast with the warm water and let it soften for 10 to 15 minutes. Combine the flour, sugar, dried milk, egg, and butter in a large bowl and stir to mix. Add the yeast and mix the dough well. Cover and let rise in a warm place for about 1 hour.

■ Prepare the filling while dough is rising. Combine the pizza sauce, tomato paste, mushrooms, onion, salt, pepper, oregano, and garlic powder in a saucepan over medium-low heat and cook until warm. Add the browned meat and stir together.

■ Turn the dough out onto a floured surface and knead for a few minutes. Roll out the dough in a rectangle about the size of a baking sheet. Place on a greased or parchment paper-lined baking sheet.

■ Pour the filling down the center of the dough and spread to within two inches of the edge. Sprinkle the cheese on top of the filling. Fold up the sides, overlapping to make a loaf shape. Fold the ends up toward the center. Roll the loaf, seam side down, onto the baking sheet. Let rise for 15 minutes.

■ Preheat the oven to 375°F and bake for 25 minutes.

—Cathaleen Hemminger
Bremen, Indiana

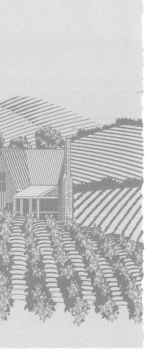

Here are some simple ideas for preparing a chicken breast. These are based on one or two chicken breasts, but you can easily increase the measurements for more. Keep in mind that it's important not to overbake them. They are done when the juices run clear when pierced.

Chicken with Dill
Wash and dry chicken breasts. Lightly dredge with mixture of flour, salt, and pepper. Sprinkle paprika heavily on both sides of breasts. Fry in extra virgin olive oil until cooked thoroughly. Remove chicken from frying pan. Reduce the heat and add enough sour cream to pan drippings to create a pink paprika sauce. Add snipped fresh dill to sauce and serve over the chicken. ***From Peggy Holupka, Dundalk, Maryland***

Creamy, Crunchy Chicken Breasts
Dip chicken breasts in yogurt, roll in seasoned bread crumbs, and bake for 20 to 25 minutes in a 350°F oven. Can be sprinkled with Parmesan cheese before baking. ***From Mike Hostetter, Englewood, Ohio***

Island Chicken Breasts
Sear breasts in a hot skillet with 1 tablespoon olive oil for 4 to 7 minutes on each side. Place in a baking dish and top with Island Fruit Relish (see page 131). Bake for 20 minutes more in a 350°F oven.

Italian Chicken Breasts
Dip chicken breasts in your favorite Italian salad dressing, then sprinkle with ½ teaspoon brown sugar. Bake in a 350°F oven for 15 to 20 minutes. ***From Hope Gebhart, Brookville, Ohio***

Moroccan Almond-Crusted Chicken Breasts
Brush mixture of ¼ cup honey, 1 teaspoon cinnamon, ½ teaspoon ginger on chicken breasts. Then roll in 1 cup crushed almonds. Bake in 350°F oven for 15 to 20 minutes. ***From Chris Fogerty and JoAnn Myers, North Manchester, Indiana***

Ranch Chicken Breasts
Dip chicken breasts in ranch salad dressing (see page 156), then roll in crushed buttery crackers. Bake in a 350°F oven for 15 to 20 minutes.

Basic Marinade for Grilled Chicken
Place ½ cup olive oil, ¼ cup cider vinegar, 2 tablespoons Worcestershire sauce, and 1 teaspoon seasoned salt mix in a resealable plastic bag. Add chicken breasts and marinate 10 minutes or more in the refrigerator. Grill indoors or outdoors for 12 to 15 minutes, turning several times.

Deli Marinade for Grilled Chicken
Place ¼ cup water, ¼ cup olive oil, 1 cup vinegar, 1 tablespoon poultry seasoning, 1 tablespoon minced garlic, 1 teaspoon salt, and 1 teaspoon pepper in a resealable plastic bag. Add chicken breasts and marinate for several hours in the refrigerator. Grill for 15 to 20 minutes, turning several times. ***From Rebecca Golladay, Harrisonburg, Virginia***

Lime Marinade for Grilled Chicken
Place 1 tablespoon olive oil, 2 tablespoons fresh lime juice, 1 teaspoon lemon pepper, and 1 teaspoon sugar in a resealable plastic bag. Add chicken breasts and marinate for at least 15 minutes in the refrigerator. Grill for 15 to 20 minutes, turning several times. ***From Stephen C. Custer, Carlisle, Pennsylvania***

OVEN CHICKEN

This is our most requested family meal. It's simple and delicious!

Serves 6 to 8

1 cup buttermilk
1 egg, beaten
1 cup soda or butter crackers, crushed (1 sleeve)
¼ cup grated Parmesan cheese
1 tablespoon dried parsley
½ teaspoon salt
½ teaspoon dried oregano
½ teaspoon dried basil
½ teaspoon celery salt
½ teaspoon onion salt
¼ teaspoon paprika
¼ teaspoon pepper
1 fryer chicken, cut up

- Preheat the oven to 350°F. Lightly grease a 13 x 9-inch baking dish with oil and set aside.

- Mix the buttermilk and egg together in a wide shallow bowl.

- Mix the crackers, Parmesan cheese, parsley, salt, oregano, basil, celery salt, onion salt, paprika, and pepper in another wide shallow bowl.

- Dip chicken pieces in the buttermilk mixture and then roll in the cracker mixture. Place the coated chicken pieces in the prepared baking dish and cover.

- Bake for 45 minutes. Remove the cover and bake an additional 15 minutes to brown the chicken.

—Ina Fike
Willow Springs, Missouri

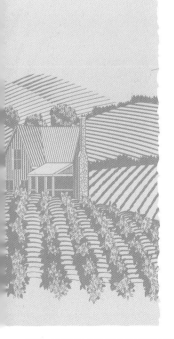

Prosciutto, Poblano Chicken over Pasta

Prosciutto is a dry-cured Italian ham that is usually thinly sliced and served uncooked. It is hard to cut in pieces for cooking, so make sure you use a sharp knife, or you can shred it by hand. If you like it spicy, use red poblano chile peppers. They are hotter than the less ripe green poblanos.

Serves 4 to 6

- ¾ pound linguine or 1 pound penne pasta
- ⅓ cup olive oil
- ¼ cup minced garlic
- 1½ skinless, boneless chicken breasts, cut into strips
- 2 poblano chiles, seeded, sliced thinly (optional)
- 3 plum tomatoes, seeded and diced
- ½ cup thinly sliced fresh basil
- 4 ounces prosciutto, chopped
- 2 tablespoons butter
- 1 cup grated or shredded Parmesan cheese, divided

- Cook the pasta in a pot of boiling, salted water until tender but firm, about 7 minutes. Drain and set aside in a large serving bowl.

- While the pasta is cooking heat the olive oil in a heavy skillet over medium heat. Add the garlic and sauté until light golden brown, about 2 minutes. Remove the garlic and set aside.

- Add the chicken strips to the skillet and sauté over medium-high heat for about 5 minutes. Add the chiles, if using, and sauté them with the chicken for about 2 minutes. Add the tomatoes, basil, prosciutto, and garlic to the skillet and sauté until the chicken is cooked through, about 5 more minutes. Remove from heat, add the butter, and stir until melted.

- Add the chicken mixture and ½ cup Parmesan cheese to the pasta and toss to coat. Sprinkle with remaining Parmesan and serve.

—Jennifer Hausfeld
Troy, Ohio

TRUE COMFORT FOOD

Potpie—there seem to be as many recipes as there are people, and chicken is not the only kind. Priscilla's mother's used ham. Carol's aunt made it with squirrel meat, Bev's family with leftover turkey. There are as many variations in the dough and vegetables. Helen's mother on the Eastern Shore made it with noodles and whatever vegetables she had on hand. Lillie added hard-boiled eggs. Anna's mother in Lancaster County baked it in a skillet with a crust on top and favored sweet potatoes. She sprinkled celery seed on top and served extra gravy on the side. Carol made it with biscuits.

One thing all potpies have in common is their ability to light up the eyes of those who remember them. No one I talked to considered them an every-day meal. Priscilla said it was one of her favorite dishes. Bev remembers it as a highlight of church dinners. She had to get in the food line early because Nancy's chicken potpie was so in demand that it disappeared quickly. Miriam ranked it first among her grandmother's dishes.

My own memory is of steamy windows on a Saturday morning, Ethel rolling out paper-thin noodle dough before she dried it a bit, cut it into squares, and dropped them into the boiling ham broth along with potatoes, parsley, and bits of ham. I cleaned her house as she worked. On those rare potpie days she always insisted that I stay for this treat. Besides, I needed to wait until she was finished with the noodles to clean up the flour on the kitchen floor. Of the many Saturday lunches I ate at her table, potpie is the only one I remember.

The 1911 *Inglenook Cook Book* bears testimony to the endless variety of potpie recipes. There are at least nineteen recipes that fall somewhere within this broad definition, made most often with chicken, but also with beef, liver, ham, pork, or fresh fruit. Recipes use different elements, from pastry dough to biscuits to dumplings to noodles. The most unusual variation is potato-filled moon pies cooked in broth. All contributors assume knowledge of basic cooking skills. For example, one recipe begins with directions that many of us would find challenging in their brevity: "Cut up and stew slightly a couple of young and tender chickens, but don't cook them soft. Make a crust with flour, lard, sweet milk and baking powder, same as for pie crust, but not quite so short" (p. 62).

The *Granddaughter's Inglenook Cookbook* has fewer recipes—"Boiled Irish Potpie" made with veal, and three chicken potpies, each with several minor variations. The directions are more complete than in the 1911 edition and the ingredients are listed at the beginning of the recipe.

Alma R. Reisinger's "Baked Chicken Pie" recipe reflects the changing expectations of today's cooks. Exact measurements are given and the directions are broken down into discrete steps with specific details. In preparing this dish I can well understand why it has always been a specialty. It is not a thirty-minute meal; however, the final product is well worth the effort. The golden, flaky crust covers a bubbling sauce filled with tender chicken and bright peas and carrots—true comfort food that calls for seconds or more.

CHICKEN POTPIE

Boil a good fat chicken quite tender. Then take 1 egg, 1 cup of sweet milk (the richer the better) and ½ cup of butter. Make a stiff dough, roll very thin, cut in small squares. Drop in the broth and let boil 10 minutes. You may think this would be a "sad" mess, but try it and you will be surprised (p. 63).

—Sister Nannie Neher, Hudson, Illinois

—Kathie Kurtz
Manassas, Virginia

BAKED CHICKEN PIE

Serves 6

FILLING
5 tablespoons butter
½ cup chopped onion
¼ cup flour
Pinch saffron (optional)
1 teaspoon salt
½ teaspoon black pepper
2 cups chicken broth
2 to 3 cups cooked and diced chicken
1 cup cooked and diced carrots
1 cup cooked peas
1 cup cooked and diced potatoes

CRUST
1½ cups flour
½ teaspoon salt
6 tablespoons shortening
¼ cup (½ stick) butter

■ Preheat the oven to 375°F. Coat a 2-quart casserole dish with butter or oil and set aside.

■ To make the filling, heat the butter in a saucepan over medium-high heat and sauté the onion until soft but not brown, about 5 minutes.

■ Add the flour, saffron, if using, salt, and pepper. Gradually stir in the broth. Cook over medium heat until the sauce starts to thicken, about 7 minutes.

■ Place the chicken, carrots, peas, and potatoes into the prepared casserole. Pour the broth mixture over the chicken and vegetables.

■ To make the crust, sift together the flour and salt. Cut in the shortening and butter. Add ice water, ¼ cup at a time, using only enough to hold the flour together. Stir until a dough forms and pulls away from the sides of the bowl.

■ Roll the dough ¼ inch thick and big enough to fit over the casserole dish. Cover the casserole dish with the flaky butter crust. Trim off any excess pastry. Place the dish on a baking sheet to catch any drips. Bake for 25 minutes until the crust is brown.

—Alma R. Reisinger
Manheim, Pennsylvania

BOTBOI

What is that—some Asian vegetable? It is the name for the Pennsylvania Dutch version of potpie. I have seen *Botboi* noodles at the grocery store and found recipes for it online. It is what Ethel made on those long-ago Saturday mornings and what Janette referred to as "northern potpie" made by her husband's mother in Pennsylvania. Although this form seems nearer to soup than to a pie, these two variations share the same English name.

—Kathie Kurtz
Manassas, Virginia

SKILLET CHICKEN

This is a family favorite, and I prepare it often for guests. It is important to use whole wheat flour for a distinctive coating and flavor. I like to use red onions for a colorful touch but yellow onions can be used too. This is a very tender and moist chicken dish and can easily be doubled for more servings.

Serves 3 to 4

> 2 tablespoons canola oil, divided
> 1 medium onion, sliced (about 1 cup)
> 6 chicken tenders or 3 skinless, boneless chicken breasts, cut in
>   half lengthwise
> 2 tablespoons whole wheat flour
> ¼ cup chicken broth
> Salt and pepper to taste
> Sprigs of parsley (optional)

■ Heat 1 tablespoon of the oil in a skillet over medium-high heat. Add the onion and sauté for about 3 minutes, stirring often. Remove the onions and set aside.

■ Coat the chicken pieces with whole wheat flour. Heat the remaining 1 tablespoon oil in the skillet over medium heat. Add the chicken and brown on both sides, about 2 minutes per side.

■ Add the chicken broth and cook for 3 minutes. Then reduce the heat to medium low, cover, and cook until the chicken is cooked through, about 15 minutes. Uncover and continue cooking until the liquid is almost gone, about 10 minutes.

■ Add the onions, salt, and pepper. Garnish with parsley, and serve from the skillet.

—Anna Leiter Lease
Walkersville, Maryland

CHICKEN 'STUFF'

I created this recipe when my children were very young and it immediately became a family favorite. When I would ask them what we should fix for dinner, the answer was usually, "Ooo, ooo, that chicken stuff!" Now they're all grown up, but when they visit and I ask them what they would like for dinner, the answer is still the same.

Serves 6

¼ cup (½ stick) butter
⅓ cup flour
1 teaspoon salt
⅛ teaspoon black pepper
2 cups chicken broth
2 cups diced cooked chicken
2 to 3 cups cooked rice
1 (4-ounce) can sliced mushrooms, drained
⅓ cup diced green bell pepper
2 tablespoons chopped pimento
¼ cup slivered or sliced almonds
Snipped parsley

■ Preheat the oven to 350°F. If you don't have a Dutch oven, lightly grease a 13 x 9-inch baking dish and set aside.

■ In a large skillet or Dutch oven melt the butter over medium-high heat. Add the flour, salt, and black pepper and stir to make a roux. Continue stirring the flour and butter mixture just till it starts to brown.

■ Gradually add the chicken broth to make a gravy, stirring till thickened, about 5 minutes. Remove from the heat.

■ Combine the gravy with the cooked chicken, rice, mushrooms, bell pepper, and pimento.

■ Transfer to the prepared baking dish or leave in the Dutch oven, if using. Top with almonds and parsley. Bake for 30 to 40 minutes.

Notes: Leftover or cooked turkey also works well in this recipe. I like to cook a whole turkey and freeze the cooked meat in 2 cup portions, ready to use. This recipe can easily be doubled or tripled as needed.

—Dianna E. Ullery
Olympia, Washington

Garlic Lover's Chicken

Serves 6

½ cup dry bread crumbs
⅓ cup grated Parmesan cheese
2 tablespoons minced fresh parsley
½ teaspoon salt (optional)
⅛ teaspoon pepper
¼ cup milk
6 skinless, boneless chicken breasts
¼ cup (½ stick) butter, melted
2 garlic cloves, minced
2 tablespoons lemon juice
Paprika to taste

■ Preheat the oven to 350°F. Coat a 13 x 9-inch baking dish with oil or butter.

■ In a large, resealable plastic bag, combine the bread crumbs, Parmesan cheese, parsley, salt, if using, and pepper.

■ Place the milk in a shallow bowl. Dip the chicken in the milk, then place in the plastic bag, seal, and shake in the bread crumb mixture. Place the coated breasts in the prepared baking dish.

■ Combine the butter, garlic, and lemon juice in a small bowl. Drizzle over the chicken. Sprinkle with paprika.

■ Bake uncovered for 30 minutes or until the juices run clear.

—Connie Burk Davis
Westminster, Maryland

CHICKEN AND FRIED RICE

Serves 4

2 tablespoons vegetable oil
¼ to ½ pound skinless, boneless chicken, cubed
3 garlic cloves, minced
1 large onion, chopped
1 teaspoon salt
1 teaspoon pepper
1 teaspoon sugar
1 tablespoon soy sauce
3 cups cooked rice
1 cup chopped vegetables (leftover or frozen broccoli, peas, carrots)

- Heat the cooking oil in a large skillet over medium-high heat. Add the chicken, garlic, onion, salt, pepper, sugar, and soy sauce.

- Stir-fry until the chicken is cooked through, about 7 minutes.

- Add the rice. Stir-fry 5 minutes more. Add the vegetables. Stir well and heat till hot.

Notes: This is gluten free if you use liquid aminos instead of the soy sauce. You can find them at most health-food stores. Leftover chicken works well too.

—Phoebe Koser Oellig
Leola, Pennsylvania

CHICKEN STIR-FRY

CUTTING UP A CHICKEN

My teenage daughter called me at work one day to ask how to cut up a chicken for dinner that night. I told her to find the joints and cut between them and to split the breast. I was very surprised to come home and find one chicken fried in twenty-eight pieces! I never figured out exactly what some of the pieces were.

—Gail C. McGlothin
Tyler, Texas

Serves 8 to 10

1 tablespoon cornstarch
¾ teaspoon garlic powder
¼ teaspoon chopped ginger
1½ teaspoons soy sauce
¼ cup hoisin sauce
1 teaspoon chicken (or beef) bouillon granules
3 tablespoons vegetable oil
1 pound skinless, boneless chicken breasts, cut into 1-inch pieces
½ cup chopped broccoli
½ cup chopped carrots
½ cup sliced mushrooms
5 cups cooked rice or chow mein noodles

■ Combine the cornstarch, garlic powder, ginger, soy sauce, hoisin sauce, bouillon, and 1 cup hot water in a large bowl. Stir and set aside.

■ Heat the oil in a large skillet over medium-high heat. Stir-fry the chicken until no longer pink, about 7 minutes. Add the vegetables and stir-fry until crisp-tender, about 5 minutes.

■ Add the sauce and stir just until it thickens, about 8 minutes.

■ Pour over the rice or chow mein noodles.

Note: Other meats like cubed beef, pork, or turkey may be substituted.

—Donna E. Stiver
Roann, Indiana

Chicken Enchiladas

Serves 6 to 8

 3 tablespoons vegetable oil
 4 skinless, boneless chicken breasts, cubed
 ½ cup chopped onion
 1 (7-ounce) can mild green chiles
 1 (4-ounce) can sliced black olives
 1 teaspoon chopped garlic cloves
 ¼ teaspoon poultry seasoning
 3 ounces cream cheese
 1 cup sour cream
 1 (15-ounce) can chili con carne without beans
 10 flour tortillas
 1 (8-ounce) package shredded Mexican blend cheese
   (Monterey Jack and Cheddar cheeses)
 1 cup whipping cream

- Preheat the oven to 350°F. Coat a 13 x 9-inch baking dish with cooking spray and set aside.

- Heat the oil in a large skillet over medium-high heat. Sauté the chicken cubes until no longer pink inside. Add the onion, chiles, olives, garlic, poultry seasoning, cream cheese, sour cream, and chili. Mix together thoroughly. Cook until heated through and then remove from the heat.

- Put a spoonful or two on each tortilla, roll, and then place in the prepared baking dish.

- Top with cheese and whipping cream and bake for 35 to 45 minutes, until bubbly.

Notes: This is gluten free if you use corn tortillas. Try using beef instead of chicken for variation.

—Karen Verner
Lacey, Washington

CHICKEN PICCATA

Serves 4

½ cup flour
3 teaspoons salt
1 teaspoon black pepper
4 chicken cutlets
2 tablespoons vegetable oil
2 tablespoons white vinegar
1 teaspoon minced garlic
½ cup chicken broth
2 tablespoons fresh lemon juice
2 tablespoons capers
2 tablespoons unsalted butter
Fresh lemon slices
Fresh parsley, chopped
12 ounces cooked angel hair pasta

■ Combine the flour, salt, and pepper in a shallow bowl. Dredge the chicken cutlets in the flour mixture.

■ Heat the vegetable oil in a sauté pan over medium-high heat. Sauté the cutlets 2 to 3 minutes on each side. Transfer to a warm plate.

■ Deglaze the pan with the vinegar and 2 tablespoons of water. Add the minced garlic. Cook until the garlic is slightly brown, about 3 minutes. Add the broth, lemon juice, and capers. Return the cutlets to the pan and cook on each side for 1 to 2 minutes. Transfer the cutlets to a warm plate.

■ Add the butter and lemons to the sauté pan to finish the sauce. Once the butter is melted, pour the sauce over the cutlets and garnish with lemon slices and chopped fresh parsley. Serve over angel hair pasta.

—Nancy Shifflett Bowman
Fishersville, Virginia

CHICKEN SALTIMBOCCA

My daughter is an associate producer for a production company. ♨ GF
They were filming a cooking program for a local TV station. The
program featured local chefs, both professional and non-professional,
who cooked their favorite dishes. One of the chefs backed out at the last
minute, so my daughter called me to see if I could fill in for him. I cooked
this dish for the program. Everyone loved it!

Serves 4

4 skinless, boneless chicken breast halves
Salt and pepper to taste
3 tablespoons extra virgin olive oil
2 tablespoons butter, divided
24 sage leaves, sliced
4 thin slices prosciutto, cut into thin strips
1 tablespoon vinegar
1 cup chicken broth
4 cups cooked mashed potatoes

- Season the chicken breasts with salt and pepper.

- Heat the olive oil and 1 tablespoon of the butter in a large saucepan over medium-high heat. Sear the chicken breasts until golden brown, 3 to 4 minutes per side. Remove the chicken from the pan and set aside.

- Add the sage leaves and prosciutto to the pan and cook until crisp and slightly brown, about 2 minutes. Transfer to a plate lined with paper towels.

- Add the vinegar with $\frac{1}{3}$ cup water to the pan and bring to a boil, scraping up any browned bits from the bottom of the pan with a wooden spoon. Cook until the mixture is almost completely reduced, about 8 minutes. Add the chicken broth and boil until reduced by half, 3 to 5 minutes. Stir in the remaining 1 tablespoon butter. Return the chicken to the pan and cook until no longer pink inside.

- Scoop a cup of potatoes onto each of four plates. Add the chicken, spoon the sauce over the chicken, and sprinkle with sage and prosciutto.

—Jane Durant
Middletown, Maryland

ANNA MOW'S PILAO

Anna Beahm Mow was born in 1893 in Daleville, Virginia. She met her husband, Baxter Mow, in Chicago while studying at Bethany Bible School. They were then called to India where they served for seventeen years. This is where Anna had a powerful encounter with Jesus. This recipe is a tribute to this Brethren saint.

Serves 6

2 tablespoons salt
1 tablespoon pepper
1 tablespoon paprika
4 large chicken breasts or
    1 whole fryer, cut up
¼ cup (½ stick) butter, divided
1½ cups chicken broth

1 cup brown rice
2 tablespoons butter
1 large onion, sliced
½ cup raisins
4 hard-cooked eggs, sliced
¼ cup almonds, slivered

■ Preheat the oven to 350°F.

■ Combine the salt, pepper, and paprika in a small bowl. Sprinkle rub over the chicken. Place the chicken in a baking dish, place 1 tablespoon butter on each piece of chicken, and bake for 1 hour.

■ Bring the chicken broth to a boil in a large pot over high heat. Add the rice, stir, and bring back to a boil. Reduce the heat to low, cover, and simmer for 45 minutes until tender. Add more water, if necessary.

■ Heat 2 tablespoons butter in a sauté pan over medium heat. Sauté the onion in the butter for about 8 minutes. Drain with slotted spoon and set aside.

■ Sauté the raisins in the butter until puffed, about 5 minutes.

■ To serve, arrange the rice, chicken, and eggs on a large platter. Top with the onion, raisins, and almonds.

Note: Dried cranberries may be substituted for raisins and peanuts for almonds.

—Maxine Mundy Ritchie
Tucson, Arizona

TURKEY SWEET AND SOUR

We usually add more carrots and stir-fry them longer. This is a good recipe for using leftover Thanksgiving turkey.

Serves 6 to 8

    2 tablespoons cornstarch
    1 cup pineapple juice
    ⅓ cup cider vinegar
    ¼ cup soy sauce
    ¼ cup ketchup or chili sauce, similar to hoisin sauce
    2 tablespoons vegetable oil
    ¾ cup carrots, cut into "coins"
    ¾ cup green bell peppers, cut in chunks
    ¾ cup drained pineapple chunks
    4 cups cubed cooked turkey
    3 to 4 cups cooked rice

- Combine the cornstarch, juice, vinegar, soy sauce, and ketchup in a small saucepan over medium heat. Cook and stir the sweet and sour sauce until thick and clear. Set aside.

- Heat a skillet, wok, or electric fry pan to medium hot. Add the oil and stir-fry the carrots for 1 minute.

- Add the bell peppers, pineapple, and turkey and stir-fry until heated through.

- Pour in the sweet and sour sauce, stir to heat, and serve over hot rice.

Note: If you use liquid aminos instead of soy sauce, this makes a great gluten-free dish.

—Merry Christina Roy
East Wenatchee, Washington

Ground Turkey Shepherd's Pie

This is a healthful swap for the traditional shepherd's pie. This recipe calls for lean ground turkey instead of beef and calcium-rich yogurt instead of milk or cream. The brightly colored carrots and peas against the white of the potatoes look great when presented on serving plates. **GF**

Serves 8

TOPPING
1½ pounds russet potatoes, peeled and cut into small pieces
3 parsnips (6 ounces), peeled and cut into small pieces
1 cup plain fat-free yogurt
¾ teaspoon kosher salt
Freshly ground black pepper to taste

FILLING
1 tablespoon plus 1 teaspoon extra virgin olive oil
1 large onion, finely chopped (about 1½ cups)
3 celery ribs, finely chopped
2 medium carrots, finely chopped
2 garlic cloves, minced
2 pounds lean ground turkey
1 tablespoon fresh thyme
¾ teaspoon chipotle or regular chili powder
1½ teaspoons kosher salt
Freshly ground black pepper to taste
2½ tablespoons cornstarch
6 ounces frozen peas (about 1½ cups)

■ To make the topping, place the potatoes and parsnips in a medium saucepan, cover with water by 2 inches, and bring to boil over high heat. Reduce the heat to low and simmer until fork tender, about 20 minutes. Drain, reserving 2 cups of the cooking liquid.

■ Purée the potatoes and parsnips by passing through a food mill, mashing with a fork, or pulsing in a food processor. Transfer to a mixing bowl and stir in the yogurt, salt, and pepper.

■ Preheat the oven to 425°F.

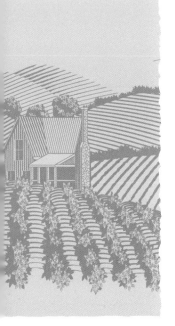

- To make the filling, heat the oil in a medium skillet over medium heat. Sauté the onion, celery, carrots, and garlic until tender, 10 to 12 minutes. Add the turkey and cook, stirring to break up any large pieces, for about 7 minutes. Stir in the thyme, chili powder, salt, and pepper.

- Whisk together the cornstarch with the reserved 2 cups cooking liquid; add to the turkey mixture. Increase the temperature to medium high and boil for 1 minute. Stir in the peas and cook for 1 minute more.

- Transfer the filling mixture to a lightly oiled 2-quart round or oval baking dish; top with potatoes and bake until bubbling and the top is browned, about 35 minutes.

—Norene E. Kanagy
Ypsilanti, Michigan

ROASTED TOMATO SPAGHETTI

This is one of my favorite summertime dishes. Watch the tomatoes carefully. Some take less time to cook than others. It depends on the moisture content of the tomatoes. This seems like a large amount of fat, but it really isn't an oily dish.

Serves 6 to 8

12 Roma tomatoes (about 1¾ pounds)
Salt and pepper
3 to 6 garlic cloves, minced
½ cup chopped Italian parsley, divided
½ cup olive oil, divided
1 pound dry spaghetti
2 tablespoons butter, at room temperature
½ cup fresh snipped basil leaves
Grated Parmigiano-Reggiano (Parmesan) cheese

■ Preheat the oven to 425°F.

■ Cut the tomatoes in half lengthwise and arrange, cut sides up, in a 13 x 9-inch baking dish. Sprinkle lightly with salt and pepper to taste. Mix the garlic, parsley, and ¼ cup of the olive oil. Drizzle over the cut sides of the tomatoes. Bake until browned on top, about 1 hour.

■ Cook the spaghetti in a large pot of boiling, salted water, uncovered, until barely tender, about 7 minutes. Drain and set aside.

■ In a large warm serving bowl, combine the butter, the remaining ¼ cup of oil, and basil. Remove and discard most of the skin from 4 roasted tomato halves. Add them to the bowl and coarsely mash them with a fork. Add the pasta and stir to mix. Add the remaining tomatoes and pan juices. Gently mix, adding more salt and pepper to taste. Add as much cheese on top as desired.

—Jan Dull Eller
Portland, Oregon

BAKED SPAGHETTI

This recipe came from a church newsletter, and it's a keeper! It makes two 13 x 9-inch pans of spaghetti, so you can bake one and freeze one. Use whole wheat pasta for a more healthful option.

Serves 10 to 12

12 ounces spaghetti
1 egg, beaten
2 cups grated Parmesan cheese, divided
1 (24-ounce) container low-fat cottage cheese
¼ cup chopped parsley
1 pound lean ground beef or turkey
1 cup chopped onion
¾ cup chopped green bell pepper
1 (26-ounce) jar spaghetti sauce
1 (8-ounce) package shredded mozzarella cheese
1 (8-ounce) package shredded sharp Cheddar cheese

- Preheat the oven to 350°F. Lightly grease two 13 x 9-inch baking dishes and set aside.

- Cook the spaghetti in a large pot of boiling, salted water until al dente, about 7 minutes; drain. Return the cooked pasta to the pot and add the egg and 1 cup of the Parmesan cheese; stir to combine.

- Divide the pasta mixture between the prepared 13 x 9-inch baking dishes.

- Using the same pan, combine the cottage cheese, remaining 1 cup Parmesan cheese, and parsley; divide this mixture and spread evenly over both dishes of pasta.

- Brown the ground beef or turkey, onion, and bell pepper in a skillet over medium-high heat. Cook until the beef is no longer pink, draining off any excess fat; add the spaghetti sauce and simmer for 2 to 3 minutes.

- Divide the sauce evenly on top of the spaghetti mixture in the dishes.

- In a large bowl, combine the mozzarella and Cheddar cheeses and then spread evenly over top of both casseroles.

- Bake, uncovered, for 35 to 40 minutes.

—Bev Anspaugh
Rocky Mount, Virginia

LIFETIME IMPRESSIONS

Every spring, the senior music majors were invited to John and Ann Barrs' house for supper. And they always served the most amazing meal: hamburger curry on rice with all the trimmings—onions, peppers, tomatoes, peanuts, coconut, bananas, pineapple, raisins, and hard-cooked eggs. You might think those things don't go together, but they do! So we gathered to eat a meal like I had never had before, accompanied by rich conversation. Before leaving, they invited us to sign the tablecloth. Later, Ann would embroider our names over our signatures. I will never forget their warm, generous hospitality that night. It made a lifetime impression.

—Paula Ziegler Ulrich
Greenville, Ohio

Spaghetti with Zucchini, Walnuts, and Raisins

This is a delicious vegetarian dish that will surprise you.

Serves 4

- 12 ounces spaghetti (¾ box)
- 3 tablespoons olive oil
- ½ cup roughly chopped walnut halves
- 4 garlic cloves, thinly sliced
- 4 to 5 small zucchini, sliced thin
- ¾ cup raisins
- ½ teaspoon kosher salt
- ¼ teaspoon black pepper
- ½ cup grated Parmesan cheese, divided

■ Cook the pasta according to the package directions, drain, reserving ³⁄₄ cup of pasta water, and return to the pot.

■ Meanwhile, heat the oil in a large skillet over medium-high heat. Brown the walnuts while stirring frequently, about 3 to 4 minutes. Add the garlic and cook, stirring frequently, until it begins to brown, about 1 minute. Add the zucchini and raisins, season with salt and pepper, and cook, tossing occasionally, until the zucchini is just tender, 4 to 5 minutes. Add the reserved pasta water and boil until reduced by half, about 5 minutes.

■ Add the zucchini mixture to the pasta and toss to combine. Sprinkle with ¼ cup of the Parmesan cheese before serving. Serve the remaining Parmesan cheese on the side.

—Darlene R. Creighton
Lancaster, Pennsylvania

Tetrazzini

Serves 6 to 8

¼ cup (½ stick) butter
½ cup chopped onion
½ cup finely chopped green bell pepper
½ cup finely chopped celery
1 tablespoon flour
1 tablespoon Worcestershire sauce
2 cups diced cooked chicken or turkey
Salt and pepper
½ cup diced Cheddar cheese
1½ cups dry macaroni, cooked and drained
1 cup chicken or turkey broth
½ cup grated Cheddar cheese

■ Melt the butter in a large saucepan over medium-high heat. Add the onion, bell pepper, and celery. Reduce the heat to medium and cook until the vegetables are soft, about 7 minutes. Do not brown.

■ Stir in the flour and Worcestershire sauce. Simmer until thickened.

■ Add the chicken or turkey, salt and pepper to taste, and diced Cheddar cheese. Stir in the cooked macaroni and broth. Top with the grated Cheddar cheese. Bring to a simmer, reduce the heat to medium low, and cook for 2 to 3 minutes more.

—Phyllis Kline
Mount Sidney, Virginia

RIGATONI WITH CHEESE

I served this to a workcamp crew of teenagers working at the Ashland City disaster site in Tennessee, and there wasn't anything left.

Serves 8 to 10

- 1 tablespoon olive oil
- 1 garlic clove, minced
- 1 pound ground beef
- 1 (24-ounce) jar spaghetti sauce
- 1 pound rigatoni, cooked according to package directions
- 8 ounces provolone cheese, sliced
- ¾ cup sour cream
- 1 cup shredded mozzarella cheese

■ Preheat the oven to 350°F. Butter a 13 x 9-inch casserole dish and set aside.

■ Heat the olive oil in a large heavy skillet over medium heat. Sauté the garlic in the oil until clear. Brown the ground beef in the oil and garlic mixture until no longer pink, about 10 minutes. Add the spaghetti sauce and simmer for 15 minutes.

■ Place half of the cooked rigatoni in the prepared casserole dish. Add a layer of provolone slices. Spread sour cream over the provolone slices. Spoon half of the spaghetti sauce mixture over the sour cream and provolone.

■ Add the rest of the rigatoni. Spoon the rest of the spaghetti sauce mixture over the pasta. Top with the mozzarella cheese and bake for 30 to 40 minutes.

Notes: I like to drain the grease after browning the ground beef. It does not harm the flavor. You can use sautéed onions and red bell peppers for added flavor and color.

—Carolyn S. Barr
Girard, Kansas

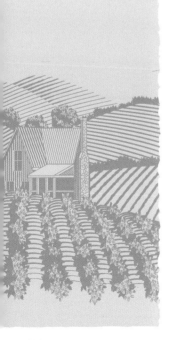

BAKED MACARONI AND CHEESE

This recipe can be made lactose free by using lactose-free milk and Cheddar cheese.

Serves 6

- **3 cups elbow macaroni**
- **2 tablespoons cornstarch**
- **1 teaspoon salt**
- **¼ teaspoon pepper**
- **2½ cups milk**
- **2 tablespoons butter**
- **2 cups shredded Cheddar cheese, divided**

■ Add the elbow macaroni to a large pot of boiling, salted water. Cook for 7 minutes, drain, and set aside in a large mixing bowl.

■ Preheat the oven to 375°F. Grease a 2- to 3-quart casserole dish with butter or oil and set aside.

■ Combine the cornstarch, salt, pepper, and milk in a medium saucepan over medium-high heat. Stir together well. Add the butter and bring to a boil, stirring constantly. Boil for 1 minute and then remove from the heat.

■ Stir in 1½ cups of the shredded cheese.

■ Pour the cheese sauce over the cooked macaroni and mix well. Pour into the prepared casserole dish and sprinkle with the remaining ½ cup cheese.

■ Bake, uncovered, for 25 minutes or until lightly browned.

—Ginny Mason
West Lafayette, Indiana

POTLUCK GATHERINGS

Imagine a warm serving of short pasta tubes, uniquely bent into familiar U-shapes and suspended in rich, creamy cheese. Who would have the nerve to discount the claim that macaroni and cheese is one of the most popular comfort foods in America? Just ask the children, or better yet, just watch them at a potluck or at a restaurant buffet where this classic is served. You will witness plates heaped high with ivory-to-yellow mounds, leaving little room for meats and vegetables. Many adults would side with the kids, though, and most Brethren fellowship dinners would be incomplete without at least one nine-by-thirteen version of this classic dish.

It is noteworthy that the 1911 *Inglenook Cook Book* dedicated an entire chapter to macaroni and cheese dishes, unlike later editions. A glimpse into history suggests that macaroni was simply a generic name for any form of the high-gluten pasta made from durum or "hard wheat," a recently introduced cash crop suited to the semiarid Dakotas and other areas of the Northwest. Before that, most of the hard wheat pasta was imported from Italy or France, making it a luxury that escaped most Brethren dining tables. However, by 1900, domestic production of hard wheat pasta (macaroni) introduced an affordable food staple known for its long shelf life and ease of preparation.

Truly a multigenerational favorite, this simple dish has changed very little over the years. The 1911 classic recipe from Luverna Sheets shows very little contrast to the modern version, except in the preparation method (p. 80). Both could be described as mildly gooey but sliceable, with a firmness of texture in the pasta. Betty L. Breidenstine's "Easy Macaroni and Cheese" recipe offers a certain ease in the steps involved, but the final product is very similar to the classic model. In fact, a quick study of macaroni and cheese dishes reveals very few digressions from the use of the simplest of ingredients. The few variations do little to alter the taste that we have grown to cherish. Even in its basic form, this classic has become a main dish for many meals—a pleasing alternative for the heartiest of meat-eaters and vegetarians alike.

Betty L. Breidenstine notes that her recipe has become a favorite at church gatherings. While any of the main dishes in this chapter would satisfy the cravings of folks at home, many of them, like Betty's, could easily grace the table at any church potluck meal. The long-standing tradition of sharing our tastiest creations brings to mind some of our fondest food memories. These community meals have served as meaningful Church of the Brethren social functions for generations. Just as "Easy Macaroni and Cheese" finds its rightful place on the table at Betty's church, so could any of these fine recipes.

While each recipe holds its own appeal, the distinctive feature of any community meal is the medley of sensory sweetness that materializes as the slow cookers jockey for position, the foil and plastic wraps are removed, the pots and pans are positioned on trivets, and the plastic containers are unburped. At that moment the meetinghouse becomes infused with an aroma that defies duplication—a delightful blend of kitchen individualities that somehow symbolizes the inimitable merger of the loving hearts and souls who have gathered there.

—Mike Fike
Morgantown, West Virginia

MACARONI

Boil about ¼ pound of macaroni in slightly-salted water until tender. Drain and put into a pan with alternate layers of cracker crumbs and bits of cheese until all the macaroni is used, add a pinch of salt with butter. Cover with sweet milk and bake twenty minutes. Serve hot in the dish in which it is baked.

—Sister Luverna Sheets, Mount Solon, Virginia

EASY MACARONI AND CHEESE

When I serve this at church gatherings, I am often asked for the recipe. This recipe can easily be doubled and placed in a 13 x 9-inch pan. It is easy to prepare because the macaroni does not have to be cooked. I serve it with stewed tomatoes.

Serves 4 to 6

2 cups milk
3 tablespoons butter, melted
1 cup uncooked macaroni
2 cups grated Cheddar cheese
1 cup chopped ham (optional)

■ Preheat the oven to 350°F.

■ Heat the milk for a couple of minutes in the microwave as the other preparations are made.

■ Put the melted butter in an 8- or 9-inch square baking dish. Add the uncooked macaroni and stir to coat. Add the cheese and ham, if using. Stir to mix well.

■ Pour the warmed milk over the macaroni and cheese and press with a spoon to make sure the ingredients are under the milk as much as possible.

■ Bake for 30 minutes. Do not cover or stir while baking.

—Betty L. Breidenstine
Hummelstown, Pennsylvania

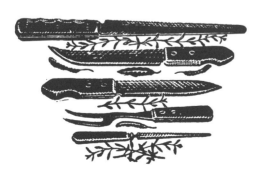

BAKED LASAGNA

Gluten-free noodles can be substituted very easily. This recipe is made simpler by not having to cook the noodles before baking the lasagna. The lasagna can be assembled early and refrigerated, but allow 15 minutes or so longer in the oven if cooking directly from the refrigerator.

Serves 12

1 pound ground beef or sausage
1 garlic clove, minced
1 tablespoon basil
1½ teaspoons salt
1 (16-ounce) can crushed tomatoes
1 (12-ounce) can tomato paste
3 cups cottage cheese or ricotta
½ cup grated Parmesan cheese

2 tablespoons dried parsley
2 eggs, beaten
½ teaspoon black pepper
1 (10-ounce) box lasagna noodles, uncooked
1 pound mozzarella cheese, grated

■ Brown the ground beef in a skillet over medium heat until no longer pink, about 10 minutes. Drain the fat. Add the garlic, basil, salt, tomatoes, and tomato paste and simmer uncovered for 30 minutes, stirring occasionally.

■ Preheat the oven to 375°F. Lightly grease a 13 x 9-inch baking dish with butter or oil and set aside.

■ In a large bowl, combine the cottage or ricotta cheese, Parmesan cheese, parsley, eggs, and pepper.

■ Pour 1 cup of the meat sauce in the bottom of the prepared baking dish. Layer in this order: noodles to cover the sauce, half the cottage or ricotta cheese mixture, half the mozzarella cheese. Repeat the same layering, topping off with the remaining mozzarella cheese.

■ Bake, covered with foil, for 45 minutes; uncover and bake 15 more minutes or until bubbly. Let stand 10 minutes before cutting into squares.

—Catherine A. Patrick
Lindsborg, Kansas

Vegetarian Lasagna

The frozen tofu has the texture of ground meat and satisfies most meat lovers. Adding a layer of thinly sliced zucchini or yellow crookneck squash before the last layer is a nice addition.

Serves 12

1 (12- to 16-ounce) package frozen extra firm tofu, thawed
2 tablespoons olive oil
¾ cup chopped onion
1 garlic clove, minced
2 (14-ounce) cans diced tomatoes, undrained
2 cups tomato sauce
1 tablespoon parsley flakes

½ teaspoon black pepper
2 teaspoons dried oregano
1 teaspoon dried basil
9 uncooked lasagna noodles
2 cups cottage cheese
8 ounces mozzarella cheese, shredded
1 cup grated Parmesan cheese

- Preheat the oven to 350°F. Lightly grease a 13 x 9-inch baking dish and set aside.

- Remove the tofu from the wrapper; place the tofu on a paper towel on a cutting board. Put another paper towel on top of the tofu and press with a plate to squeeze out the liquid. Continue with another set of paper towels until the block is as dry as possible. Tear the tofu into bite-size pieces.

- Heat the oil in a large skillet over medium heat. Sauté the onion and garlic in the oil. When the onion is translucent, add the tofu and stir for 2 to 3 minutes.

- Add the diced tomatoes with their juice, tomato sauce, parsley, pepper, oregano, and basil. Simmer uncovered, stirring occasionally, for 30 minutes or until thickened.

- Meanwhile, cook the lasagna noodles in boiling, salted water; rinse and drain.

- Spread about 1 cup of the tomato sauce over the bottom of the dish and then layer as follows: three lasagna noodles side by side to cover the sauce, $\frac{1}{3}$ of the remaining sauce, $\frac{1}{2}$ of the cottage cheese, $\frac{1}{3}$ of the mozzarella and Parmesan cheeses. Repeat for two more layers, ending with the mozzarella and Parmesan cheese.

- Bake for 40 to 50 minutes or until lightly browned and bubbling.

- Allow to stand 15 minutes, then cut into squares and serve.

—Peggy Reiff Miller
Milford, Indiana

SAUSAGE VEGGIE GRILL

Our garden always has an abundance of zucchini and yellow squash,  *so naturally this is one of our favorite recipes. If you like it spicy, try hot Italian sausage. Experiment with the vegetable choices and amounts. They can be varied to accommodate your family's preferences.*

Serves 4

1 pound Italian sausage links, cut into ½-inch slices
1 zucchini, cut into 1-inch slices
1 yellow summer squash, cut into 1-inch slices
1 red bell pepper, sliced
1 onion, cut into wedges
1 cup quartered fresh mushrooms
¼ cup olive oil
1 tablespoon dried oregano
1 tablespoon dried parsley flakes
1 teaspoon garlic salt
1 teaspoon paprika

- Prepare a charcoal grill or heat a gas grill to medium hot.

- Brown the sausage in a skillet over medium heat. Cook until just browned, about 5 minutes. In a large bowl, combine the sausage, zucchini, squash, red pepper, onion, and mushrooms.

- In a small bowl, combine the oil, oregano, parsley, garlic salt, and paprika and stir to mix. Pour over the sausage mixture; toss to coat.

- Lay two pieces of heavy-duty foil about 14 x 12 inches onto a work surface. Divide the sausage mixture evenly between the two pieces of foil. Fold the foil around the sausage mixture and seal tightly.

- Grill, covered, for 25 to 30 minutes, or until the sausage is no longer pink on the inside and the vegetables are tender. When checking open the foil carefully to allow steam to escape.

Note: To bake in an oven, place the mixture in a covered casserole dish and bake at 350°F for 30 to 40 minutes until the vegetables are tender.

—Donna L. Straub
Taneytown, Maryland

Sausage Stir-Fry

Serves 3

½ pound pork sausage
½ cup chopped onion
½ cup chopped bell pepper (green, yellow, or red)
1½ cups chopped cabbage
1 cup chopped broccoli
½ cup chopped carrots

■ Cook and crumble the sausage in a large skillet over medium heat until no longer pink, about 8 minutes.

■ Add the onion, bell pepper, cabbage, broccoli, carrots, and ½ cup water. Bring to a boil. Cover the skillet and reduce the heat to low. Simmer for 5 to 10 minutes or until the vegetables are at desired doneness. Stir often.

Variations: You can add one large potato, chopped into small pieces. One cup of chopped cauliflower can also be added. Frozen mixed vegetables may be also be substituted for the fresh ones. Ground beef or chicken pieces may be substituted for the sausage.

—Beth Keihl
Versailles, Ohio

BLACK BEANS AND SAUSAGE WITH RICE

This can be a vegetarian main dish, or a side dish, if you leave out the sausage. You could use a different variety of beans to suit your taste.

Serves 6 to 8

1 teaspoon vegetable oil
1 small onion, chopped
2 garlic cloves, finely chopped
½ teaspoon thyme
½ teaspoon salt
¼ teaspoon cayenne pepper (or to taste)
1 (15-ounce) can diced tomatoes, undrained
1 cup long-grain white rice
½ to 1 pound kielbasa or sausage
2 (15-ounce) cans black beans

■ Heat the oil in a large skillet over medium-high heat. Add the onion and garlic and sauté until softened, 3 to 4 minutes. Add the thyme, salt, cayenne pepper, tomatoes, and 2 cups water and stir. Bring to a boil.

■ Stir in the rice and return to a boil. Reduce the heat to medium low and simmer, covered, for 20 minutes.

■ Meanwhile, slice the sausage and lightly brown in a skillet over medium-high heat.

■ Drain and rinse the beans and pour them on top of the rice mixture. Don't stir. Cover and let stand 5 minutes. Then stir in the beans and the sausage slices and serve.

—Jill D. Fike
Willow Springs, Missouri

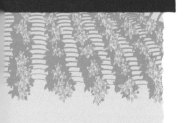

Jeff's Tamale Pie

My husband's mother used to make this delicious "pie" when he was growing up. We eat this several times a year and enjoy it every time, even though it seems to be different each time my husband makes it. Any meat will work depending on your taste. If a milder dish is preferred, leave out the chiles. If you want more spice, add chili powder or paprika. **(GF)**

Serves 6 to 8

¼ cup (½ stick) butter
2 pounds spicy Italian sausage
1 large white onion, chopped
1 cup chopped celery
1 (16-ounce) can corn, drained
2 (16-ounce) cans beans (pinto, black, kidney), drained
1 (6-ounce) can whole pitted black olives, drained (optional)
1 (10-ounce) can enchilada sauce
1 (5-ounce) can green mild chiles
Salt and black pepper to taste
Chili powder to taste
¾ to 1 cup yellow cornmeal
2 cups grated Cheddar cheese

- In a large ovenproof skillet, melt the butter over medium-high heat. Brown and crumble the Italian sausage in the butter. After about 4 minutes, add the onion and celery. Reduce the heat to medium and continue cooking for another 4 to 5 minutes or until the sausage is cooked through. Drain.

- Add the corn, beans, olives, if using, enchilada sauce, and chiles to the sausage mixture. Season with salt, pepper, and chili powder.

- Preheat the oven to 375°F.

- Add 2 cups water to the sausage mixture. Add ¾ cup yellow cornmeal. If it seems a bit thin add more cornmeal.

- When thickened, cover with Cheddar cheese and bake for 25 minutes or until a toothpick inserted into the center comes out clean. Cool slightly before serving.

—Sandy Isaacs
Waterloo, Iowa

PORK BARBECUE FOR SANDWICHES

This recipe freezes well.

Serves 12

¼ cup (½ stick) butter
6 to 8 pounds pork butt or shoulder
Salt and pepper to taste
2 (12-ounce) bottles chili sauce
1 teaspoon Worcestershire sauce
1 teaspoon mustard
1 tablespoon cider vinegar
½ to 1 cup packed brown sugar

■ Melt the butter in a large pot over medium-high heat. Brown the pork in the butter, turning to sear all over for about 5 minutes per side. Add salt and pepper and enough water to almost cover the pork. Bring to a boil; then reduce the heat to medium low and simmer for 3 hours or until the meat falls from the bone. Reserve 1 cup of the cooking liquid or pork juice.

■ Shred the pork when cool.

■ Combine the chili sauce, Worcestershire sauce, mustard, vinegar, brown sugar, and pork juice in a bowl. Pour over the shredded meat and heat over medium low.

—Jean C. Myers
Sinking Spring, Pennsylvania

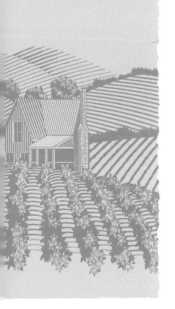

Classic Glazed Hamloaf

This makes a large loaf. It can be divided in half, with one half frozen for later use.

Serves 8 to 10

1½ pounds ground pork
1½ pounds ground smoked ham
4 eggs, beaten
¾ cup milk
1 teaspoon salt
3 tablespoons ketchup
1½ cups cracker crumbs
¼ cup sugar
¼ cup pineapple juice
2 tablespoons butter
3 to 4 pineapple rings for garnish
Maraschino cherries for garnish

■ Preheat the oven to 350°F.

■ In a large bowl, combine the pork, ham, eggs, milk, salt, and ketchup. Stir in the cracker crumbs and mix well. Transfer to a 13 x 9-inch glass baking dish and shape into a loaf and bake for 1¼ hours.

■ Meanwhile, prepare a glaze. Dissolve the sugar in the pineapple juice and butter in a small saucepan over medium heat, stirring occasionally. After the loaf has cooked for 15 minutes, remove it from the oven and spoon the glaze over the top. Return the loaf to oven. After cooking for 30 more minutes, remove from the oven and baste with the glaze in the baking dish. Return the loaf to the oven and cook for a final 30 minutes.

■ Garnish with pineapple rings and maraschino cherries on top.

Note: Have a local meat market grind and mix together the pork and ham into a three-pound package.

Variation: For a slightly spicier option, use all ground pork and add 2 to 3 teaspoons mustard to the glaze. Thanks to Joyce R. Fike of Doylestown, Ohio.

—Becky Flory Glick
Bridgewater, Virginia

REAL FOOD, MINDFUL FOOD

In the early twentieth century every part of a pig was useful. Looking through the pork recipes in the 1911 *Inglenook Cook Book*, we find familiar dishes such as "Bacon and Eggs" and "Pork and Beans" alongside other, less familiar ones such as "Head-Cheese" and "Pigs' Feet Souse." With modern eyes we recognize cuts of meat from the loin and leg, the shoulder and the belly, but our forebears would have been familiar with other edible parts too—head, feet, and tail. Brethren were thrifty, and it showed through their practical methods of cooking.

One of the recipes for the traditional "Snitz and Knep," a dish of pork with apple dumplings, instructs the reader that this recipe is "to be made only on bread-baking day," presumably because the making of dumplings would require time, effort, and dough that would be too much trouble to rouse on any other day (p. 68). Other recipes offer precise timing instructions: "Put on a piece of bacon to cook about 9 o'clock . . . . About 10 o'clock put the snitz [apples] in with the bacon" (p. 67).

In contrast, the more modern "Baked Hamloaf with Tomato Sauce," sent in by Donna E. Mallott, requires no such special day, and declines to provide the cook with hourly instructions as to its creation. It also calls for canned soup and other easily prepared or purchased ingredients, meaning that if you have an hour and access to the local grocery store, you could prepare the meal at any time of day or night.

These classic Inglenook recipes seem quaint to us, now. Their precise instructions, offering the cooks of the time helpful hints and guidance, make little sense in our own lives shaped by convenience and availability. Why bake bread all day when you can pick up a loaf on the way home from work? Why spend your morning cooking pork when you could drive down the street to the local barbecue joint? And yet, isn't the scent of baked dumplings worth a morning of kneading and rolling? Isn't the experience of a slow-baking ham growing golden in the oven and filling the house with its savory aroma a reward worthy of the effort put forth? In our overreliance on grocery stores and processed foods, we may have lost a little wisdom about the relationship between effort and result, the beauty involved in cooking and creating, the satisfaction of working to nourish our friends and families, and ourselves.

So, maybe we don't need to wait until baking day to make a hamloaf. Maybe we're not tied to the 9 o'clock hour for putting tonight's dinner in the oven. But we can still take the time to be just a little more attentive, a little more present, a little more engaged in our cooking and our baking.

Take a minute, as you break the eggs for the ham-loaf, to give thanks for the chickens that laid them—wherever they may be. Remember the farmers who milked the cows for the milk. Offer a prayer for the pigs, lives lived and ended in order to provide nourishment. Think even of those factory workers, spending their days labeling soup cans so that you might eat. Take another minute, as dinner is cooking, to pray for those who will eat it. Think of their bodies, and their physical health. Remember their spirits, and bless them with nourishment. Hold these loved ones in God's light and love.

There's a lot to learn from the cooks who came before us: how to spend time, attention, and care in the kitchen, creating nourishment and doing it mindfully and intentionally. Thanks be to God.

—Dana Cassell
Manassas, Virginia

SNITZ AND KNEP

For a small family take ½ pound smoked bacon, or 1 pound smoked ham, wash, put on the fire at 9 o'clock. Soak ½ pint dried sweet apple snitz with or without paring. At 10 o'clock put the snitz in with the meat, when soft, take 1½ pints of flour, 1 heaping teaspoonful baking powder. Stir well together, using enough water or sweet milk to make a stiff batter. Drop on top of snitz and meat and boil 15 minutes without uncovering.

—Sister Chloe Goughnour, Middlebranch, Ohio

Baked Hamloaf with Tomato Sauce

This recipe was made by Mrs. John D. Metzler when she entertained in Chicago in the late 1940s. The Metzlers lived in one of the Bethany apartments, and it was always a joy to share the warmth and friendship of the Metzler home. CROP began in their apartment at Bethany Seminary, before moving to an office in downtown Chicago.

Serves 10 to 12

HAMLOAF
2 pounds ground pork shoulder
1 pound ground smoked ham
1 cup dry bread crumbs
1 cup milk
2 eggs, beaten
½ can condensed tomato soup

SAUCE
½ cup sugar
½ cup cider vinegar
1 egg, beaten
2 tablespoons butter
2 tablespoons mustard
½ can condensed tomato soup

■ Preheat the oven to 350°F.

■ To make the hamloaf, combine the pork, ham, bread crumbs, milk, eggs, and soup in a bowl. Mix well and transfer to a 13 x 9-inch baking dish. Shape into a loaf and bake for 1 hour.

■ While the hamloaf is baking make the sauce. Combine the sugar, vinegar, egg, butter, mustard, and soup in a saucepan over medium heat. Cook the sauce until thick and creamy, about 10 minutes. Serve with the hamloaf.

—Donna E. Mallott
Pittsburgh, Pennsylvania

PORK DELICACIES

I have always loved eating pig stomach! And it's surprisingly lean. There are ways of making it that are good and ways that are not. My mother used to cut it into strips after it was baked and the sausage, potato, and onion filling (seasoned simply with salt and pepper) was taken out of it. I like it when it is good and brown and put through a food grinder. Sprinkle the ground-up pig stomach over the filling and mix them together, so that the browned-meat flavor permeates through it all. That's the way I love it.

—Anna N. Buckwalter
Lancaster, Pennsylvania

BARBECUED PORK CHOPS

This dish was always my favorite birthday meal.

Serves 6 to 8

¼ cup (½ stick) butter, divided
8 (1-inch thick) pork chops
1 cup ketchup
2 teaspoons salt
2 teaspoons celery seeds
1 teaspoon ground nutmeg
⅔ cup cider vinegar

■ Preheat the oven to 325°F. Coat a 13 x 9-inch baking dish with butter or oil and set aside.

■ Heat 2 tablespoons of the butter in a large skillet over medium-high heat. Brown 4 pork chops in the butter, without crowding, for about 4 minutes per side. Repeat with the remaining butter and pork chops. (You may need to do this in three batches.) Place the pork chops in the prepared baking dish.

■ Combine the ketchup, salt, celery seeds, nutmeg, vinegar, and 2 cups water in a container with a tight lid. Shake to blend the ingredients together. Pour the mixture over the pork chops.

■ Bake for 1½ hours. Turn the chops once while baking.

—Melinda Renee Kohlhorst
Greenville, Ohio

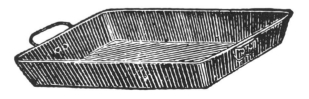

PORK LOIN CHOPS WITH ONION SAUCE

Serves 4

½ cup plus 2 tablespoons flour, divided
¼ to ½ teaspoon dried rosemary
Kosher salt
Freshly ground black pepper
4 (1-inch thick) pork chops
3 tablespoons olive oil

4 small onions, chopped
2 garlic cloves, minced
2 cups chicken broth
1 tablespoon white vinegar
2 tablespoons butter

- Preheat the oven to 300°F.

- Combine ½ cup of the flour and rosemary on a dinner plate. Sprinkle salt and pepper to taste on both sides of the chops, then dredge in the flour mixture, retaining any leftover flour for later.

- Heat the olive oil in a Dutch oven over medium-high heat. Brown the pork chops in the oil, about 4 minutes on each side. Transfer to a clean plate.

- Add the onions and garlic to the Dutch oven, adding more olive oil if needed, and cook until the onions are translucent, about 7 minutes.

- Heat the chicken broth in the microwave for about 30 seconds and add to the onions along with the vinegar and ¼ cup of water. Stir to scrape up the browned bits from the bottom of the pan (deglazing). Simmer until the sauce is smooth. Adjust the seasoning to taste.

- Place the pork chops in the sauce, including any juices that may have accumulated on the plate. Cover with the lid and cook for about 2 hours, or until the chops are fork-tender.

- Melt the butter in a small saucepan over medium heat. Add the remaining 2 tablespoons flour, turn off the heat, and mix well to make a roux.

- Remove the chops from the Dutch oven and place the pan on the stove over medium-high heat. Let the mixture come to a slight boil. Add the roux and stir vigorously to thicken the sauce. Serve with the chops.

—Sharon Vore Schwanitz
Troy, Ohio

CRANBERRY PORK ROAST IN A SLOW COOKER

I like to serve mashed potatoes with the pork roast. The cranberry gravy tastes good on the potatoes as well as the roast.

Serves 4 to 6

> 2½ to 3 pounds boneless pork loin roast
> 1 (16-ounce) can cranberry sauce
> ¼ cup sugar
> ½ cup cranberry juice or water
> 1 teaspoon dry mustard
> ¼ teaspoon ground cloves
> 2 tablespoons cornstarch

■ Trim the fat off the pork and place in a slow cooker.

■ Mash the cranberry sauce in a bowl. Add the sugar, cranberry juice, dry mustard, and cloves. Mix well and pour over the pork.

■ Cook on low for 6 to 8 hours, or until the roast is tender. Transfer the roast to a plate and cover with foil to keep warm.

■ Skim the fat from the juices in the slow cooker. Measure 2 cups of the juice, adding water if needed to make 2 cups. Pour into a saucepan and bring to a boil over medium heat.

■ Mix the cornstarch in 2 tablespoons cool water. When juice in the saucepan begins to boil, gradually add the cornstarch mixture and stir until thickened, about 4 minutes. Serve the cranberry gravy with the roast.

—Betty L. Breidenstine
Hummelstown, Pennsylvania

Slow-Roasted Honey Mustard Pork

Serves 12

1 (5-pound) pork roast
1 cup honey
3 tablespoons mustard
½ tablespoon salt
½ tablespoon black pepper

- Preheat the oven to 275°F.

- Place the roast in a large Dutch oven or slow cooker.

- Combine the honey, mustard, salt, and pepper in a mixing bowl. Stir to mix. Drizzle the sauce over the pork.

- Cover and bake for 5 hours or if using a slow cooker, cook on low for 6 to 8 hours.

—Lester E. Kesselring
Sebring, Florida

BABY BACK PORK RIBS

Serves 4 to 6

2 racks baby back pork ribs
⅓ cup ketchup
2 tablespoons soy sauce
1 teaspoon grated ginger or ¼ teaspoon ground ginger
1 garlic clove, minced
3 tablespoons pineapple, peach, or apricot preserves

■ Trim the fat from the ribs and cut into serving size pieces. Put into a large soup pot and cover with water. Boil for 30 minutes over medium-high heat and then drain.

■ Prepare a grill to hot.

■ Place on the hot grill for 10 minutes, turning once, until the ribs register 160°F on a meat thermometer.

■ While the ribs are cooking, mix the ketchup, soy sauce, ginger, garlic, and preserves together in a bowl. Brush the ribs with the sauce after 5 minutes of grilling. Cook 5 minutes more. Serve with any remaining sauce.

Note: If you do not have a grill you can bake these at 350°F until the ribs reach 160°F on a meat thermometer.

—Patricia Mae Marshall
Masontown, Pennsylvania

MARYLAND CRAB CAKES

Serves 8

1 pound crabmeat
1 large egg
1½ teaspoons Dijon mustard
1½ teaspoons seafood seasoning (like Old Bay)
1 teaspoon lemon juice
½ teaspoon Worcestershire sauce
1¼ cup bread crumbs

- Combine the crabmeat, egg, mustard, seafood seasoning, lemon juice, Worcestershire sauce, and bread crumbs in a sealable container. Mix well, cover, and refrigerate for 1 to 3 hours.

- When ready to prepare the crab cakes, preheat the oven to 350°F. Line a baking sheet with parchment paper or lightly grease with oil.

- Shape the mixture into 8 crab cakes and place on the prepared baking sheet.

- Bake for 20 to 25 minutes or until brown.

—Anne S. Harvey
Easton, Maryland

WHAT'S FOR DINNER?

The question was written on my worship bulletin by my best friend. The rest of the congregation was singing a hymn while Annie and I were thinking about Sunday dinner at Grandma Millie's house. I sometimes wondered if Annie was my friend solely to earn a seat at Grandma's table. Sunday dinners were legendary with more than enough food for my large family and any friends we brought along. "Roast duck and chicken," I wrote back. She answered by drawing a smiley face.

—Christy J. Waltersdorff
Lombard, Illinois

COD CREOLE

You can serve this dish right from the baking dish. It goes well with baked red potatoes and thin cucumber slices as side dishes.

Serves 6

> 2 (16-ounce) packages frozen cod fillets, partially thawed
> ¼ cup (½ stick) butter
> 1 large green bell pepper, diced
> 1 medium onion, chopped
> ½ cup thinly sliced celery
> 1 (8-ounce) can tomato sauce
> 1 teaspoon dried thyme
> 1 teaspoon salt
> ⅛ teaspoon black pepper

- Preheat the oven to 350°F.

- Lightly grease a 13 x 9-inch baking dish. Place the cod fillets in a single layer in the baking dish.

- Heat the butter in a skillet over medium heat. Sauté the bell pepper, onion, and celery in the butter until tender, about 7 minutes. Stir in the tomato sauce, thyme, salt, and black pepper and bring to a boil, stirring occasionally. Spoon the mixture over the fish. Cover and bake for 45 minutes or until the fish flakes easily with a fork.

—Virginia M. Barrows
Waterloo, Iowa

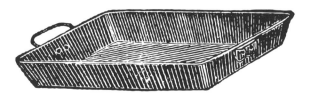

SALMON WITH COLORFUL ORIENTAL SAUCE

Everyone oos and ahs when this dish is presented at the table. It is a very easy and colorful dish that works well with other mild fish as well as chicken.

Serves 4

1½ cups uncooked rice
4 (4-ounce) salmon steaks
4 tablespoons olive oil
1 garlic clove, minced
½ red bell pepper, chopped
2 green onions, chopped
2 tablespoons soy sauce
1 tablespoon sesame oil
2 tablespoons rice vinegar
2 tablespoons fish sauce (found in most Asian food sections)
2 tablespoons capers
3 tablespoons fresh cilantro (optional)

■ Boil the rice in 2 to 3 cups of water in a saucepan over high heat. (Less water will make the rice firmer.) Reduce the heat to low and cook for 20 minutes.

■ Grill or broil salmon steaks for 7 minutes or until they flake easily when pierced with a fork. Cover and keep warm in a 120°F oven.

■ Heat the olive oil in a small saucepan over medium heat. Sauté the garlic, bell pepper and the white parts of the onions (reserving the green parts for later) in the olive oil for 5 minutes, until hot but still crisp. Add the soy sauce, sesame oil, vinegar, and fish sauce. Cook until the mixture is heated but still crisp, about 3 minutes. Remove from the heat and add the capers.

■ Mound the rice on a serving platter. Place the salmon on top of the rice. Pour the sauce over the entire dish. Sprinkle with the green onion tops and cilantro, if desired, and serve immediately.

—Marilyn E. Lerch
Bedford, Pennsylvania

PAN-SEARED TILAPIA WITH ROASTED TOMATOES

This recipe is simple, quick, and healthful. The lemon zest really adds pizzazz to the spinach.

Serves 2

> 1½ cups cherry tomatoes
> 1 tablespoon chopped parsley
> 2 tablespoons plus 1 teaspoon olive oil, divided
> Salt and ground black pepper to taste
> 2 fresh tilapia fillets, 1-inch thick, about 5 to 7 ounces
> 1½ tablespoons fresh thyme leaves
> 1 garlic clove, pressed or minced
> 9 ounces baby spinach, rinsed
> Zest of 1 lemon

- Preheat the oven to 375°F.

- Combine the tomatoes, parsley, 1 tablespoon of the olive oil, and salt and pepper in a bowl. Toss to mix and then transfer to a baking sheet. Bake for about 10 minutes or until the tomatoes start to brown.

- Meanwhile, rinse and dry the tilapia. Rub with the thyme leaves and season with salt and pepper.

- Heat another tablespoon of olive oil in an ovenproof sauté pan over high heat. Add the tilapia fillets. Turn the heat down to medium and cook until golden, about 3 minutes. Turn the tilapia over and place the pan in the oven. Cook for 5 minutes.

- In another medium sauté pan heat the remaining teaspoon of olive oil over high heat. Sauté the garlic in the oil and then add the spinach. Toss and add the lemon zest, heating just till the spinach is slightly wilted. Remove the spinach mixture from the heat.

- To serve, divide the spinach between two plates and top with the tilapia and roasted tomatoes.

—Renee R. Staab
Warrensburg, Missouri

MARINATED SALMON

This marinade will make farmed salmon taste divine. It's great grilled, broiled, baked, steamed, or pan fried.

Serves 4

4 (4-ounce) salmon fillets
½ cup olive oil
½ cup soy sauce
½ cup Dijon mustard
3 tablespoons horseradish
¼ cup packed brown sugar
3 teaspoons cider vinegar

■ Rinse and pat dry the salmon fillets, and put in a sealable container.

■ Combine the oil, soy sauce, mustard, horseradish, brown sugar, and vinegar together in a bowl. Mix well and pour over the salmon fillets.

■ Cover and marinate for 2 to 4 hours in the refrigerator.

■ Fifteen minutes before cooking, prepare a grill to hot. Remove the salmon from the refrigerator and grill for about 4 minutes per side. An alternative is to bake for about 20 minutes in a 350°F oven.

Note: Use gluten-free soy sauce to turn this into a gluten-free dish.

—Jeff Lennard
Elgin, Illinois

SHRIMP SCAMPI

Serves 4

3 tablespoons butter
2 tablespoons minced garlic
1 pound shrimp, shelled and deveined
1 (8-ounce) can tomato sauce
¼ cup chicken or vegetable broth
1 tablespoon white vinegar
1 cup cream
½ teaspoon dried basil
½ teaspoon dried oregano
Salt and pepper to taste
8 ounces dry pasta, cooked and drained

■ Heat the butter in a sauté pan over medium heat. Cook the garlic in the butter for 2 minutes. Add the shrimp and cook until pink.

■ Pour the tomato sauce, broth, and vinegar over the shrimp. Continue to cook for 10 minutes more.

■ Add the cream, basil, and oregano. Cook until thickened, about 7 minutes. Season with the salt and pepper. Serve over pasta.

—Jane Durant
Middletown, Maryland

FEEDING THOUSANDS

Our kitchen table could always expand for one or two or four more people who dropped in around mealtime. My mother, Geraldine Shifflett, would somehow create "fishes and loaves" out of whatever was on the table. Her openness to inviting people to eat with us helped fill the stomachs of literally hundreds of guests.

—Barb Myers
Mechanicsburg,
Pennsylvania

SPINACH FETA RICE

My teenage daughter likes this dish even though it is a departure
from pizza, burritos, and burgers. This dish tastes even better
when made with brown rice. Because the feta and broth are
somewhat salty, there is no need for additional salt.

Serves 4

1 cup uncooked rice
1 cup chicken or vegetable broth
1 teaspoon vegetable oil
1 medium onion, chopped
1 cup sliced button or baby bella mushrooms (about 4 ounces)
2 garlic cloves, minced
1 tablespoon lemon juice
½ teaspoon dried oregano
6 cups shredded fresh spinach leaves (about ¼ pound)
4 ounces feta cheese, crumbled
Freshly ground black pepper to taste

- Combine the rice, broth, and 1 cup water in a medium saucepan and bring to boil over high heat; stir once or twice. Cover the pan, reduce the heat to low, and simmer until the rice is tender and the liquid is absorbed.

- Heat the vegetable oil in a large skillet over medium-high heat. Cook the onion, mushrooms, and garlic in the oil until the onion is tender but not brown, about 7 minutes. Stir in the lemon juice and oregano. Stir in the cooked rice. Add the spinach and cheese and toss lightly until the spinach is wilted. Season lightly with pepper during this process.

—Cady Laycook
Long Beach, California

DANIEL'S CHOICE

When we think of Daniel, we think of the lion's den or the fiery furnace, not the first chapter on refusing the king's food. This story is about many things, but principally it's about the clash of the kingdoms. It's not really about becoming a vegetarian or even being kosher. Daniel is about resisting the dominant culture that is diametrically opposed to the reign of God. It's about refusing to be polluted by a system that starves an underclass and reserves choice meats and spirits for the elite. It's about making decisions that honor God.

—Paula Bowser
Englewood, Ohio

RAVIOLI WITH PEA SHOOT PESTO

Serves 4 to 6

1 garlic clove
1½ quarts (6 cups) lightly packed tender pea shoots, divided
½ cup mint leaves
½ cup extra virgin olive oil
4 ounces Parmigiano-Reggiano (Parmesan) cheese, finely grated
1 pound fresh cheese ravioli
2 cups sugar snap peas

■ Place the garlic in a food processor and mince. Add 2 cups of the pea shoots, the mint, and oil; pulse until coarsely puréed. Scrape into a small bowl and stir in the cheese; press plastic wrap against the pesto to keep the color bright.

■ Cook the ravioli according to the package directions, adding the snap peas during the last 2 minutes. Drain and return to the pot.

■ Whisk the pesto, then gently toss with the pasta. Add the remaining 4 cups pea shoots and toss gently. Serve immediately.

—Jan Dull Eller
Portland, Oregon

ZUCCHINI FRITTATA

There is a joke about zucchini. It grows so abundantly where we live that when it's ready to be harvested, don't go to town and leave your vehicle windows open; you may return to a vehicle full of zucchini!

Serves 4

- 1 teaspoon vegetable oil
- 1 cup shredded zucchini
- ½ cup chopped onion
- 3 eggs, beaten
- ¼ teaspoon salt
- 1 cup (4 ounces) shredded Swiss cheese

■ Preheat the oven to 350°F.

■ Heat the oil in an 8-inch skillet over medium heat. Sauté the zucchini and onion for 2 to 3 minutes or until tender. Pour the eggs over top, add the salt, and stir to mix.

■ Cook until almost set, 6 to 7 minutes. Sprinkle with the Swiss cheese.

■ Bake, uncovered, for 4 to 5 minutes or until the cheese melts. Serve hot.

—Ruth A. Clark
Froid, Montana

FLAVORS AROUND THE WORLD

For decades now we have awakened not only to the dynamic flavors of vegetarian fare, but also to the added benefits for consumers, farmers, and the planet. Although previous generations were unlikely to have prepared Brenda M. Wagner's vegetarian "Filipino Rice and Lentils," we can recognize the recipe as one of our own. The dish is warming, hearty, and unassuming, but not without flavor—perhaps similar to our Brethren ancestors.

Like this recipe, I am new to the Church of the Brethren. I joined this faith community long after God chose me and I chose to be a Christian. Though I am not dyed-in-the-wool Brethren, the core values resonate with my understanding of how God calls me to live in faith. Vegetarian recipes are a natural fit for this new era in Brethren history. As Brethren have become more involved in the world, our horizons have expanded to relationships around the globe. Our lives are richer, but so are our palates!

As the global population increases, so does our demand for more food to eat. We in the United States, however, consume a tremendous amount of resources for a relatively modest number of people. Our ostensible availability of resources and consumption patterns are the envy of some countries; yet these patterns of consumption are not sustainable or healthy for us or the world God created. As Christians, as Brethren, we're called to do things differently. Eating this lentil dish, with its subtle yet rich flavors, offers a chance for another way of living—living closer to faraway neighbors, living lighter on the land, and living in community around a common table. It becomes a sacred act that holds us together in conversation and gives us common nutrition and flavors to savor.

As my family and friends shared this dish, I thought of how soothing it is—like an introduction to a new comfort food. Despite the oft-perceived "spicy" additions, the earthy sweetness of the rice, cinnamon, and coconut milk makes this a mild, calming dish with the texture of sticky rice. It is not unlike "Beans Sambal," a classic recipe from the 1942 *Granddaughter's Inglenook Cookbook* (p. 165).

Eating vegetarian meals, particularly ones featuring beans or other legumes, honors people around the globe who do not choose this staple food but are grateful for what is available. When we choose to live more simply so that others might simply live, we not only enhance the lives of indigenous people of many lands but also honor the entire created world as a gift of God. When we choose to forgo meat for some or all of our meals, we honor a weary food system. When we choose plant-based diets, the corporate incentive for factory farming is deterred. When demands for animal production are down, precious land, water, and forests are better protected. As you discover new vegetarian recipes here, how might you consider adapting your weekly menu? Eat one well-balanced vegetarian meal each day, set aside one vegetarian day per week, or use this opportunity as a Lenten practice for one year. You may find this a creative, invigorating, even prayerful experience.

In my family, one way we remember other peoples around the world is by preparing dishes from other cultures. Somehow these dishes taste better with the mindfulness of those who eat these foods on a daily basis. As I prepared this lentil dish, I was mindful of my relative from the Philippines and her family. May you be enriched in a similar fashion as you prepare this meal and others. May you be nourished in body and spirit, encouraged by the gift of earthy flavors and the company around our tables that adds spice to our lives.

—Kimberly Koczan-Flory
Fort Wayne, Indiana

BEANS SAMBAL (INDIA)

Green beans
Vinegar
Salt
Pepper powder
Thick coconut milk

Boil green beans till soft in salt water; drain well. Put in dish; add vinegar, salt to taste and sufficient thick coconut milk to cover the bits. Sprinkle pepper powder over and serve.

—Anetta C. Mow, Elgin, Illinois

FILIPINO RICE AND LENTILS

This is a simple, complete meal. I wouldn't substitute any of the whole spice items. After it is fully cooked, make sure to remove the bay leaves, cinnamon stick, and whole cloves. For more flavor substitute chicken broth for the water, and for more substance add grilled salmon or albacore tuna.

Serves 6 to 8

- ½ cup dry lentils
- 2 small onions, chopped
- 2 garlic cloves, chopped
- 2 bay leaves
- 2 whole cloves
- 1 (13-ounce) can coconut milk
- 2 cups brown rice
- 1 cinnamon stick
- ¼ teaspoon turmeric
- ¼ teaspoon curry powder

■ Sort and wash the lentils. Boil the lentils in a medium saucepan with enough water to cover for 20 minutes. Drain and set aside.

■ In a large stock pot over high heat, combine the onions, garlic, bay leaves, cloves, coconut milk, rice, cinnamon stick, turmeric, curry powder, and 3¼ cups water. Bring to a boil. Reduce the heat to medium low and cook the rice until the liquid is absorbed, approximately 40 minutes.

■ Add the softened, drained lentils. Keep the lid on for 5 to 10 more minutes, toss then serve.

—Brenda M. Wagner
Kleinfeltersville, Pennsylvania

ROUNDING OUT THE MEAL

This is a wonderful dish that is more than a side dish, but not quite a full main course. Consider cooking a full pound of lentils and, after taking the portion out for this dish, make a savory curried lentil side dish to add to each plate. In addition, stir-fried mixed vegetables, lightly seasoned (perhaps a dash of curry tossed with coconut oil or a dash of sesame oil and sesame seeds with a bit of sea salt) can round out the meal and add great color without distracting from the other flavors.

—Kimberly Koczan-Flory
Fort Wayne, Indiana

CHEESE AND NUT LOAF

I found this delicious recipe when my son was a vegetarian. My husband was a rice farmer, so I have many recipes that include brown rice. It freezes well.

Serves 8 to 10

¼ cup wheat germ, divided
3 tablespoons vegetable oil
1 medium onion, chopped
1½ cups chopped celery
1 cup chopped cashews
1 cup chopped walnuts
2 cups cooked brown rice
2 cups cottage cheese
2 tablespoons chopped chives
¼ cup toasted sesame seeds
2 tablespoons chopped parsley
½ teaspoon thyme
1 teaspoon sea salt
3 eggs, lightly beaten
½ pound diced tofu
1 cup sliced mushrooms
½ cup grated Parmesan cheese
1 (14-ounce) can cream of mushroom soup
1 tablespoon white wine vinegar
Sautéed mushrooms (optional)

- Preheat the oven to 375°F. Grease a 9 x 5-inch loaf pan, dust with some of the wheat germ, and set aside. Reserve the remaining wheat germ.

- Heat the oil in a saucepan over medium heat. Sauté the onion and celery in the oil until soft, about 7 minutes.

- Combine the cashews, walnuts, rice, cottage cheese, chives, sesame seeds, parsley, thyme, salt, eggs, tofu, and mushrooms in a large bowl. Stir in the cooked onion and celery.

- Press the mixture into the prepared pan and sprinkle the remaining wheat germ on top.

- Bake for 1 hour. Top with grated cheese during the last 15 minutes of baking. Remove from the oven and let stand 5 to 10 minutes to firm up.

- Meanwhile, prepare a sauce by combining the soup, vinegar, ¼ cup water, and mushrooms, if using, in a saucepan over medium heat. Cook until heated through, about 5 minutes.

- Serve the loaf with warmed sauce.

—Pauline Fillmore
Live Oak, California

Tomato-Basil Pie

Serves 4

1 (9-inch) prebaked piecrust
1½ cups shredded mozzarella cheese, divided
5 Roma (or 4 slicer) tomatoes
1 cup loosely packed fresh basil leaves
4 garlic cloves
½ cup mayonnaise or salad dressing
¼ cup grated Parmesan cheese
⅛ teaspoon ground white or black pepper

- Preheat the oven to 375°F.

- Heat the prebaked piecrust in the preheating oven for about 5 minutes. Add ½ cup of the mozzarella cheese and bake for 2 minutes to melt the cheese; remove from the oven.

- Cut the tomatoes into wedges, scoop out the seeds, and arrange the wedges on top of the melted cheese in the piecrust.

- Combine the basil leaves and garlic cloves in a food processor to chop coarsely, or chop by hand. Sprinkle over the tomatoes.

- Combine the remaining 1 cup mozzarella cheese, mayonnaise, Parmesan cheese, and pepper in a bowl and stir to mix. Spoon over the basil mixture, spreading to evenly cover the top.

- Bake for 35 to 40 minutes or till golden brown and bubbly. Serve warm.

—Rachel Gross
North Manchester, Indiana

VEGETABLES
AND RICE

Potatoes come from far Virginia;
Parsley was sent us from Sardinia;
French beans, low growing on the earth,
To distant India trace their birth;
But scarlet runners, gay and tall,
That climb upon your garden wall—
A cheerful sight to all around—
In South America were found.
The onion traveled here from Spain;
The leek from Switzerland we gain,
Garlic from Sicily obtain.
Spinach in far Syria grows;
Two hundred years or more
Brazil the artichoke sent o'er.
And Southern Europe's sea-coast shore
Beet-root on us bestows.

When 'Lizabeth was reigning here,
Peas came from Holland, and were dear.
The south of Europe lays its claim
To beans, but some from Egypt came.
The radishes, both thin and stout,
Natives of China are, no doubt;
But turnips, carrots, and sea-kale,
With celery, so crisp and pale,
Are products of our own fair land,
And cabbages, a goodly tribe,
Which abler pens might well describe—
Are also ours, I understand.

—London Young Folks' Rural
The Inglenook magazine (Jan. 12, 1904)

QUICK
& EASY

SPECIAL
OCCASION

GLUTEN
FREE

VEGETARIAN

VEGAN

Hobo Beans

Serves 6

½ pound ground beef
1 small onion, chopped
1 (15-ounce) can pork and beans
1 (15-ounce) can black beans, drained
⅓ cup dark molasses
½ cup ketchup
1 teaspoon chili powder
⅛ teaspoon cumin

- Brown the ground beef in a skillet over medium heat until no longer pink, about 10 minutes, and drain off the fat. Add the onion and sauté about 5 minutes. Turn off the heat and set aside.

- Preheat the oven to 350°F.

- Combine the pork and beans and black beans in a 13 x 9-inch baking dish.

- Add the cooked ground beef, onion, molasses, ketchup, chili powder, and cumin. Stir gently until all the ingredients are well combined.

- Bake uncovered for 25 to 30 minutes.

—Jeff Bach
Mount Joy, Pennsylvania

Rocky Mountain Sweet and Sour Beans

Serves 8 to 10

8 bacon slices, cut and cooked, but not crisp
1 medium onion, chopped
¾ cup packed brown sugar
⅓ to ½ cup vinegar
Salt to taste
1 teaspoon dry mustard
1 (15-ounce) can kidney beans, drained
1 (15-ounce) can yellow lima beans or Great Northern beans, drained
1 (15-ounce) can green lima beans, drained
1 (15-ounce) can pork and beans

■ Preheat the oven to 350°F. Grease a 3-quart casserole dish and set aside.

■ Combine the bacon and onion in a large bowl. Add the brown sugar, vinegar, salt, and mustard. Stir until well mixed. Add all the beans, stir well, and pour into the prepared casserole dish. Bake for 1 hour.

—Susan Kinsel Fitze
New Lebanon, Ohio

Sautéed Kale

Experiment with other types of greens and vegetables for a different sauté.

Serves 4 to 6

2 tablespoons olive oil
½ cup chopped onion
1 garlic clove, minced
½ cup chopped mushrooms (optional)
5 to 6 cups chopped kale, chard, or other greens
¾ cup frozen corn
⅓ cup chopped red or yellow bell pepper
Salt and pepper to taste

■ Heat the oil in a large skillet over medium heat. Sauté the onion, garlic, mushrooms, if using, and greens until the onions are translucent and the greens are slightly wilted.

■ Mix in the corn, bell peppers, and salt and pepper. Reduce the heat to low and cook for about 10 minutes, stirring as necessary. Add a small amount of water to steam, if needed.

—Pearl Fruth Miller
Warrensburg, Missouri

SHAVED BRUSSELS SPROUTS WITH PANCETTA

Serves 8 to 10

2 pounds Brussels sprouts
1 tablespoon olive oil
8 ounces pancetta or bacon, cut crosswise into ½-inch-wide strips and separated
Salt and freshly ground black pepper

■ Using a sharp knife or mandoline, thinly slice the Brussels sprouts crosswise, discarding the ends.

■ Heat the olive oil in a large skillet over high heat; add the pancetta or bacon and stir. Cook until slightly crisp, about 5 minutes.

■ Reduce the heat to medium high; add the Brussels sprouts, and cook, stirring often, until they are bright green and tender, 3 to 5 minutes.

■ Add salt and pepper to taste. Serve hot.

—Jan Dull Eller
Portland, Oregon

Green Beans with Spicy Peanut Sauce

Our daughter's college friend asked me to send this recipe to his mother because they were the best beans he'd ever eaten. I prefer leaving the beans whole, but it's fine to snap them into pieces if you wish.

Serves 4 to 6

   1 pound green beans, washed and trimmed
   2 tablespoons butter (see note)
   ¼ cup chunky peanut butter
   ¼ teaspoon ground nutmeg
   Pinch of salt and pepper
   ¾ teaspoon red pepper flakes (or less to taste)

■ Cook the green beans in boiling water until crisp-tender, about 8 minutes, and drain.

■ Melt the butter in a saucepan over medium heat and add the peanut butter, nutmeg, salt and pepper, and red pepper flakes. Cook until the peanut butter is melted, about 4 minutes and pour over the hot green beans.

Notes: To make the sauce in the microwave, place all the sauce ingredients in a glass measuring cup or bowl. Microwave on high for about 1 minute and then stir to mix. If you use oil instead of butter, this is a vegan recipe.

—Carol Compton Spangler
Vienna, Virginia

HONEY-ROASTED CARROTS AND PARSNIPS

Serves 4

1 tablespoon honey
3 tablespoons olive oil
2 cups sliced carrots (about 4 carrots)
2 cups sliced parsnips
Pinch fresh thyme sprigs

- Preheat the oven to 350°F.

- Combine the honey and oil together in a saucepan over medium-low heat. Add the carrots and parsnips and toss to coat the vegetables evenly.

- Spread the mixture into a shallow baking pan and sprinkle the thyme on top.

- Bake until the vegetables are tender, about 30 minutes.

—Janet Maldet
Johnstown, Pennsylvania

HONEY-MUSTARD CARROTS

Serves 4

2 cups sliced carrots (about 4 carrots)
½ teaspoon salt
1 tablespoon butter (see note)
1 teaspoon prepared mustard
½ teaspoon curry powder
1 tablespoon honey
Dill weed (optional)

- Briefly cook the carrots in boiling water until just tender, about 7 minutes. Drain and return to the pot. Stir in the salt, butter, mustard, curry powder, and honey. Garnish with dill weed, if desired, and serve warm.

Note: If you use oil instead of butter, this is a vegan recipe.

—Marie Hoover Willoughby
North Manchester, Indiana

Scalloped Carrots

This recipe freezes well. If baking from frozen, bake for an hour. Otherwise, thaw before baking.

Serves 6 to 8

  4 cups sliced carrots (about 8 medium carrots)
  3 tablespoons butter
  1 medium onion, chopped
  1 (10-ounce) can cream of celery soup
  Salt to taste
  Pepper to taste
  ½ cup grated Cheddar cheese
  3 cups croutons
  ⅓ cup butter, melted

■ Preheat the oven to 350°F. Lightly grease a 2½-quart baking dish.

■ Boil the carrots in a pot of water over high heat until tender, about 8 minutes. Drain.

■ Heat the butter in a large saucepan over medium heat. Cook the onion until translucent, about 5 minutes.

■ Stir in the soup, salt, pepper, cheese, and carrots. Pour the carrot mixture into the prepared baking dish. Toss the croutons with the melted butter and spoon over the carrot mixture.

■ Bake for 20 minutes.

—Karen Stocking
South Elgin, Illinois

MEXICAN FRIED CORN

This is wonderful served with chicken enchiladas.

Serves 6

> 2 tablespoons olive oil
> 1 small onion, finely chopped
> ½ green bell pepper, cut in rings
> ½ red bell pepper, cut in rings
> 1 green chile pepper, seeded and finely chopped
> 2 tablespoons chopped fresh cilantro (reserving some leaves for garnish)
> 1¾ cups whole kernel corn
> 1 (4-ounce) jar sliced mushrooms or ½ cup fresh sliced mushrooms
> Salt and black pepper to taste

■ Heat the oil in a heavy skillet over medium heat. Add the onion, bell peppers, chile pepper, and cilantro. Cook for 5 minutes or until the peppers are soft, stirring occasionally.

■ Stir in the corn, mushrooms, and salt and pepper. Cook another 5 minutes or till hot, stirring occasionally. Transfer to a warmed serving dish. Garnish with cilantro leaves, if desired.

—Jeannie Campbell
Beavercreek, Ohio

WHITE HOMINY AND CORN DISH

This is a family favorite at holiday meals in lieu of corn pudding.

Serves 6 to 8

- 2 cups canned white hominy
- 2 cups frozen yellow corn, thawed
- 1 garlic clove, minced
- 6 ounces sharp Cheddar cheese, shredded
- 2 cups milk
- 4 eggs, beaten
- 1 teaspoon salt
- ¼ teaspoon cayenne pepper

■ Preheat the oven to 350°F. Lightly grease a 2-quart baking dish or casserole dish with butter or cooking spray.

■ Combine the hominy and corn and stir to mix. Pour into the prepared baking dish, leveling off the top of the mixture with a spoon. Sprinkle the garlic and cheese on top.

■ Whisk together the milk, eggs, salt, and cayenne pepper in a medium bowl and pour over the mixture in the baking dish.

■ Bake for 50 to 60 minutes, or until set and the top is bubbling.

■ Remove from the oven and let rest for 5 to 10 minutes before serving.

—Christine S. Ontiveros
Roanoke, Virginia

ORZO VEGGIES

This has been a huge hit at our Cancer Center's frequent breakfast potlucks.

Serves 8

1 pound asparagus, trimmed
3 bell peppers (red, green, or yellow)
6 green onions, chopped
1 cup grape tomatoes, cut into halves
1 medium zucchini, sliced
¼ cup extra virgin olive oil, divided
1 garlic clove, crushed
1 tablespoon Italian seasoning
¾ teaspoon salt
⅛ teaspoon coarsely ground black pepper
1 cup orzo (see note)
2 cups reduced-sodium vegetable or chicken broth
½ cup pine nuts, toasted
¾ cup crumbled feta cheese

■ Preheat the oven to 350°F.

■ Cut the asparagus, bell peppers, and onions into bite-size pieces. Place the asparagus, peppers, onions, tomatoes, and zucchini into a 13 x 9-inch baking dish.

■ Add two tablespoons of the olive oil, garlic, Italian seasoning, salt, and pepper. Toss well.

■ Roast for 30 minutes or until the vegetables are tender.

■ Add the remaining 2 tablespoons olive oil to a large saucepan over medium-high heat. Add the orzo and sauté until brown. Add the broth and bring to a boil. Reduce the heat to low and cook, covered, until the liquid is absorbed, about 15 minutes.

■ Add the orzo to the roasted vegetables. Mix well. Sprinkle pine nuts and cheese over top.

■ Cover with foil and bake for 30 minutes. Serve hot or at room temperature.

Note: Use quinoa and/or lentils to make the recipe gluten free.

—Susan Sweigard Balcarcel
Sonora, California

OVEN-FRIED ZUCCHINI IN A CRUNCHY PARMESAN CRUST

Serves 4

1 tablespoon extra virgin olive oil
½ cup fine dried bread crumbs
⅓ cup grated Parmigiano-Reggiano (Parmesan) cheese
½ teaspoon dried rosemary
⅛ teaspoon cayenne pepper
½ teaspoon salt
¼ teaspoon freshly ground black pepper
2 large eggs
4 to 6 small green or golden zucchini squash

■ Preheat the oven to 400°F. Lightly grease a heavy baking sheet with the oil and set aside.

■ In a shallow dish, combine the bread crumbs, cheese, rosemary, cayenne, salt, and pepper and mix well. In a second shallow dish, lightly beat the eggs.

■ Trim the ends of the squash. Cut each squash in half lengthwise. Lay the halves flat and cut in half lengthwise again. Then cut the strips in half crosswise. Dredge each piece first in the egg and then in the cheese mixture, coating evenly. Arrange well-spaced in a single layer on the prepared baking sheet.

■ Bake for 5 to 7 minutes, then turn the squash over and bake for 5 to 7 minutes longer, or until crisp and lightly browned. Serve hot or at room temperature.

—Jan Dull Eller
Portland, Oregon

SUMMER STILL LIFE

Whether it takes a trip to the garden or to the farmer's market, I love to compose a still life of our supper's ingredents— red tomatoes, satin-finished purple eggplants, skinny green zucchini, golden-skinned onions, plump green peppers, paper-white garlic cloves. Sometimes I add a bouquet of crinkly parsley, smooth-leaved basil, and variegated thyme. All day I enjoy the still life, with all its God-given colors, shapes, and textures. Then I transform it into a stew that is equally alluring, bubbling in my big black cast-iron pot.

—Kathie Kurtz
Manassas, Virginia

Summer Squash Skillet

Serves 4

- **2 tablespoons butter**
- **½ cup chopped onion**
- **½ cup chopped green bell pepper**
- **1 tablespoon sugar**
- **1 tablespoon flour**
- **1 teaspoon salt**
- **¼ teaspoon black pepper**
- **2 cups cubed summer squash**
- **3 medium tomatoes, peeled and cut into small wedges**
- **½ cup grated Cheddar cheese**

- Preheat the oven to 350°F. Lightly grease a 13 x 9-inch baking dish and set aside.

- In a large skillet melt the butter over medium heat. Add the onion and bell pepper. Sauté until tender, about 7 minutes, but do not brown. Stir in the sugar, flour, salt, and pepper.

- Add the squash and tomatoes. Cook over low heat until tender, about 8 minutes. Transfer to the prepared baking dish, sprinkle the cheese on top, and bake until the cheese is melted, about 5 minutes.

—Phyllis Kline
Mount Sidney, Virginia

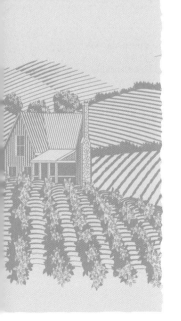

Summer Southern Creole Zucchini

I had more zucchini in my garden than I could use, so I brought some to church. My African American friend gave me this recipe that came from his mother. You can add corn or other vegetables, and you can omit the tomatoes. You can also vary the amount of seasoning you use.

(GF)(🥕)(V)

Serves 2 to 4

- 1 tablespoon olive oil
- 1 medium zucchini, thinly sliced
- 1 onion, chopped
- 2 garlic cloves, crushed
- 1 teaspoon Creole or Cajun seasoning
- 1 tablespoon brown sugar
- ¼ teaspoon salt
- 2 tomatoes, chopped

■ Heat the olive oil in a skillet over medium heat and sauté the zucchini, onion, and garlic until the zucchini is tender and the onion is translucent, about 8 minutes.

■ When the vegetables are softened, add the Creole or Cajun seasoning, brown sugar, salt, and tomatoes and cook until heated through, about 5 minutes.

■ Remove from the heat and serve.

—Waneta I. Benson
Mechanicsburg, Pennsylvania

SWEET POTATOES REVISITED

A classic addition to many Brethren tables over the years has been sweet potatoes. Baked, fried, or boiled, they've been standard fare for many family celebrations, a food that signifies the beginning of autumn, cooler weather, and preparations for winter. A favorite sweet potato dish from my childhood in Pennsylvania was candied sweet potatoes. The potatoes were melt-in-your-mouth soft with a gooey sauce on the outside that when cooled, tasted and behaved like caramel.

Earlier recipes commonly required cooks to make sweet potato dishes *sweet*, with butter, nuts, and large amounts of sugar. One savory version, "Baked Sweet Potatoes Southern Style" from the 1942 *Granddaughter's Inglenook Cookbook*, calls for lard, salt, and pepper (p. 282). A sweet variation includes brown sugar, crushed pineapple, ground nuts, and marshmallows—a sweet potato casserole very similar to those many of us have seen on Thanksgiving tables, past and present. While sweet potatoes are delicious when prepared with butter and sugar, maple syrup, or honey, savory preparations move toward healthful, more wholesome additions to autumn meals.

A savory recipe that combines flavors once perhaps unknown to most Brethren cooks is "Curried Sweet Potatoes" from Sylvia Hess' recipe box. In this recipe, Sylvia combines healthier olive oil with curry, salt, and pepper. The inclusion of this recipe speaks to many culinary and societal changes throughout the years. Many cooks these days opt for olive oil or other better-for-you fats, looking to distance themselves from animal-based fats such as lard or butter, whose link to heart disease has been studied frequently in recent decades. The inclusion of curry, a spice blend that often contains cumin, turmeric, cayenne pepper, and black pepper, demonstrates a greater desire for cooks to expand their repertoire and try new flavors from different cultures. Preparation and baking time is minimal; present-day cooks are so often looking for quick and easy recipes that can be on the table in less than half an hour.

My mother's go-to preparation for sweet potatoes is to scrub them well, wrap them in aluminum foil, and bake them until soft. To serve, she peels off the aluminum foil, slices the potato, and adds a bit of butter—perhaps a simple way to prepare a very versatile tuber, but nonetheless delicious.

While living in El Salvador, however, I have learned other ways to prepare sweet potatoes. Here, we have access more to yams than sweet potatoes, but dare I say it, I find them nearly interchangeable. I will never forget trying to make a Thanksgiving dinner during my first November as a BVS volunteer, asking in various market stalls for a yellow sweet potato—literally in Spanish, *papas dulces*. People looked at me like I was crazy. Several months later, a friend of mine gave me something called *camote en miel*, and eating the first bite was a revelation. I jumped up and down with joy, having finally found my comfort food that brought back so many soothing memories from childhood autumn meals.

Like sweet potato casserole or baked sweet potatoes, Sylvia's recipe is an up-and-coming comfort food. Curry adds dimension to a root vegetable so often prepared in a sweet side dish or dessert, expanding cooks' horizons to include new flavors and aromas from around the world.

BAKED SWEET POTATOES SOUTHERN STYLE

Select enough potatoes for the servings desired. Wash and dry thoroughly. Rub lard over skins with wax paper. Place in hot oven on pan and bake until done. In this method the sweet potatoes form their own sugar. When taken from oven remove skins, cut to desired size and season to taste with salt, pepper and butter. Serve while hot.

—Mrs. Ruby Morningstar, Howe, Indiana

—Sarah Hall
San Salvador, El Salvador

CURRIED SWEET POTATOES

Feel free to use more olive oil, if you like, and you may not need to spray the baking sheet. With the smaller, bite-size pieces, I toss them in the oil and seasonings to get all the surfaces coated. The proportions of all the ingredients can be adjusted to individual taste.

Serves 4

> **2 large sweet potatoes**
> **2 teaspoons olive oil**
> **1 teaspoon curry powder**
> **½ teaspoon salt**
> **½ teaspoon black pepper**

■ Preheat the oven to 450°F. Spray a baking sheet with cooking spray.

■ Scrub the sweet potatoes and peel if desired. Cut the sweet potatoes in half, and then cut each half into quarters. Depending on the size of your potatoes, the quarters can be cut into smaller, bite-size pieces.

■ Place the sweet potatoes on the baking sheet, drizzle with olive oil, and sprinkle with the curry powder, salt, and pepper, turning to coat.

■ Roast until the sweet potatoes are fork-tender, about 15 minutes. They will not become crisp like white potatoes.

—Sylvia M. Hess
Xenia, Ohio

CAMOTE EN MIEL

Camote en miel (yams in honey) is a favorite afternoon snack common in El Salvador. Adults and children alike enjoy it with a cup of coffee or a thick corn- or flour-based hot beverage, perfect on a cool day in the mountains

—Sarah Hall
San Salvador, El Salvador

CREAMY POTATO CASSEROLE

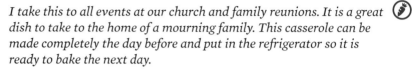

I take this to all events at our church and family reunions. It is a great dish to take to the home of a mourning family. This casserole can be made completely the day before and put in the refrigerator so it is ready to bake the next day.

Serves 8 to 10

CASSEROLE
2 pounds (32 ounces) frozen shredded hash brown potatoes
½ cup (1 stick) butter, melted
½ teaspoon salt
½ teaspoon pepper
1 (8-ounce) container sour cream
2 tablespoons minced onion
1 (10¾-ounce) can cream of chicken soup
2 cups shredded Cheddar cheese

TOPPING
¼ cup (½ stick) butter, melted
2 cups crushed corn flakes

■ Preheat the oven to 425°F. Lightly grease a 13 x 9-inch glass casserole dish with cooking spray and set aside.

■ For the casserole, combine the potatoes, butter, salt, pepper, sour cream, onion, soup, and cheese in a bowl. Mix well and then press into the prepared dish.

■ For the topping, combine the butter and corn flakes in a bowl. Mix well and spread over the top of the potatoes.

■ Bake for approximately 45 minutes, until bubbly and golden brown on top.

Note: For a creamier casserole, add ½ to ¾ cup milk with the soup.

—Doris T. Quesenberry
Floyd, Virginia

RANCH POTATO CASSEROLE

This recipe is from my Aunt Kathy Lechlider's kitchen. She loved cooking so much she put together her own recipe book and gave them out as gifts. She loved cooking for large groups especially at our family gatherings. This recipe is submitted in memory of her with love.

Serves 8

CASSEROLE
6 to 8 medium red potatoes
½ cup sour cream
½ cup ranch dressing (see page 156)
¼ cup cooked crumbled bacon
2 teaspoons fresh or 1 teaspoon dried parsley
1 cup shredded Cheddar cheese

TOPPING
½ cup shredded Cheddar cheese
2 cups slightly crushed corn flakes
¼ cup (½ stick) butter, melted

■ Preheat the oven to 350°F. Grease a 13 x 9-inch baking dish with butter or cooking spray and set aside.

■ Wash and dice the potatoes. Cook in boiling, salted water over high heat until tender, about 15 minutes. Drain and set aside.

■ In a large bowl, combine the sour cream, ranch dressing, bacon, parsley, and cheese. Add the potatoes and toss until completely coated. Pour into the prepared baking dish.

■ For the topping, combine the cheese, corn flakes, and butter. Spread over the casserole.

■ Bake for 40 to 45 minutes, until the potatoes are bubbly and browned on top.

—Barbara L. Helmick
Bridgewater, Virginia

RED CABBAGE

Serves 6

1 medium head red cabbage, shredded
½ cup vinegar
3 tablespoons butter
¼ cup sugar
1 teaspoon salt
Dash of nutmeg

■ Bring ½ cup water to a boil in a large saucepan over high heat. Add the cabbage, vinegar, and butter. Reduce the heat to medium low, cover, and cook for 45 minutes.

■ Add the sugar, salt, and nutmeg. Continue cooking, uncovered, until the liquid has evaporated.

—Mildred D. Teets
Aurora, West Virginia

SAUTÉED BABY SPINACH

Serves 3 to 4

2 tablespoons olive oil
¼ cup chopped red onion
¼ cup chopped red and orange bell pepper
2 tablespoons minced garlic
1 pound baby spinach
Salt and pepper to taste

■ Head the oil in a large skillet over medium heat. Add the onion, bell peppers, and garlic. Sauté until the garlic is fragrant, about 1 minute.

■ Add the spinach and stir until wilted, about 3 minutes. Salt and pepper to taste.

—Chris Fogerty and JoAnn Myers
North Manchester, Indiana

COLORFUL ROASTED VEGETABLES

This recipe can be adapted to accommodate individual tastes. Omit what you don't like and add any vegetables you prefer.

Serves 6 to 8

2 medium carrots, julienned
½ large green bell pepper, julienned
½ large red bell pepper, julienned
½ medium onion, sliced and separated into rings
2½ cups broccoli florets
2½ cups cauliflower florets
¾ pound asparagus, trimmed and halved
⅛ to ¼ cup olive oil
1½ tablespoons lemon juice
2 garlic cloves, minced
1½ teaspoons dried rosemary, crushed
½ teaspoon salt

■ Preheat the oven to 400°F. Grease a baking sheet with cooking spray or butter and set aside.

■ Combine the carrots, bell peppers, onion, broccoli, cauliflower, and asparagus in a large bowl. Toss to mix.

■ In a small bowl, combine the olive oil, lemon juice, garlic, rosemary, and salt. Whisk to mix, drizzle over the vegetables, and stir to coat. Transfer the vegetables to the prepared baking sheet.

■ Roast uncovered for 20 to 25 minutes, to desired crispness.

—Betty L. Breidenstine
Hummelstown, Pennsylvania

NIGERIAN MIXED GREENS

In Nigeria they call this Aleho and Yacua Soup, which means spinach and greens soup. We usually use spinach, but we have substituted the stronger mustard greens with turnip greens, collards, and kale. This meal is great just as it stands, but meat could be added to the sautéing onions. It also makes a great side dish for a favorite meat dish.

Serves 10

2 cups uncooked rice
1½ tablespoons olive oil
1 cup chopped onion
2 garlic cloves
1 chile pepper, chopped
4 large tomatoes, chopped
8 to 12 ounces mustard greens, washed and chopped
10 to 16 ounces spinach, fresh or frozen
2 vegetable bouillon cubes
Salt and black pepper

■ Prepare the rice according to package directions.

■ Heat the oil in a sauté pan over medium heat. Sauté the onion until clear, about 5 minutes. Add the garlic, chile pepper, and tomatoes. Cook until the tomatoes soften, about 3 minutes. Add a little water if necessary to keep it moist.

■ Add the mustard greens and cook for about 10 minutes. Do not let the vegetables cook dry.

■ If the spinach is fresh, rinse and trim the stems. Chop the spinach into 2-inch square pieces. Baby spinach leaves are fine whole. Add the bouillon and spinach leaves. Cook for about 5 minutes. The fresh greens are bulky until they cook down. You may need a larger pot or to add greens in small increments until they soften from the heat. Add salt or black pepper to taste.

■ Serve the mixed greens over cooked rice.

—Bonnie Jean Rager Bohrer
South Bend, Indiana

NOT JUST FOR DINNER

Vegetables are not just for dinner anymore. For a wonderful smoothie to help your day start smoothly, try adding a handful of spinach or kale into the blender with fruit and the milk, kefir, or yogurt of your choice. By adding blueberries, the drink turns purple rather than green and disguises the hidden vegetable goodness. Plus, your body will thank you.

—Kimberly Koczan-Flory
Fort Wayne, Indiana

Spanish Rice

Serves 8 to 10

1 cup uncooked rice
¼ cup (½ stick) butter
1 onion, finely minced
1 medium green bell pepper, finely minced
¼ cup finely diced celery
1 (15-ounce) can diced tomatoes, drained
½ teaspoon salt
⅛ teaspoon pepper
Shredded Cheddar cheese (optional)
Crumbled bacon (optional)

■ Cook the rice in a pot with 1¾ cups boiling, salted water for 20 minutes or until the water is absorbed.

■ Meanwhile, melt the butter in a large skillet over medium heat. Sauté the onion, bell pepper, and celery until softened, about 8 minutes. Add the tomatoes, salt, and pepper. Reduce the heat to low and simmer for 15 minutes. Gently stir in the hot, cooked rice.

■ Sprinkle cheese and bacon on top before serving, if desired.

—Jill D. Fike
Willow Springs, Missouri

Dislikes and Likes

With eight children in our family, Mom would not allow us to be picky. Each of us was permitted to dislike only one food. Mine was sweet potatoes. Fifty years after the fact, my taste buds have matured. Now I dearly love these colorful bastions of vitamins.

—Jeanne Jacoby Smith
McPherson, Kansas

CORNBREAD AND WILD RICE STUFFING WITH CRANBERRIES

Serves 8 to 10

2 (12-ounce) boxes cornbread mix
1 (6-ounce) package wild rice blend
1 pound dried cranberries
3 celery ribs
2 carrots
1 red onion
2 cups vegetable or chicken broth

■ Preheat the oven to 350°F. Grease a 13 x 9-inch baking dish with cooking spray or oil and set aside.

■ Prepare the cornbread mix and wild rice according to the package directions.

■ Combine the cooked cornbread and wild rice in a large bowl. Add the cranberries and toss to mix.

■ Chop the celery, carrots, and onion in a food processor until finely minced. Add the vegetables to the cornbread mixture and toss to combine.

■ Add the vegetable or chicken broth and stir to wet the mixture. You may need a little more broth if the mixture still seems dry. It should be completely wet but not submerged.

■ Transfer to the prepared baking dish, cover with foil, and bake for 35 minutes. Remove the foil and bake an additional 15 minutes, until browned and set in the middle.

—Chris Fogerty and JoAnn Myers
North Manchester, Indiana

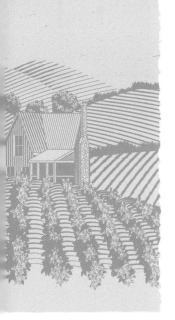

LEMON RICE

This is a nice side dish for fish.

Serves 6

1 cup uncooked rice
¼ cup chopped onion
2 tablespoons lemon juice

1 teaspoon salt
1 teaspoon dried parsley
½ teaspoon dried thyme

■ Combine the rice, onion, lemon juice, salt, parsley, and thyme in a 2-quart saucepan. Add 1¾ cups water. Bring to a boil over high heat; then reduce the heat to low and cook for 20 minutes, or until the rice absorbs all the water.

—Norma Ross Sexton
Auburn, California

WILD RICE CRANBERRY SALAD

This dish keeps well for several days. It's great for potlucks and carry-ins.

Serves 6 to 8

1 (6-ounce) package long-grain and wild rice mix
1 cup dried cranberries
1 cup chopped fresh broccoli florets
4 green onions, chopped
3 celery ribs, thinly sliced
1 (2-ounce) jar diced pimento, drained
½ cup sweet and sour sauce (see page 151)
1 cup dry roasted peanuts

■ Cook the rice according to package directions and set aside to cool.

■ In a salad bowl, combine the cranberries, broccoli, onions, celery, pimento, and sauce. When cool, add the rice and stir gently.

■ Chill for 2 hours in the refrigerator. Stir in the peanuts just before serving.

—Velma A. Meador
Rocky Mount, Virginia

PUMPKIN RISOTTO

Risotto is often thought of as a fancy dish, but really it's standard Italian comfort food. In Italy risotto is normally considered a first course, served before the main course. It is a high-starch, round grain that is stickier than typical rice. The most common kind used in America is Arborio rice, found in most supermarkets.

Serves 6 to 8

> 2 tablespoons butter
> 2 tablespoons olive oil
> ½ cup finely diced carrots
> ½ cup finely diced celery
> ½ cup finely diced onions
> 1 teaspoon crushed garlic
> Salt and pepper to taste
> 1½ cups diced pumpkin or winter squash (½-inch cubes)
> 1½ cups hot vegetable or chicken broth (hot water may be used)
> ½ cup uncooked rice (not minute rice)
> 2 tablespoons butter
> ⅓ cup grated Pecorino Romano cheese
> Toasted pumpkin seeds (optional)

- Melt the butter and the oil in a heavy pan over medium-high heat. When hot add the carrots, celery, onions, and garlic. Cook until the onions begin to turn translucent, about 7 minutes.

- Add the salt, pepper, and pumpkin and stir together. Add the hot broth and bring to boil. Cover and cook for 5 minutes.

- Add the rice and stir. Cover the pan, reduce the heat to low, and simmer for 18 to 20 minutes, until the rice is tender and the pumpkin is soft. Season with additional salt and pepper if necessary.

- Stir in the butter and cheese.

- Garnish with additional cheese and toasted pumpkin seeds, if desired.

Notes: This is great with leftover ham mixed in at the end. To make it easier, use a food processor to chop the carrots, celery, and onions. Chop them all at once until the vegetables are small and roughly chopped.

—Steve Dodge
Harrisburg, Pennsylvania

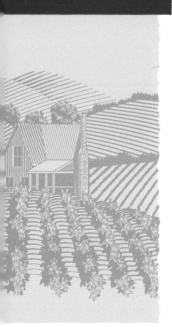

DESSERTS

The appetite recalls
a first, blissful bite—
froth of meringue,
smooth pool of custard,
forkful of cake
cloaked in rich
chocolate frosting.
Oh, it remembers
the way grandmother's
piecrust shattered
into flakes, how the sliced
apples nestled in their
warm cinnamon bath.

And somewhere
on a high shelf or counter
in the recesses of the mind
stands a cookie jar
filled to the brim
with chewy perfection—
oatmeal raisin, peanut butter,
chocolate chip.
We measure and sift,
stir, roll, and bake
to re-create
time and place,
to taste again
such utter sweetness.

—Karen Allred McKeever
Elgin, Illinois

QUICK
& EASY

SPECIAL
OCCASION

GLUTEN
FREE

VEGETARIAN

VEGAN

Swiss Chocolate Bars

Makes 36 bars

2 cups flour
2 cups sugar
1 teaspoon baking soda
½ teaspoon salt
2 eggs, beaten
½ cup sour cream
½ cup (1 stick) butter
1½ ounces unsweetened chocolate

- Preheat the oven to 375°F. Grease a 15 x 10-inch jelly-roll pan and set aside.

- Combine the flour, sugar, baking soda, and salt in a bowl and stir to mix.

- In a separate bowl combine the eggs and sour cream.

- Heat 1 cup water in a saucepan over medium heat. Add the butter and chocolate and heat until just melted, about 5 minutes. Remove from the heat and add the sour cream mixture to the chocolate mixture and mix well.

- Stir in the flour mixture. Mix well and then pour into the prepared jelly-roll pan.

- Bake for 25 minutes.

- Top with your favorite icing and cut into bars to serve.

—Sara L. Ellison
Greenville, Ohio

CRANBERRY BLISS BARS

Makes 18 bars

1 cup (2 sticks) butter, at room temperature
1¼ cups packed light brown sugar
3 eggs
1½ teaspoons vanilla
1 teaspoon ground ginger
¼ teaspoon salt
1½ cups flour
¾ cup chopped dried cranberries
6 ounces white chocolate, cut into chunks

■ Preheat the oven to 350°F. Grease a 13 x 9-inch pan and set aside.

■ Beat the butter and brown sugar until creamy. Add the eggs, vanilla, ginger, and salt and beat well.

■ Gradually add the flour, stirring after each addition. Mix in the cranberries and chocolate chunks. Pour into the prepared pan.

■ Bake for 35 to 40 minutes. Cool before cutting into bars.

—Melanie A. Miller
Carrboro, North Carolina

HIGHLAND OATMEAL-TOFFEE BARS

My mom Mary (Mitzi) Diehl got this recipe from a member of the *Flower Hill Church of the Brethren in Gaithersburg, Maryland, sometime around 1949. I make this all the time for the grandkids. We call it healthy since it has oatmeal in it.*

Makes 20 to 25 bars

⅔ cup (1½ sticks) butter, melted
4 cups quick-cooking oats
1 cup light brown sugar
1 teaspoon salt
1 tablespoon vanilla
½ cup light corn syrup
1 (12-ounce) package semisweet chocolate chips
½ cup chopped walnuts

■ Preheat the oven to 400°F. Line a 15 x 10-inch baking sheet with parchment paper, spray with cooking spray, and set aside.

■ Combine the butter and oats and mix well. Add the brown sugar and salt and mix well. Add the vanilla and corn syrup and continue mixing.

■ Press firmly in the prepared baking sheet. Bake for 15 minutes.

■ When done, sprinkle chocolate chips over the baked oatmeal and spread when melted. Sprinkle with nuts.

■ Cool. Break into pieces and store in an airtight container.

—Ethel Diehl Lough
Dayton, Virginia

APRICOT COCONUT BALLS

These are a good treat to serve at Christmastime.

Makes 36 balls

1 (10-ounce) package dried apricots, finely chopped
2½ cups flaked coconut
¾ cup sweetened condensed milk
1 cup finely chopped walnuts
Powdered sugar

■ Line a baking sheet with wax paper and set aside.

■ Combine the apricots, coconut, condensed milk, and walnuts in a large bowl. Stir to mix.

■ Form into balls with a small cookie scoop and roll in powdered sugar.

■ Place the balls on the prepared baking sheet.

■ Let stand for at least 2 hours before serving.

—Helen May Rocha
Northwood, Ohio

S'MORES

Makes 24 bars

18 plain graham crackers, about 2 sleeves
¼ cup sugar
½ teaspoon sea salt
1 cup (2 sticks) unsalted butter, melted
2 cups milk or semisweet chocolate chips
½ teaspoon chipotle pepper powder (optional)
3½ cups mini marshmallows

- Preheat the oven to 350°F. Line the bottom and sides of 13 x 9-inch baking dish with foil and coat with cooking spray or butter and set aside. Leave a 4-inch overhang on each end to use as handles to remove the bars from the pan in one piece.

- Crush the crackers or grind them into fine crumbs in a food processor to make about 2 cups.

- Add the sugar, salt, and melted butter and mix until a coarse crumb texture forms. Set aside a heaping ¼ cup of crumb mixture for the topping. Evenly press the remaining crumbs into the prepared baking dish.

- Bake for 12 to 15 minutes. Remove from the oven and cool slightly.

- Melt the chocolate in a saucepan over low heat or in the microwave for 40 to 60 seconds. Stir often.

- When the chocolate is melted, add the chipotle pepper, if desired.

- Preheat the broiler.

- Pour the melted chocolate over the baked cracker crust and spread evenly. Sprinkle the marshmallows over the chocolate and press them lightly into the chocolate. Sprinkle the reserved crumbs over the marshmallows.

- Broil the bars six inches from the heat until golden brown, 1 to 2 minutes. Watch carefully to prevent the marshmallows from burning.

- Refrigerate until the chocolate is hard, about 2 hours, before cutting.

—Samuel Vannatta
Guthrie Center, Iowa

ANTICIPATION

Cookies made from the last of the dough, the little test pancake, a lick of the beater before it is scoured in the dish water: this is the world of the child in the kitchen who is not old enough to cook yet, and who feels too grown up to play with the little kids.

—Dena Lee
Churchill, Ontario

BUSY DAY RAISIN BARS

*My grandmother, Fanny Hood, often had a pan of these raisin bars
ready for an afterschool snack when I was a girl. When I was older,
my three boys enjoyed sharing a pan of raisin bars with their friends after
school, but my family doesn't like the nuts. Now I take them for the coffee
hour after church.*

Makes 24 bars

BARS
1 cup raisins
½ cup (1 stick) butter or
   shortening
1 cup sugar
1 egg, beaten
1 teaspoon baking soda
2 cups flour
1 teaspoon ground cinnamon

¼ teaspoon ground nutmeg
¼ teaspoon ground cloves
½ cup chopped nuts (optional)

ICING
1 cup powdered sugar
2 tablespoons water

■ For the bars, combine the raisins and 2 cups water in a saucepan
over medium-high heat. Cook down to 1 cup liquid, about 10
minutes (or while you eat your morning oatmeal).

■ Preheat the oven to 350°F. Grease a 15 x 10-inch jelly-roll pan and
set aside.

■ While the raisins are still hot, add the butter or shortening and
sugar. Stir until the butter is melted and the sugar is dissolved. Add
the egg, baking soda, flour, cinnamon, nutmeg, and cloves and mix
until well blended. Spread into the prepared jelly-roll pan. Sprinkle
the nuts on top, if using.

■ Bake for 15 to 18 minutes, or until a toothpick inserted into the
center comes out clean.

■ For the icing, combine the powdered sugar and water, ½ tablespoon at a time, and stir until a pourable consistency. Drizzle the
icing over the raisin bars. Cut into squares and serve.

Notes: Sometimes I make this with 1 cup white flour and 1 cup whole wheat
flour. And you can get away with reducing the sugar to ¾ cup.

—Shirley Jean Downhour
Scottsdale, Arizona

DATE SNACKS

This is a quick and easy recipe that is well-loved in our family. My
mother brought this recipe to our family reunions and church social
events from the 1930s through the 1980s. The dish was always empty
when she took it home.

Makes 24 squares

1 (8-ounce) package pitted dates, chopped
1 cup granulated sugar
1 cup firmly packed dark brown sugar
½ cup butter
1½ cups flour
½ teaspoon salt
1 teaspoon baking soda
1¾ cups quick-cooking oats

- Preheat the oven to 350°F. Grease a 13 x 9-inch baking dish with cooking spray or butter and set aside.

- Combine the dates, granulated sugar, and 1 cup water in a saucepan over medium-low heat. Cook for about 5 minutes until it becomes like a thick applesauce; set aside to cool.

- Thoroughly mix the brown sugar and butter together in a bowl. Set aside.

- Combine the flour, salt, baking soda, and oats in a large bowl and mix. Add the brown sugar mixture to the oat mixture and stir to make a crumble.

- Pat half of the crumbly oat mixture into the prepared baking dish. Spread the date mixture on top and then cover with the remaining oat mixture. Pat lightly into the filling.

- Bake for 25 minutes or until lightly browned. Cool slightly before cutting into squares.

—Ruth Rishel Gleim
York, Pennsylvania

TANDY CAKES

Substitute butterscotch chips, semisweet chocolate chips, or white chocolate chips for the milk chocolate to vary the flavor of the bars.

Makes 20 to 25 bars

4 eggs, beaten
1 teaspoon vanilla
⅛ teaspoon salt
2 cups sugar
2 cups flour
1 cup milk
1 teaspoon baking powder
2 tablespoons vegetable oil
¾ cup peanut butter
1 (12-ounce) package milk chocolate chips
6 tablespoons butter

■ Preheat the oven to 350°F. Grease a 15 x 10-inch jelly-roll pan with cooking spray, butter, or oil and set aside.

■ Combine the eggs, vanilla, salt, sugar, flour, milk, baking powder, and oil. Mix well and pour into the prepared jelly-roll pan.

■ Bake for 20 to 25 minutes.

■ Spread the peanut butter over the cake as soon as it comes out of the oven. Set aside to cool.

■ Combine the chocolate chips and butter. Melt in the microwave just until melted, about 1 minute. Stir until smooth, and immediately spread the chocolate mixture over the peanut butter. Chill for at least 1 hour before cutting into bars.

—Vivian S. Ziegler
Lancaster, Pennsylvania

DOUBLE CHOCOLATE BROWNIES

Makes 24 brownies

1 cup (2 sticks) butter
2 ounces (4 squares) unsweetened chocolate
2 cups sugar
3 eggs
1 teaspoon vanilla
1 cup flour
1½ cups coarsely chopped walnuts, divided
6 ounces semisweet chocolate chips

- Preheat the oven to 350°F. Grease a 13 x 9-inch baking dish with cooking spray or butter and set aside.

- Melt the butter and chocolate in a large glass dish in the microwave. Check after 45 seconds and keep heating in 10-second increments until melted.

- Beat in the sugar a little at a time until thoroughly mixed. Add the eggs one at a time, beating well after each addition. Stir in the vanilla and flour until well mixed.

- Add 1 cup of the walnuts and stir to mix. Spread the batter in the prepared baking dish.

- Combine the remaining ½ cup nuts and chocolate chips. Sprinkle over the top of the batter, pressing down lightly to secure the topping.

- Bake for 35 minutes. Cool, and then cut into bars.

—Gladys E. Crawford
Greenville, Ohio

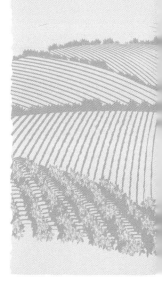

DOUBLE CHOCOLATE MINT BROWNIES

These brownies are expected at church potluck meals. When I don't take them to a meal, I am a very unpopular pastor!

Makes 15 to 20 brownies

BATTER
1 cup flour
1 cup sugar
½ cup (1 stick) butter
4 eggs
1½ cups chocolate syrup

FILLING
2 cups powdered sugar
½ cup (1 stick) butter
½ teaspoon mint extract
3 drops green food coloring

TOPPING
6 tablespoons butter
1 cup semisweet
  chocolate chips

- Preheat the oven to 350°F. Spray a 13 x 9-inch baking dish with cooking spray and set aside.

- For the batter, combine the flour, sugar, butter, eggs, and chocolate syrup in a large bowl and mix well with an electric mixer on low speed until completely combined, about 1 minute. Pour the batter into the prepared dish and bake for 25 to 30 minutes, or until a toothpick inserted in the center comes out clean. Cool completely.

- For the filling, combine the powdered sugar, butter, 1 tablespoon water, mint extract, and food coloring in a bowl. Mix with an electric mixer on low speed until completely combined. Spread over the cooled brownies.

- For the topping, melt the butter and chocolate chips in the microwave for 1 minute. Check to see if the chocolate has melted. It may need another 20 or 30 seconds. When melted stir until smooth. Spread over the filling and refrigerate until firm, about 1 hour.

—Christy J. Waltersdorff
Lombard, Illinois

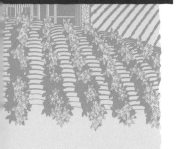

FARMER'S BROWNIES

Makes 25 to 30 brownies

BROWNIES
½ cup cocoa
½ cup (1 stick) butter
2½ cups flour
1 teaspoon baking soda
½ teaspoon salt
2 cups sugar
2 eggs, lightly beaten
½ cup buttermilk
1 teaspoon vanilla
1 cup chopped nuts (walnuts, pecans, almonds)

FROSTING
½ cup cocoa
1 cup powdered sugar
2 tablespoons butter, softened
Powdered sugar for dusting

■ Preheat the oven to 375°F. Grease a 17 x 12-inch baking sheet or jelly-roll pan with butter and set aside.

■ To make the brownies, mix the cocoa in 1 cup hot water. Stir in the butter and let the mixture cool.

■ Sift the flour, baking soda, salt, and sugar into a separate bowl. Add to the cocoa mixture and stir. Add the eggs and stir again.

■ Beat in the buttermilk and vanilla; then fold in the nuts.

■ Spread on the prepared baking sheet or jelly-roll pan.

■ Bake for 16 to 20 minutes, or until a toothpick inserted in the center comes out clean. Be careful not to overbake the brownies or they will be dry.

■ To make the frosting, combine the cocoa, powdered sugar, and butter in a bowl. Add 1 tablespoon of hot water at a time, stirring continuously, until smooth and desired consistency is achieved. Spread the frosting over the brownies and dust with powdered sugar.

—Kathleen Graber
Wooster, Ohio

COOKIE DOUGH BROWNIES

All of my friends love my grandma's Cookie Dough Brownies.

Makes 18 brownies

BROWNIES
2 cups granulated sugar
1½ cups flour
½ cup cocoa
½ teaspoon salt
¾ cup vegetable oil
4 eggs
2 teaspoons vanilla
½ cup chopped walnuts (optional)

FILLING
½ cup (1 stick) butter
½ cup packed brown sugar
¼ cup granulated sugar
2 tablespoons milk
1 teaspoon vanilla
1 cup flour

GLAZE
1 cup (6 ounces) semisweet chocolate chips
1 tablespoon butter
¾ cup chopped walnuts

■ Preheat the oven to 350°F. Lightly grease a 13 x 9-inch baking dish and set aside.

■ For the brownies, combine the sugar, flour, cocoa, and salt in a bowl and stir. Add the oil, eggs, and vanilla; beat with an electric mixer at medium speed for 3 minutes. Stir in the walnuts, if desired.

■ Pour the batter into the prepared dish. Bake for 30 minutes, or until a toothpick inserted into the center comes out clean. Cool completely.

■ For the filling, beat together the butter and sugars. Add the milk and vanilla; mix well. Beat in the flour. Spread over the cooled brownies. Chill until firm.

■ For the glaze, melt the chocolate chips and butter in a saucepan over medium-low heat, stirring until smooth. Spread over the filling. Immediately sprinkle with nuts, pressing down slightly.

Note: You may substitute a family-size brownie mix if you are in a hurry.

—Kacie M. Brous
Hays, Kansas

SUGAR COOKIES

Generations have treasured these light and tender cookies, perfect for decorating. I adapted this recipe from the Granddaughter's Inglenook Cookbook (p. 55).

Makes about 36 cookies

- **3 cups flour**
- **1 teaspoon baking powder**
- **¼ teaspoon salt**
- **1¼ cups sugar**
- **1 cup (2 sticks) butter, at room temperature**
- **3 eggs**
- **1 teaspoon flavoring (vanilla, almond, or lemon)**

■ Preheat the oven to 375°F. Lightly grease baking sheets or line them with parchment paper and set aside.

■ Sift the flour, baking powder, and salt into a bowl and set aside.

■ Beat the sugar and butter until light and fluffy. Continue beating and add the eggs, one at a time. Add the flavoring.

■ Stir in the flour mixture to make a firm dough.

■ Roll the dough to about ½ inch thick and cut into shapes. Place the cookies 1 inch apart on the prepared baking sheets.

■ Bake for 8 to 10 minutes, until the edges are just beginning to turn light brown. Cool on the baking sheets for 2 minutes before transferring the cookies to cooling racks.

—Karen Crim Dillon
Vandalia, Ohio

THE BEST PEANUT BUTTER COOKIE

This cookie recipe came out of the Dayton Daily News *many years* *ago. It is a great recipe. You may add chocolate chips, if desired.*

Makes 24 cookies

> **1 cup creamy peanut butter**
> **1 cup sugar**
> **1 large egg**
> **1 teaspoon baking soda**

- Preheat the oven to 350°F and grease 2 baking sheets with nonstick cooking spray and set aside.

- Beat together the peanut butter and sugar until combined. Beat in the egg. Sprinkle baking soda over the mixture and beat until combined.

- Roll heaping teaspoon-size pieces of dough into small balls. Arrange on the prepared baking sheets and with the tines of a fork, flatten the balls.

- Bake the cookies in batches in the middle of the oven until puffed and pale golden, about 10 minutes.

- Cool the cookies on the baking sheets for 2 minutes before transferring to cooling racks. This is important because they are very fragile when hot from the oven.

—Sharon A. Walker (Brumbaugh)
Clayton, Ohio

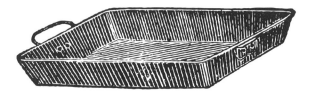

HEALTHY OATMEAL PEANUT BUTTER COOKIES

This was one of my prized recipes. When I began eating healthier, *I cut the fat and sugar and added more oats, some wheat germ, and whole wheat flour. These also make a good breakfast cereal.*

Makes about 60 cookies

1 cup plus 2 tablespoons butter	1 cup whole wheat flour
¾ cup peanut butter	1 cup untoasted wheat germ
¾ cup granulated sugar	2 teaspoons ground cinnamon
¾ cup packed brown sugar	1 teaspoon salt
3 eggs	2 teaspoons baking soda
½ cup skim milk	1 teaspoon baking powder
3 teaspoons vanilla	2 cups raisins
¾ cup all-purpose flour	5½ cups rolled oats

- Preheat the oven to 350°F. Lightly grease 2 baking sheets or line with parchment paper and set aside.

- Beat together the butter, peanut butter, granulated sugar, and brown sugar until well mixed. Beat in the eggs, skim milk, and vanilla.

- Stir the flours, wheat germ, cinnamon, salt, baking soda, and baking powder together in a bowl. Add it to the peanut butter mixture, and stir to combine.

- Stir in the raisins and oats and then drop by the teaspoonful onto the prepared baking sheets.

- Bake for 8 to 12 minutes, until lightly browned on the edges. Allow to cool for 5 minutes on the baking sheets before transferring to cooling racks.

Note: Almond butter or soynut butter may be substituted for the peanut butter.

—Vernon F. Merkey
Ankeny, Iowa

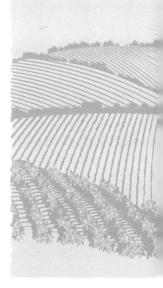

FOR THE LOVE OF COOKIES

It's hard to find someone who will turn down a cookie. They're so satisfying with their sweetness and irresistible crunch or chewiness. We love eating and sharing them with others. Think of all the cookie exchanges you've participated in, where each person brings in a favorite recipe. Remember the care packages or gift boxes filled with home-baked goodness you've mailed to loved ones or friends, and how they became tangible symbols of your thoughtfulness and concern.

On a personal level, cookies are quite practical—easily portable and requiring no utensils or plates, thus great for snacks, packed lunches, or picnics. They are filling enough for on-the-go breakfast meals, paired with a cup of tea or coffee, and simple enough to be a dessert placed next to a scoop of your favorite ice cream. And don't forget about the best way to eat them—dunked in a glass of milk!

Cookies are a treat, whether they're packed with exotic ingredients like chocolate, dried fruits, and spices, or simple ingredients like molasses, flour, and butter. And sometimes it's simple ingredients, like oats, that bring us back for more. Although oatmeal cookies may not have any less sugar in them, we tell ourselves they're healthier than others. But there is some truth to it. One serving of oatmeal per day increases the body's insoluble fiber intake, which assists in lowering cholesterol and may prevent certain kinds of cancer. The addition of dried fruits such as raisins and cranberries provide natural fruit-based sweetness, allowing you to reduce the amount of processed sugars in your diet.

Both the 1911 *Inglenook Cook Book* and the 1942 *Granddaughter's Inglenook Cookbook* place oatmeal cookies within the chapter on cakes, which harks back to their simplest definition as small handheld cakes. Reviewing the various oatmeal cookie recipes reveals only slight changes through the years, with recipes based on simple, easy-to-find ingredients. While early recipes called for lard, perhaps with half butter, later recipes used all butter or shortening. As far as sweeteners, earlier recipes traditionally called for molasses, when more refined sugars were not available. This became especially true during World War II when sugar was rationed. Present-day recipes for oatmeal cookies typically use half brown sugar and half granulated white sugar, sometimes substituting molasses for brown sugar.

Comparing the "Coconut Macaroons" recipe from the 1942 edition (p. 52) with Carol Meador's recipe, I was curious to see if they'd be similar. By definition a "macaroon" is a small meringue-like cookie made from egg whites, sugar, and almonds (no flour). These recipes don't fit that picture; rather, they are akin to a typical oatmeal cookie. I found the recipes to be very similar, and the cookies baked up nearly the same. Both versions are chewy and delicious. And when I compared Carol's recipe with my own for "Oatmeal Crispies," I was pleasantly surprised to find them to be exactly the same! These aren't "macaroons" in the technical sense, but I guess there can be more than one name for a cookie.

All in all, oatmeal cookie recipes are versatile and simple to make, contain readily available ingredients, and always produce a deliciously chewy cookie, which is very popular with people of all ages. They're so simple, why not make them yourself? I'd recommend taking a basic recipe like this one from the 1942 cookbook and make it your own. I get a bit adventurous, and with this one I sometimes add $1/2$ teaspoon of almond flavoring and 1 cup of toffee bits. In another variation I omit the coconut and add 1 cup of raisins or semisweet chocolate chips. Do something creative, but make sure you take time to enjoy these with friends and family. It will do you a world of good.

—Susan B. Hertzog
Lebanon, Pennsylvania

COCONUT MACAROONS

1 c. brown sugar
1 c. white sugar
⅔ c. melted shortening
2 eggs
1 c. coconut

1 c. flour
4 c. quick rolled oats
1 tsp. soda
4 tb. milk

Have eggs beaten well; combine all ingredients.

—Mrs. J. L. Bagwell, Union City, Indiana

Oatmeal Macaroons

A friend from McPherson College served these cookies at her home in Waterloo, Iowa, when I visited her there. I liked them so much I asked for the recipe. Now I make them for potluck dinners at the church.

Makes 3 dozen cookies

1 cup shortening or 2 sticks butter
1 cup packed brown sugar
1 cup granulated sugar
½ teaspoon vanilla
2 eggs
1½ cups flour
½ teaspoon salt
½ teaspoon ground cinnamon
3 cups quick-cooking oats
1 cup chopped nuts
1 cup coconut

- Preheat the oven to 360°F. Lightly grease 2 baking sheets with cooking spray and set aside.

- Beat together the shortening, sugars, and vanilla until creamy. Add the eggs and continue mixing.

- In a separate bowl combine the flour, salt, cinnamon, and oats. Fold into the sugar mixture. Add the nuts and coconut and stir to combine.

- Drop rounded teaspoons of batter about 1 inch apart onto the prepared baking sheets. Bake for 10 minutes, or until the tops are lightly browned.

—Carol Meador
Maggie Valley, North Carolina

Cookie Bazaars

Bazaars, which are popular fundraisers among Brethren, provide a great opportunity for people to come together in a community effort. Combined with sales of crafts, nuts, candy, and cookies, these annual events can net thousands of dollars, often used toward relief efforts. Lebanon Valley Brethren Home hosts a bazaar each fall, featuring a chicken barbecue and quilt sale, as well as a concert given by a local symphony. You will also find a huge room full of cookies of all sorts, sold by the pound. The cookies are donated by bakers from the twenty-one churches which support the home. The profits from this day-long event go toward auxiliary projects.

—Susan B. Hertzog
Lebanon, Pennsylvania

SWEDISH BISCOTTI

This is from my Swedish heritage. It is good for breakfast, dessert, or a snack.

Makes 4 to 5 dozen biscotti

1 cup (2 sticks) butter
1 cup sugar
2 eggs
1 teaspoon vanilla or almond extract
3 cups flour
⅛ teaspoon baking soda
1 teaspoon baking powder
Pinch of salt
3 tablespoons sour cream
Cinnamon sugar for topping

- Preheat the oven to 350°F. Line two baking sheets with parchment paper.

- Beat the butter, sugar, eggs, and vanilla or almond extract in a bowl until creamy. Add the flour, baking soda, baking powder, and salt. Blend in the sour cream. Mix well. The batter will be stiff.

- Transfer the dough to a lightly floured work surface and divide in fourths. Form each piece into a long rectangle the length of a baking sheet and about 3 inches wide. Lay two rectangles of dough on each baking sheet, placing them about 2 inches apart. Dough will spread while baking. Sprinkle the tops with cinnamon sugar.

- Bake for 20 to 25 minutes. Don't let them get too brown.

- Immediately after baking, cut each rectangle into strips about ½ to ¾ inch wide. Separate all strips from each other so that no pieces are touching.

- Turn off the oven. Return the biscotti to the oven and let sit there overnight to dry.

—Margaret Drafall
Elgin, Illinois

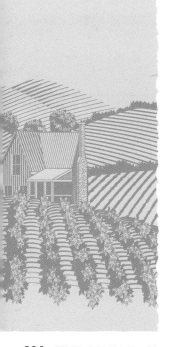

Chocolate Chip Cookies

I first started making these cookies using the recipe from my mother's Granddaughter's Inglenook Cookbook. *I made them for my husband while we were dating, and I tell people they are the reason he married me. I have changed it a bit since then.*

Makes about 48 cookies

1 cup (2 sticks) butter
¾ cup firmly packed brown sugar
¾ cup granulated sugar
2 eggs
1½ cups flour
1 teaspoon baking soda
1 teaspoon ground cinnamon
¼ teaspoon ground nutmeg
2 cups rolled oats
2 cups (12 ounces) chocolate chips
1 teaspoon vanilla

■ Preheat the oven to 350°F. Grease 2 or 3 baking sheets with cooking spray or butter or line with parchment paper and set aside.

■ Beat the butter and sugars until creamy. Add the eggs and beat.

■ Mix in the flour, baking soda, cinnamon, and nutmeg; then add the oats, chocolate chips, and vanilla, and mix thoroughly.

■ Drop by heaping tablespoonsful onto the prepared baking sheets.

■ Bake for 8 to 10 minutes, or until golden brown.

—Barbara K. McNally
Phoenixville, Pennsylvania

GINGERBREAD COOKIES

This crisp, firm cookie holds its shape quite well. It is especially good for making gingerbread houses or gingerbread people. Although it is a dry cookie, when served with coffee, tea, or fresh milk, the spicy flavor is rich and delightful. I've adapted it from the ginger snap variation in the Granddaughter's Inglenook Cookbook *(p. 52).*

Makes 12 gingerbread people and 1 large house

1 cup sugar
1 cup (2 sticks) butter
1 cup molasses
2 teaspoons baking soda
2 eggs
1 teaspoon ground cinnamon
½ teaspoon ground nutmeg
½ teaspoon ground ginger
5 to 6 cups flour

■ In a medium saucepan combine the sugar, butter, and molasses, bring to a boil over medium-high heat, and cook for 1 minute or until the butter is melted and the sugar dissolved. Remove from the heat and cool to lukewarm.

■ Dissolve the baking soda in ¼ cup water and add to the molasses mixture. Add the eggs, cinnamon, nutmeg, and ginger. Beat together until smooth and glossy.

■ Preheat the oven to 350°F. Lightly grease two baking sheets with oil or line with parchment paper and set aside.

■ Stir in the flour 1 cup at a time until a stiff dough forms, stirring between each addition. Roll the dough very thin on a lightly floured surface. Cut the dough with cookie cutters. Place on the prepared baking sheets about 1 inch apart. Bake for 10 to 12 minutes until firm to the touch.

—Karen Crim Dillon
Vandalia, Ohio

GINGER CRINKLES

Makes 36 cookies

- 2¼ cups flour
- 2 teaspoons baking soda
- 1 teaspoon ground ginger
- 1 teaspoon ground cinnamon
- ½ teaspoon ground cloves
- ¼ teaspoon salt
- 1 cup packed brown sugar
- ¾ cup shortening
- ¼ cup mild molasses
- 1 egg
- 1 cup granulated sugar

■ Sift the flour, baking soda, ginger, cinnamon, cloves, and salt into a large bowl.

■ In a separate bowl combine the brown sugar, shortening, molasses, egg, and beat well.

■ Add the dry ingredients to the sugar mixture and beat well.

■ Refrigerate for 30 minutes to 1 hour.

■ Preheat the oven to 375°F.

■ Pour the granulated sugar into a shallow dish. Remove the dough from the refrigerator and pull off tablespoon-size pieces and form 1-inch balls. Roll in sugar and place 2 inches apart on ungreased or parchment paper-lined baking sheets.

■ Bake for 8 to 10 minutes.

—Irene Frick
Modesto, California

MOTHER'S MODEL OF LIVING

Hospitality was a way of life growing up—a way of life my mother learned from her mother. We regularly welcomed people from diverse backgrounds into our home—sometimes for a meal, sometimes for an extended stay. Our dining room opened into our living room and the table could be extended to accommodate forty. Whether it was one guest or forty, a meal or an extended stay, I don't remember their presence producing stress. Rather my mother, and following her lead our whole family, joyfully embraced the guests, welcoming them into our home and integrating them into our lives.

—Rhonda Pittman Gingrich
Minneapolis, Minnesota

PUMPKIN GOBS

Traditionally made with chocolate cake cookies and filled with white frosting or marshmallow crème, gobs are the Amish version of whoopie pies. This is the pumpkin version. No matter when you serve these gobs, they are always a hit!

Makes 30 to 36 gobs

COOKIES
6 cups flour
2 teaspoons cinnamon
2 teaspoons ground ginger
2 teaspoons ground cloves
2 teaspoons salt
2 teaspoons baking soda
2 teaspoons baking powder
4 cups firmly packed
   brown sugar
2 cups vegetable oil

4 eggs
4 cups pumpkin
2 teaspoons vanilla

FILLING
1 (3-ounce) box vanilla instant
   pudding
1 cup sugar
1 cup (2 sticks) butter
1 teaspoon vanilla
1 cup whole milk

- Preheat the oven to 350°F. Lightly grease 2 baking sheets with cooking spray and set aside.

- For the cookies, combine the flour, cinnamon, ginger, cloves, salt, baking soda, and baking powder. Mix well and set aside.

- In a separate bowl beat the brown sugar, oil, eggs, and pumpkin until well mixed. Add the vanilla and dry ingredients and stir until thoroughly mixed.

- Drop tablespoonsful on the prepared baking sheets about 1 inch apart. Using a cookie scoop will help make the cookies more uniform in size.

- Bake for 12 to 15 minutes.

- Meanwhile, make the filling. Combine the instant pudding, sugar, and butter. Add the vanilla and then slowly add the milk, beating until thick enough to spread between the cookies.

- Make cookie sandwiches by spreading the filling on one cookie and placing another on top. Continue until all the cookies are "filled." Store in an airtight container in the refrigerator.

—Linda M. Deal
Meyersdale, Pennsylvania

AUNT ESSIE'S SOFT RAISIN COOKIES

This recipe came from my great-aunt Essie. When I was growing up  *these cookies were made as a special treat at Christmastime. My husband enjoys these cookies even though he's not a fan of raisins. We sometimes add 1 cup chopped nuts, but the original recipe did not include them. We have used black walnuts, English walnuts, and pecans.*

Makes 5 dozen cookies

1 (15-ounce) box raisins
4 eggs, separated
1 cup (2 sticks) butter
1½ cups sugar
2 teaspoons vanilla
3½ cups flour
1 teaspoon baking soda
½ teaspoon salt
1 cup chopped nuts (optional)

- Preheat the oven to 375°F. Line a few baking sheets with parchment paper.

- Cook the raisins in 2 cups water in a saucepan over medium heat until soft, about 10 minutes. Drain and let cool.

- Beat the egg whites and save for folding in later.

- Beat the butter and sugar in a bowl until creamy. Add the egg yolks and vanilla. Beat well. Mix in the flour, baking soda, and salt. Fold the raisins and egg whites into the batter. Add the chopped nuts, if using.

- Drop spoonsful of batter about 1 inch apart onto the prepared baking sheets.

- Bake for 8 to 12 minutes, or until the cookie has lost its glossy look.

- Cool and store in an airtight container. They should stay soft. These are good to freeze.

—Dorothy Liller
Hollidaysburg, Pennsylvania

Banana Nugget Cookies

My husband, Henry Hunsberger, was in the free ministry at the Welsh Run Church of the Brethren. He traveled around the tri-state area and held evangelistic services in many Brethren congregations. I received this recipe from Anna Nyce of the Indian Creek Church of the Brethren when Henry held a series of services there in 1970. Raisins can be used in place of the chocolate chips.

Makes 3 dozen cookies

    1 cup sugar
    ½ cup (1 stick) butter
    1 egg, beaten
    ½ teaspoon baking soda
    1 teaspoon salt
    ½ teaspoon ground nutmeg
    ½ teaspoon ground cinnamon
    1½ cups flour
    1½ cups rolled oats
    1 cup soft bananas (3 bananas)
    6 ounces chocolate chips

- Preheat the oven to 375°F. Lightly grease 2 baking sheets.

- Beat the sugar, butter, and egg until creamy. Add the baking soda, salt, nutmeg, and cinnamon. Stir to mix.

- Add half of the flour and oats and mix well. Add half of the bananas and stir. Repeat until all the flour, oats, and bananas are used.

- Stir in the chocolate chips.

- Drop spoonsful of batter about 1 inch apart onto the prepared baking sheets.

- Bake for 15 minutes. Cool slightly on the pan before transferring to a cooling rack.

—Martha G. Hunsberger
Mercersburg, Pennsylvania

WALNUT CHEWS

We are walnut farmers, so I always use lots of walnuts in my
recipes. Many people have asked me to share this cookie recipe.
These cookies don't have any shortening in them. A double batch
goes nicely in a 13 x 9-inch baking pan.

Makes 12 to 15 chews

- **1 egg**
- **1 cup packed brown sugar**
- **½ teaspoon salt**
- **1 teaspoon vanilla**
- **⅛ teaspoon baking soda**
- **½ cup flour**
- **1 cup chopped walnuts**

■ Preheat the oven to 350°F. Grease an 8 x 8-inch baking pan with cooking spray and set aside.

■ Beat the egg until light and fluffy. Add the brown sugar and beat until well blended. Add the salt and vanilla. Mix well.

■ Sift the baking soda and flour together in a separate bowl and add to the sugar mixture. Mix well. Stir in the chopped walnuts.

■ Spread the mixture into the prepared pan. Bake for 20 minutes, or until puffy. Cut into squares while warm.

—Pauline Fillmore
Live Oak, California

STRAWBERRY MERINGUES

Our daughter chose these meringues instead of cake for her graduation reception. We have served them often for a light, colorful dessert.

Makes about 24 meringues

3 egg whites
¼ teaspoon cream of tartar
¾ cup granulated sugar
¾ cup whipping cream
2 tablespoons powdered sugar
Fresh sliced strawberries or other fresh fruit
Mint sprigs (optional)

■ Preheat the oven to 225°F. Line 2 large baking sheets with heavy brown paper or parchment paper and set aside.

■ With an electric mixer, beat the egg whites and cream of tartar until foamy. Beat in the sugar, 1 tablespoon at a time; continue beating until stiff, glossy peaks form.

■ Drop by the tablespoonful onto the prepared baking sheets and shape into ovals or circles; make an indentation into each one with a spoon.

■ Bake for 1 hour. Turn off the oven and leave the meringues in the oven with the door closed for 1 additional hour.

■ When ready to serve, beat the whipping cream and powdered sugar in a chilled bowl until stiff. Fill the indentations on the meringues with the whipped cream, then top with fresh strawberries or other colorful fresh fruit. Garnish with fresh mint sprigs, if desired.

Notes: These meringues freeze well. You can use store-bought frozen whipped topping instead of the fresh whipped cream if you prefer.

Variations: Fill the meringues with lemon or chocolate pudding and dot with whipped cream or fruit.

—Pearl Fruth Miller
Warrensburg, Missouri

GRANDMA'S COOKIES

Other people make cookies but grandma's cookies, while they are made of the same kind of flour and sugar, have some extra good taste to them that no other cookies have. It may be only the generous smile and the sweet spirit that accompanies the giving, but whatever it is, it makes grandma's cookies the best in the world.

—*The Inglenook* magazine December 3, 1907

Buttermilk Cookies with Frosting

Makes about 36 cookies

COOKIES
1 cup (2 sticks) butter or shortening
2 cups sugar
3 eggs
1 teaspoon vanilla
1 teaspoon lemon or orange juice
1 cup buttermilk or sour cream
4 cups flour
2 teaspoons baking powder
1 teaspoon baking soda
1 teaspoon salt

FROSTING
⅓ cup butter
3 cups powdered sugar
1½ teaspoons lemon or orange juice
2 tablespoons milk

- Preheat the oven to 350°F. Lightly grease baking sheets or line with parchment paper and set aside.

- To make the cookies, combine the butter or shortening with the sugar and stir until well mixed. Add the eggs and beat well.

- Add the vanilla, lemon or orange juice, and buttermilk and beat until well mixed.

- Stir in the flour, baking powder, baking soda, and salt until well blended. Drop by the teaspoonful, about 1 inch apart, onto the prepared baking sheets.

- Bake for 10 or 12 minutes or until slightly browned.

- To make the frosting, beat the butter and sugar until creamy. Stir in the lemon or orange juice and milk. Beat to form a smooth, spreadable consistency. Frost the cookies when cool.

—Linda Q. Long
Mount Solon, Virginia

COMFORT FOOD

I remember eating by kerosene light in my grandmother's kitchen, where she would beat her cake batter by hand—they had no electricity. She heated water on a wood cook stove and baked in its oven with recipes handed down from that German-speaking side of my family. She is gone now, along with most of my relatives that I should have spoken to more. She held out until ninety-two years of age. But I still have some of her recipes. They are the physical memories of my childhood, my comfort food.

—David L. Farmer
Elizabethtown,
Pennsylvania

GRANDMOM'S BUTTERSCOTCH COOKIES

Makes 6 to 8 dozen cookies

  2 cups (4 sticks) butter, softened
  4 cups packed brown sugar
  4 eggs
  5 cups flour
  1 tablespoon baking soda
  1 tablespoon cream of tartar
  1 cup chopped nuts

- Beat the butter and sugar in a bowl until creamy. Add the eggs and mix.

- Sift together the flour, baking soda, and cream of tartar. Add to the butter mixture. Add the chopped nuts. Stir until well combined. Refrigerate overnight.

- Preheat the oven to 350°F. Line 2 baking sheets with parchment paper.

- Drop spoonsful of dough about 2 inches apart on the baking sheets. Be careful; these cookies will spread. Bake for 10 minutes, or until done.

Note: The dough can be frozen and baked later.

—Nancy Harvey
Waterloo, Iowa

TRIPLE CHOCOLATE ESPRESSO COOKIES

I added espresso, lots of nuts, and dark chocolate chips to make these *cookies even more flavorful. For additional decadence, top each cookie with a chocolate kiss immediately after removing from the oven.*

Makes about 4 dozen cookies

¾ cup flour
½ teaspoon baking powder
¼ teaspoon salt
3 ounces bittersweet chocolate
1 cup semisweet chocolate chips
½ cup (1 stick) butter
3 large eggs

1 tablespoon instant espresso
  powder
1 tablespoon vanilla
1 cup plus 2 tablespoons sugar
1 cup walnut pieces
1 cup pecan pieces
1 cup dark chocolate chips

■ Preheat the oven to 350°F. Grease baking sheets with cooking spray or line them with parchment paper.

■ Combine the flour, baking powder, and salt and set aside.

■ Melt the bittersweet chocolate, semisweet chocolate chips, and butter in a saucepan over medium-low heat, about 7 minutes or in a microwave at minute intervals. Remove from the heat and let cool.

■ Beat the eggs in a large bowl. Add the espresso powder, vanilla, and sugar and continue beating.

■ While stirring the egg mixture, slowly add the cooled chocolate mixture.

■ Add the flour mixture and blend well. Gently stir in the nuts and dark chocolate chips.

■ Drop teaspoons of dough onto the prepared baking sheets.

■ Bake for 8 to 10 minutes, until the edges are slightly cracked. Cool a few minutes before moving to cooling racks.

—Martha Swinger Burkholder
Verona, Pennsylvania

Raspberry Almond Shortbread Thumbprints

This has become my favorite cookie. My eleven-year-old grandson,  *Wyatt, likes them so much, he asked for the recipe so he could make them at home. I like to prepare these cookies the day I want to serve them because after about a day, the red of the jam seeps into the white glaze. It doesn't affect the taste, only the appearance.*

Makes about 4 dozen cookies

COOKIES
⅔ cup granulated sugar
1 cup (2 sticks) butter, at room temperature
½ teaspoon almond extract
2 cups flour
1 cup raspberry jam, divided

GLAZE
1 cup powdered sugar
1½ teaspoons almond extract

- Preheat the oven to 350°F. Grease 2 baking sheets with cooking spray or butter, or line with parchment paper, and set aside.

- To make the cookies, beat the sugar, butter, and almond extract until smooth and creamy. Gradually add the flour and beat until well blended.

- Shape the dough into 1-inch balls and place 2 inches apart on the prepared baking sheets.

- Make an indentation in the center of each cookie. The edges may crack slightly, but that's okay. Fill each indentation with ¼ teaspoon raspberry jam.

- Bake for 14 to 18 minutes, or until the edges are lightly browned.

- Remove from the oven and let stand for 1 minute before transferring to a cooling rack.

- To make the glaze, combine the sugar, almond extract, and 2 tablespoons warm water in a small bowl. Stir to combine. The glaze should be thin. Add an extra tablespoon of water if necessary. Spoon the glaze into a plastic bag. Cut off a bit of one corner and pipe the glaze over the cooled cookies. Let the glaze set before placing the cookies on a plate or in tins.

—Betty L. Breidenstine
Hummelstown, Pennsylvania

PEPPERMINT CRUNCH COOKIES

I have been making these cookies since I was ten years old. I
usually make several batches during Christmas. I like to use Andes
Peppermint Crunch Baking Chips, which are available around the
holidays. You can use crushed peppermint candies in a pinch.

Makes 24 cookies

½ cup granulated sugar
½ cup packed light brown sugar
½ cup (1 stick) butter, softened
1 egg
1 teaspoon almond extract
1½ cups flour
½ teaspoon baking soda
½ teaspoon salt
1 cup peppermint crunch baking chips

- Preheat the oven to 375°F. Grease 2 baking sheets with cooking spray or line them with parchment paper and set aside.

- In a large mixing bowl, combine the granulated sugar, brown sugar, butter, egg, and almond extract and with an electric mixer beat at medium speed until light and fluffy.

- Sift the flour, baking soda, and salt together and add to the sugar mixture; mix thoroughly.

- Stir the peppermint crunch baking chips into the dough.

- Drop the dough by rounded tablespoons onto the prepared baking sheets.

- Bake for 10 to 12 minutes or until the cookies are light brown. Cool cookies on the baking sheets for one minute. Then transfer to a wire rack to cool completely.

—Kristi L. Matthews
Rocky Mount, Virginia

REDEEMING THE RECIPE

Culinary skills are not my forte, but one summer I served as a counselor for culinary camp at Camp Mack. One day I was put in charge of making dessert: a double-crust apple pie. Following the recipe, I added several cups of what I thought was flour but instead was very similar-looking powdered sugar. I kept wondering why the mixture was gloppy rather than solidifying as it was supposed to. Fortunately the director, an accomplished chef, came by and was able to salvage my disaster by turning it into a delicious butter cream frosting for an apple cake. Thank God for those who can bring redemption, whether in our cooking or our faith.

—Walt Wiltschek
North Manchester, Indiana

GRANDMA BEAVERS' CHOCOLATE CAKE

This recipe has been in our family for well over a century. My grandmother Anna Deckert Beavers was born in Orient, Ohio, on May 27, 1867. In 1893 she moved to Lamar, Colorado, where she spent the rest of her life. This was her mother's recipe, so I have no idea how old it is, but I know my family and friends think it is the best chocolate cake ever.

Serves 18

CAKE
2½ cups flour
2 cups sugar
½ cup cocoa powder
1 teaspoon salt
2 teaspoon baking soda
1 cup (2 sticks) butter
1 cup sour cream
2 eggs, beaten
1 teaspoon vanilla

FROSTING
⅓ cup milk
1 square dark unsweetened chocolate
¼ cup (½ stick) butter
1 teaspoon vanilla
2 to 3 cups powdered sugar

■ Preheat the oven to 350°F. Grease a 13 x 9-inch baking pan (or three 9-inch cake pans) and set aside.

■ To make the cake, sift the flour, sugar, cocoa powder, salt, and baking soda into a large bowl. Add the butter, sour cream, eggs, vanilla, and 1 cup boiling water. Mix until the batter turns from a dark to a light brown.

■ Pour into the prepared pan and bake for 30 to 40 minutes, or until a toothpick inserted into the center comes out clean. Place the pan on a wire rack to cool completely.

■ To make the frosting, combine the milk, chocolate, and butter in a saucepan over medium heat. Bring to a boil and then remove from the heat. Add the vanilla and powdered sugar, a cup at a time, and stir until the mixture is spreadable. Spread the frosting over the cooled cake.

—Anna M. Everett
Fort Collins, Colorado

JIFFY CHOCOLATE FEATHER CAKE

This cake has become somewhat famous at our church's annual summer chicken barbecue. To make enough cake for the big event, I triple the recipe and frost each layer with chocolate butter cream frosting. Not even a crumb is left. It has been adapted from the Granddaughter's Inglenook Cookbook *(p. 45).*

Serves 8

1 egg
½ cup cocoa powder
1 cup sugar
½ cup oil
1½ cups flour
1 cup buttermilk
1 teaspoon baking soda
1 teaspoon vanilla
½ teaspoon salt

- Preheat the oven to 350°F. Cut circles of wax paper to fit a 9- or 10-inch cake pan. Grease the sides of the cake pan and set aside.

- Break the egg into a large mixing bowl. Without stirring, add the cocoa, sugar, oil, flour, buttermilk, baking soda, vanilla, and salt. Then beat the ingredients to make a smooth batter.

- Pour into the prepared cake pan. Bake for 30 minutes, or until a toothpick inserted into the center comes out clean. Let cool for 7 or 8 minutes on a wire rack. Run a thin knife around the edges to loosen the cake from the pan. Invert on the wire rack to cool completely before frosting it.

- Frost with your favorite butter cream frosting or see page 386.

Note: This cake can be easily doubled, or tripled, to make a layered cake.

Hint: Sometimes cakes get too dry while baking. To bring back moistness, stir 1 to 2 teaspoons sugar with 2 tablespoons warm water until the sugar dissolves. Using a pastry brush, paint the top of the cake with sugar water before frosting it. It makes a big difference.

—Karen Crim Dillon
Vandalia, Ohio

ON BEING A HOSTESS

Our family has sat in the same seats at our kitchen table for as long as I can remember: my dad at the head, my sisters to my left, my mom to the right, and me at the foot. I never really gave it much thought until as an adult, a friend told me the host sits closest to the kitchen so he or she can get whatever additional things are needed for the meal, such as drink refills and dessert. My mom was a great hostess to our family, and I now find myself sitting closest to the kitchen with my own family.

—Emily LaPrade Van Pelt
Dayton, Virginia

WARM CHOCOLATE MELTING CAKE

My husband and I enjoyed this on a cruise. It is our favorite dessert.

Serves 8

8 ounces semisweet chocolate
1 cup (2 sticks) butter
7 eggs, divided
6 tablespoons sugar
½ cup flour

■ Preheat the oven to 375°F. Grease 8 individual ramekins with butter or cooking spray and set aside.

■ Melt the chocolate and butter in a microwave for 45 seconds or in a double boiler for 5 minutes, until melted. Cool for 10 minutes.

■ Beat 4 of the eggs with the sugar. Add the flour and beat again. Add the remaining three eggs and beat until well mixed. Add the egg mixture to the chocolate mixture and stir to mix.

■ Divide the combined mixture evenly among the individual ramekins.

■ Bake until just done, about 15 minutes, until the edges begin to brown. Be careful not to overbake. Serve with vanilla ice cream.

—Sharon I. Hausenfluck
Stephens City, Virginia

EASY CHOCOLATE CAKE

Serves 8

CAKE
1½ cups flour
1 teaspoon baking soda
1 cup sugar
3 tablespoons cocoa powder
1 teaspoon salt
¼ cup plus 2 tablespoons vegetable oil
1 teaspoon vanilla
1 tablespoon white vinegar

FROSTING
1 (16-ounce) bag powdered sugar
¾ cup (1½ sticks) butter, softened
1 tablespoon vanilla

■ Preheat the oven to 350°F. Grease a 9-inch cake pan with cooking spray or butter and set aside.

■ To make the cake, sift the flour, baking soda, sugar, cocoa powder, and salt into a bowl. Stir until well mixed. Add the oil, vanilla, and vinegar and stir until smooth.

■ Pour into the prepared cake pan and bake for 30 minutes. Remove from the oven and let cool for 7 or 8 minutes in the pan on a wire rack. Loosen the sides of the cake with a thin knife. Invert the cake on the wire rack to cool completely.

■ Meanwhile, make the frosting. Combine the powdered sugar, butter, and vanilla. Stir until smooth and then spread over the cooled cake.

—Miriam Over
Williamsburg, Pennsylvania

Zucchini Chocolate Cake

This cake may also be baked in two round cake pans or in cupcake tins.

Serves 12

4 ounces unsweetened chocolate
½ cup vegetable oil
½ cup (1 stick) butter, at room temperature
2 cups sugar
3 eggs, beaten
1 tablespoon vanilla
2 cups flour
⅓ cup cocoa
2 teaspoons baking soda
2 teaspoons baking powder
1 teaspoon salt
⅓ cup buttermilk, sour cream, or plain unsweetened yogurt
3 cups coarsely grated zucchini
½ cup chopped nuts (optional)

■ Preheat the oven to 350°F. Grease and flour a 13 x 9-inch cake pan and set aside.

■ Heat the chocolate and oil in the microwave or over very low heat in a small saucepan until the chocolate is melted.

■ Beat the butter and sugar in a large bowl until creamy. Add the eggs and vanilla and beat well. Add the melted chocolate and mix well.

■ Sift the flour, cocoa, baking soda, baking powder, and salt together. Stir it into the batter with the buttermilk. Stir in the zucchini and nuts, if using.

■ Pour the batter into the prepared pan. Bake for 50 to 60 minutes or until a toothpick inserted into the center of the cake comes out clean.

■ Cool completely. Serve as is or top with whipped cream or a favorite frosting.

Variation: You can use ½ cup whole wheat cake flour for part of the flour.

—Pearl Fruth Miller
Warrensburg, Missouri

RED VELVET CUPCAKES

My family loves these cupcakes. We prefer cream cheese frosting on these but any frosting will work.

Serves 24

½ cup (1 stick) butter
1½ cups sugar
2 eggs
1 cup buttermilk
1 ounce red food coloring
1 teaspoon vanilla
1½ teaspoons baking soda
1 tablespoon distilled white vinegar
2 cups flour
⅓ cup cocoa

■ Preheat the oven to 350°F. Insert paper liners in the cups of the muffin tin.

■ Beat the butter and sugar in a large bowl until light and fluffy. Mix in the eggs, buttermilk, food coloring, and vanilla. Stir in the baking soda and vinegar.

■ Sift the flour and cocoa in a separate bowl. Then mix into the buttermilk batter and stir until well blended.

■ Spoon the batter into the muffin cups, filling about two-thirds full. An ice cream scoop works well.

■ Bake until the tops spring back when lightly touched, about 20 minutes.

■ Cool in the pan on a wire rack. Frost with cream cheese frosting (page 386) and then arrange on a large serving platter.

—Kacie M. Brous
Hays, Kansas

Pumpkin Wedding Cake

I made up the recipe for my daughter's wedding. She met her husband at National Youth Conference. This recipe can also be baked as cupcakes. You may substitute other dried fruits or add nuts.

Serves 14

CAKE
3 cups flour
2 teaspoons baking soda
2 teaspoons baking powder
3 teaspoons pumpkin pie spice
1 teaspoon salt
1½ cups vegetable oil
2 cups granulated sugar
4 eggs
2 cups packed pumpkin purée
1 teaspoon butterscotch extract
½ cup dried cherries
½ cup golden raisins
½ cup dried apricots, chopped

GLAZE
⅔ cup powdered sugar
2 teaspoons milk
1 teaspoon butterscotch extract

- Preheat the oven to 375°F. Grease and flour a 10-inch tube pan and set aside.

- To make the cake, mix the flour, baking soda, baking powder, pumpkin pie spice, and salt. Set aside.

- In a large bowl, combine the oil and sugar. Add the eggs one at a time and mix well. Add the dry ingredients and beat until smooth. Stir in the pumpkin and butterscotch extract until the mixture is smooth. Fold in the cherries, raisins, and apricots.

- Pour the batter into the prepared pan. Bake for 1 hour or until a toothpick inserted in the center of the cake comes out clean. Cool in the pan for 10 minutes on a wire rack. Run a thin knife around the sides and center of the tube pan to loosen the cake. Invert the cake onto a cake plate and cool completely.

- Meanwhile, make the glaze. Combine the powdered sugar, milk, and butterscotch extract and stir. Drizzle over the cooled cake.

—Cheryl Snavely Allen
Woodland, Michigan

Teeth Marks in a Tube Pan

I remember Grandpa Dennis Rupel deciding to make marsh hay. One day Grandma Mary Ann prepared a lunch for him and the boys. For dessert she baked custard in a tube pan. After lunch Grandpa saw a pig running blindly across the marsh with that tube pan in its mouth. He salvaged the pan, but the pig left its mark. Literally. And the teeth marks are on that pan to this day!

—Alice Rohrer
North Manchester, Indiana

CARROT CAKE

This recipe is my husband's favorite dessert. I make it in memory of my mother, Mary Vesta Sumner Slusher.

Serves 12 to 16

CAKE
2 cups flour
1 teaspoon baking soda
1 teaspoon baking powder
1 teaspoon ground cinnamon
¼ teaspoon salt
2 cups sugar
1 teaspoon vanilla
1½ cups vegetable oil
4 eggs
2 cups grated carrots

CREAM CHEESE FROSTING
½ cup (1 stick) butter
8 ounces cream cheese
4 cups powdered sugar
1 teaspoon vanilla
1 cup chopped nuts

- Preheat the oven to 350°F. Grease and flour three 8-inch round cake pans and set aside.

- To make the cake, sift together the flour, baking soda, baking powder, cinnamon, salt, and sugar. Add the vanilla, oil, eggs, and carrots. Beat well. Divide the batter evenly into the prepared cake pans.

- Bake for 20 minutes. Let cool for 7 or 8 minutes in the pan on a wire rack. Invert the cakes on the wire rack after loosening the sides with a thin knife. Cool completely.

- To make the frosting, beat the butter and cream cheese until creamy. Add the powdered sugar and beat well. Stir in the vanilla and nuts.

- To frost the cake, place the first layer, rounded side down, on a cake plate. Spread ⅓ cup frosting over the layer. Repeat with the next layer. Top layer should be rounded side up. Spread remaining frosting on sides and top of cake.

—Brenda S. Hylton
Floyd, Virginia

TRUE HUMILITY

Favorably impressed with the stuffing at the family gathering, Peggy's mother probed to determine the source of the recipe, the list of ingredients, the manner of mixing and baking. Peggy replied simply, "Mom, I used your recipe." True humility is this, that one forgets the fabulous nature of one's own cooking!

—Sandy Bosserman
Peace Valley, Missouri

FAVORITE NUT CAKE

My grandfather loved this cake. I entered this cake at the Frederick Fair and won an award.

Serves 16

CAKE
2 cups sugar
⅔ cup butter, at room temperature
3 eggs
2½ cups flour
⅛ teaspoon salt
2 teaspoons baking powder
1 cup milk
1 teaspoon vanilla
1 cup hickory nuts, walnuts, or pecans, chopped

PENUCHE FROSTING
½ cup (1 stick) butter
1 cup packed brown sugar
¼ cup milk or cream
2 cups powdered sugar
1 teaspoon vanilla

■ Preheat the oven to 325°F. Grease and flour a 13 x 9-inch pan (or two 8-inch round pans) and set aside.

■ To make the cake, combine together the sugar and butter. Add the eggs and, using an electric mixer on medium speed, beat for 2 minutes.

■ Combine the flour, salt, and baking powder and lightly mix with a fork. Add to the egg mixture alternately with the milk, stirring constantly.

■ Stir in the vanilla and nuts. Pour into the prepared pan and bake for 45 to 50 minutes. Let cool completely in the pan on a wire rack.

■ To make the frosting, melt the butter in a saucepan over medium-low heat. Add the brown sugar and boil for 2 minutes. Add the milk, increase the heat to medium, and bring just to a boil. Remove from the heat and cool to lukewarm. Then beat in the powdered sugar and vanilla. Frost the cooled cake.

—Ashley L. Nonemaker
Shepherdstown, West Virginia

PINEAPPLE-NUT CAKE

Serves 20

CAKE
2 cups flour
2 cups sugar
1 (20-ounce) can crushed pineapple, undrained
2 eggs
2 teaspoons baking soda
1 cup crushed walnuts
1 teaspoon vanilla

FROSTING
8 ounces cream cheese
½ cup (1 stick) butter
1½ cups powdered sugar
1 teaspoon vanilla
Chopped walnuts for garnish (optional)

■ Preheat the oven to 350°F. Grease a 13 x 9-inch pan and set aside.

■ To make the cake, combine the flour, sugar, pineapple, eggs, baking soda, walnuts, and vanilla. Beat with a wooden spoon by hand. Pour into the prepared pan. Bake for 45 minutes. Let cool completely.

■ To make the frosting, mix the cream cheese, butter, powdered sugar, and vanilla. Beat with a wooden spoon by hand. Spread the frosting on the cooled cake. Sprinkle walnuts on top, if desired.

—Gloria Baugher Miller
York, Pennsylvania

PINEAPPLE-COCONUT CAKE

When my husband and I were dating, I made this cake for a church potluck. He liked it and asked for the recipe. He added the coconut, which we both thought greatly improved the cake. I teased him saying he couldn't have any more of my recipes because he always experimented with them. So he married me and now has access to all the recipes.

Serves 24 to 30

CAKE
2 cups flour
2 cups sugar
2 teaspoons baking soda
1 teaspoon vanilla
2 eggs
½ cup chopped pecans
1½ cups coconut
1 (20-ounce) can crushed pineapple with juice

FROSTING
½ cup (1 stick) butter, softened
1 (8-ounce) package cream cheese
2 cups powdered sugar
1 teaspoon vanilla

■ Preheat the oven to 350°F. Grease and flour a 15 x 11-inch baking pan and set aside.

■ To make the cake, combine the flour, sugar, baking soda, vanilla, eggs, pecans, coconut, and pineapple in a large mixing bowl. Mix well.

■ Pour the batter into the prepared pan. Bake for 25 to 30 minutes.

■ For the frosting, beat the butter and cream cheese until creamy. Add the powdered sugar and vanilla and continue beating until smooth. Frost the cake once it has cooled. You will have frosting left over. Store any extra frosting in an airtight container in the refrigerator. It will keep for up to six months.

■ Refrigerate frosted cake overnight.

Note: The frosting recipe makes a lot of frosting and can be easily cut back. Just halve all the ingredients.

—Jim and Clareen Dunn
Mulberry Grove, Illinois

ANGEL FOOD CAKE

Serves 12 to 15

18 eggs, separated
2½ teaspoons cream of tartar
2 cups sugar, divided
1 teaspoon vanilla
1 tablespoon almond extract
¼ teaspoon coconut extract (optional)
1¼ cups flour

- Preheat the oven to 350°F.

- Let the egg whites come to room temperature; save the yolks for another use. Beat the egg whites with an electric mixer on high until frothy, about 3 minutes. Gradually add the cream of tartar and 1¼ cups of the sugar and continue to beat until stiff peaks form.

- Fold in the vanilla, almond extract, and coconut extract, if using.

- Sift the flour and the remaining ¾ cup sugar together 3 times. Slowly fold the flour mixture into the stiff egg whites about ¼ cup at a time.

- Pour into an ungreased angel food cake pan (tube pan). Run a knife around the edge to remove any air bubbles.

- Bake for 45 minutes, or until spongy to the touch. Invert on a plate to cool.

Variation: For a chocolate chip angel food cake, add ⅓ cup mini chocolate chips with the flour.

—Gloria B. Dell
West Alexandria, Ohio

SAUERKRAUT APPLE CAKE

This wonderfully moist apple cake is of German origin. The secret is the sauerkraut, which goes well with the cinnamon and gives the cake its moistness, as well as a nice coconut-like texture.

Serves 18 to 24

CAKE
2 cups flour
2 teaspoons baking powder
2 teaspoons ground cinnamon
1 teaspoon baking soda
1 teaspoon salt
½ teaspoon grated nutmeg
1 cup granulated sugar
½ cup packed light brown sugar
4 eggs
1 cup vegetable oil
1 (15-ounce) can shredded sauerkraut, chopped, rinsed, and drained
1 apple (Gala or Yellow Delicious), peeled, cored, and finely chopped
1 cup coarsely chopped walnuts or pecans

FROSTING
1 (8-ounce) package cream cheese, at room temperature
½ cup (1 stick) butter, at room temperature
1 (16-ounce) bag powdered sugar (4 cups)
1 teaspoon vanilla
2 teaspoons ground cinnamon
1 tablespoon grated orange zest
⅛ teaspoon salt

■ Preheat the oven to 325°F. Grease a 13 x 9-inch baking dish and set aside.

■ To make the cake, whisk together the flour, baking powder, cinnamon, baking soda, salt, and nutmeg; set aside.

■ In another large mixing bowl, combine the sugars and whisk in the eggs, and then the oil; blend well. Stir in the sauerkraut, apple, and nuts. Add the dry ingredients and stir until just moistened.

■ Pour into the prepared baking dish and bake for 35 minutes, or until the top of the cake springs back when touched with your finger, and the cake is just beginning to pull away from the sides of the dish. Cool the cake completely before frosting.

■ To prepare the frosting, in a large mixing bowl, beat the cream cheese and butter until blended and creamy. Gradually add the powdered sugar, stirring to mix. Then add the vanilla, cinnamon, orange zest, and salt; beat well. Spread on the cooled cake. Keep the cake refrigerated until serving time or the frosting becomes too soft.

—Mary Lou Van Dyke
Lincoln, Nebraska

SHOOFLY CAKE

This is a recipe that my mother made quite often.

Serves 12 to 16

- 4 cups flour
- 2 cups sugar
- ½ cup (1 stick) butter, softened
- 1 cup dark molasses
- 2 teaspoons baking soda

■ Preheat the oven to 350°F. Grease a 13 x 9-inch baking pan and set aside.

■ Combine the flour, sugar, and butter and mix with a pastry blender or fork to form small crumbs. Save 1½ cups for the topping.

■ In another bowl combine 2 cups boiling water with the molasses and baking soda. Add to the flour mixture and stir.

■ Pour into the prepared pan. Top with the reserved crumbs.

■ Bake for 45 minutes. Cool before cutting.

—Bettina Balmer
Big Creek, Kentucky

WATCH THE SPELLING

Whenever I think of pies, I am reminded of the Amish family who had a bakeshop and a roadside stand. When they started making mincemeat pies, no one bought them. They couldn't understand why nobody was buying their pies until someone asked a question about the sign they had displayed beside them. To their surprise, when they looked closely at the sign, they knew why. The letter "n" was missing and they had been advertising "Micemeat Pies for Sale"! Would you have bought any?

—Anna N. Buckwalter
Lancaster, Pennsylvania

EASY OATMEAL CAKE

Serves 14

CAKE
1 cup quick-cooking oats
½ cup (1 stick) butter
1 cup light brown sugar, not packed
1 cup granulated sugar
2 eggs, slightly beaten
1⅓ cups flour
1 teaspoon baking soda
½ teaspoon ground cinnamon

TOPPING
½ cup (1 stick) butter
1 cup grated coconut
¼ cup milk
½ cup light brown sugar, not packed
1 cup chopped walnuts

- For the cake, pour 1¼ cups boiling water over the oats and butter. Let stand for 20 minutes.

- Preheat the oven to 350°F. Grease and flour a 13 x 9-inch baking dish and set aside.

- Stir the brown sugar, granulated sugar, eggs, flour, baking soda, and cinnamon into the oat mixture.

- Pour into the prepared dish, and bake for 35 minutes.

- For the topping, combine the butter, coconut, milk, brown sugar, and walnuts in a saucepan and cook over low heat until the butter is melted, about 5 minutes. Spread over the hot cake. Put under the broiler until the topping is browned and bubbly, about 3 minutes. Serve warm.

—Mary Ann Saffer
Arriba, Colorado

Mom's Old-Fashioned Gingerbread Cake

This sweet, spicy cake is quite popular with our family in the fall and at Thanksgiving. It's great topped with whipped cream and a piece of candy corn.

Serves 20

> 2 eggs, beaten
> ¾ cup sugar
> ¾ cup vegetable oil or applesauce
> 1½ cups (12 ounces) mild-flavored molasses
> 3¾ cups flour
> ¾ teaspoon salt
> 1½ teaspoons baking powder
> ¾ teaspoon baking soda
> 2¼ teaspoons ground ginger
> 1½ teaspoons ground cinnamon

- Preheat the oven to 350°F. Grease a 13 x 9-inch cake pan and set aside.

- Beat the eggs, sugar, and oil or applesauce in a large bowl until fluffy. Add the molasses and beat again until well blended.

- In a separate bowl, mix the flour, salt, baking powder, baking soda, ginger, and cinnamon. Add to the egg mixture and stir until blended. Then add 1½ cups boiling water to the mixture and stir until smooth. This will make a thin batter.

- Pour the batter into the prepared pan. Bake for 40 minutes or until a toothpick inserted into the center comes out clean.

- Let it cool for 7 or 8 minutes in the pan and then transfer to a wire rack to cool completely. Cut and serve.

Note: This cake may be served with whipped cream, lemon sauce (page 383), or ice cream.

—Martha J. Angle
Waynesboro, Pennsylvania

APPLESAUCE CHRISTMAS CAKE

This cake was baked every Christmas by my grandmother, Maggie Danie Moran (1915–1965). Today it's baked every Christmas by my mother and daughter. Needless to say my family loves this recipe.

Serves 12 to 16

- 2 cups granulated sugar
- 1 cup (2 sticks) butter
- 2 cups applesauce
- 1 teaspoon baking soda
- 3 eggs
- 3½ cups flour
- 1 teaspoon ground nutmeg
- 1 teaspoon ground cinnamon
- 1 teaspoon ground cloves
- 1 pound raisins
- 1¼ cups chopped walnuts, divided
- 2 tablespoons brown sugar

- Preheat the oven to 300°F. Grease an 8-inch tube pan and set aside.

- Beat the sugar and butter until creamy. Combine the baking soda and applesauce and add to the sugar mixture. Beat in the eggs.

- Sift the flour, nutmeg, cinnamon, and cloves in a bowl. Toss the raisins and 1 cup of the walnuts into the flour mixture. Add the flour mixture to the applesauce batter, and stir to blend.

- Pour the batter into the greased tube pan.

- Combine the remaining ¼ cup walnuts and brown sugar. Sprinkle the topping over the batter.

- Bake for 1½ hours or until a toothpick inserted into the center comes out clean.

—Anne Price Fike
La Verne, California

LEMON ZUCCHINI CAKE

Serves 10 to 15

 - **2 cups sugar**
 - **2 cups self-rising flour**
 - **1 (3-ounce) package instant lemon pudding (see variation)**
 - **3 eggs**
 - **1 cup vegetable oil**
 - **2 cups grated zucchini (about 2 medium zucchini)**
 - **1 teaspoon vanilla (see variation)**
 - **1 cup chopped nuts (optional)**

■ Preheat the oven to 350°F. Grease and flour a 9-inch Bundt pan and set aside.

■ Combine the sugar, flour, pudding mix, eggs, oil, zucchini, vanilla, and nuts, if using. Mix well.

■ Pour the batter into the prepared Bundt pan. Bake for 1 hour or until a toothpick inserted into the center comes out clean.

■ Top with lemon sauce (page 383) or sprinkle with powdered sugar.

Variation: Use coconut pudding and flavoring for a different taste.

—Judith F. Stoddard
Bridgewater, Virginia

MADE FROM SCRATCH

We are all tempted when it comes to cake," declares Mma Ramotswe in Alexander McCall Smith's *In the Company of Cheerful Ladies*. That wise observation certainly applies to the Brethren, though we might want to add Cand ice cream"! We strive to resist temptation in many forms, but long dessert tables at our carry-ins and the number of cake recipes in our cookbooks give testimony to our wholehearted, happy indulgence when faced with sweets.

Cakes have been crowning meals and social occasions for millennia. Early Greeks and Egyptians added sweetening to form honey cakes, similar to today's baklava. The Bible refers to cakes several times. When Aaron's sons are preparing for priesthood, they are offered "unleavened cakes mixed with oil," made from "choice wheat flour" (Exodus 29:2, *NRSV*), and when Elijah meets a widow with just a smidgen of grain and oil, he commands her to "first make me a little cake of it" (1 Kings 17:13). Not until the middle of the eighteenth century did cakes, with the addition of beaten eggs, finely ground flour, and refined sugar, begin to resemble what we know today.

For me, the warm, rich smell enveloping the house as a cake unfolds its mysteries in the oven evokes childhood memories filled with love—Aunt Elsie's Easter coconut cake, baked in a lamb mold; the birthday when Mother traced my profile onto the cake; and my four-layer wedding cake, topped with fresh flowers and decorated with sugar doves, created and gifted to us by one of my dad's parishioners.

Grandma's sunny farmhouse kitchen and the spacious kitchen in the parsonage where I grew up were always open and welcoming to children. Mother created matching aprons out of checked red gingham. Mine had a bib, cut and embroidered like a cat's face. Thus attired, I felt like a "real" baker from the time I was very small. Who could resist helping bake a cake when dipping a finger into the sugary batter was so easy?

I stirred up my first "made from scratch" chocolate cake at the tender age of nine. It was very similar to Mrs. Lawrence Thompson's recipe, which is taken from the 1942 *Granddaughter's Inglenook Cookbook* (p. 40). Powdery flour, grainy sugar, bitter Baker's Chocolate, and gooey eggs gave way to a rich, deep velvety-brown beauty, and the air seemed to pulsate with the sweet chocolaty scent. I was enchanted. Today the cake I stir up most often is "Hot Milk Sponge Cake," and Faye Shaver's recipe is a classic. Fresh and warm from the oven, it melts in your mouth. You can also use it as shortcake with berries.

Yes, we Brethren are tempted by cake. It's not by towering fondant cakes or brightly colored attention-grabbers, though, but by the very act of loving intention that goes into assembling simple ingredients and baking a cake from scratch. We're lured by the way our kitchen fills with tantalizing smells and by the mystery of thin, grainy batter transforming into light, airy cake. But mostly we are tempted by the fellowship shared with others around simple slices of cake.

Delight yourself by creating one of the cakes in this cookbook. Make the simple "Jiffy Chocolate Feather Cake," or an ethereal "Angel Food Cake." Branch out and try the recipe for "Pumpkin Wedding Cake" or "Sauerkraut Apple Cake." Revel in the process. Be beguiled by the delicate texture and delectable smells. Brew a pot of tea. Cut generous pieces of cake, and sit down in the company of cheerful friends and family. Give into temptation, just a little, and enjoy!

—Susan Kinsel Fitze
New Lebanon, Ohio

CHOCOLATE CAKE

1 c. brown sugar	½ c. milk
2 tb. cocoa	2½ c. flour
1 egg yolk	3 egg whites
½ c. milk	Vanilla
1 c. brown sugar	1 tsp. soda
½ c. butter	1 tb. hot water
2 egg yolks	

Boil first 4 ingredients together; cool. Cream sugar, butter and 2 egg yolks; add boiled mixture. Add milk and flour, which has been sifted 3 times, alternately. Mix well. Add 3 egg whites and vanilla. Last, add soda dissolved in hot water. Bake in layers in moderate oven.

—Mrs. Lawrence Thompson, Story City, Iowa

Hot Milk Sponge Cake

Sponge cakes date back to at least the nineteenth century when eggs were used as a rising agent instead of yeast. The cakes were popular throughout European colonies. This is a famous recipe among the Brethren. It's very similar to the recipe in the Granddaughter's Inglenook Cookbook *(p. 46).*

Serves 16

4 eggs
2 cups sugar
2 teaspoons baking powder
¼ teaspoons salt
2 cups flour
1 cup milk
1 tablespoon butter
1 teaspoon vanilla

- Preheat the oven to 350°F. Grease and flour a 13 x 9-inch pan and set aside.

- Beat the eggs in a bowl. Add the sugar, a little at a time, and beat for 10 to 15 minutes.

- In a separate bowl, combine the baking powder, salt, and flour and sift 3 times. Add to the egg mixture a little at a time, stirring well after each addition.

- Heat the milk in a saucepan over medium heat. Add the butter and stir until melted.

- Add the vanilla and hot milk mixture to the batter. Stir to incorporate. Pour into the prepared pan.

- Bake for 40 minutes or until the cake springs back when touched.

Variation: Lemon extract is also good in place of vanilla.

—Faye Shaver
Staunton, Virginia

APPLE-CREAM CHEESE BUNDT CAKE

Here is an excellent cake to make in the fall when apples are ripe. You can tell my family really enjoys this cake because it doesn't last long at family gatherings.

Serves 12

CREAM CHEESE FILLING
1 (8-ounce) package cream cheese, softened
¼ cup (½ stick) butter, softened
½ cup sugar
1 large egg
2 tablespoons flour
1 teaspoon vanilla

CAKE
3 cups flour
1 cup granulated sugar
1 cup firmly packed light brown sugar
2 teaspoons ground cinnamon
1 teaspoon salt
1 teaspoon baking soda
1 teaspoon ground nutmeg
½ teaspoon ground allspice
3 large eggs, lightly beaten
¾ cup canola oil
¾ cup applesauce
1 teaspoon vanilla
3 cups peeled, cored, and finely chopped apples
   (about 1½ pounds)
1½ cups finely chopped toasted pecans, divided

PRALINE FROSTING
½ cup firmly packed light brown sugar
¼ cup (½ stick) butter
3 tablespoons milk
1 teaspoon vanilla
1 cup powdered sugar

- Preheat the oven to 350°F. Grease and flour a 10-inch Bundt pan and set aside.

- To make the filling, beat the cream cheese, butter, and sugar with an electric mixer on medium until creamy. Add the egg, flour, and vanilla; beat just until blended. Set aside.

- To make the cake, stir together the flour, sugars, cinnamon, salt, baking soda, nutmeg, and allspice in a large bowl. Stir in the eggs, oil, applesauce, and vanilla just until moistened. Fold in the apples and 1 cup of the pecans.

- Spoon two-thirds of the apple mixture into the prepared Bundt pan. Spoon the cream cheese filling on top and gently swirl the filling through the center part of the apple mixture using a fork or knife, keeping a 1-inch border filling free. Spoon the remaining apple mixture over the filling.

- Bake for about 1 hour, or until a toothpick inserted in the center comes out clean. Cool the cake in the pan for 15 minutes and then transfer to a wire rack to cool completely, about 2 hours.

- To make the frosting, combine the brown sugar, butter, and milk in a saucepan over medium heat and bring to a boil, whisking constantly. Boil for 1 minute, whisking constantly. Then remove from the heat and stir in the vanilla.

- Gradually whisk in the powdered sugar until smooth; stir gently for 3 to 5 minutes or until the mixture begins to cool and thickens slightly. Pour immediately over the cooled cake. Sprinkle the remaining ½ cup chopped pecans on top.

—Nancy Gay Thompson
Elkins, West Virginia

MOTHER'S RHUBARB CAKE

My mother, Eula Fyock, got a rhubarb cake recipe from a television show and found it too bland for our tastes, so she spruced it up. She added orange juice, cinnamon, and coconut, and this has been a family favorite ever since. This cake is even better after a day or two, if you can wait that long.

Serves 15 to 18

½ cup granulated sugar
½ teaspoon ground cinnamon
½ cup (1 stick) plus 1 tablespoon butter, softened, divided
1⅓ cups coconut, divided
¼ cup chopped walnuts or pecans (optional)
1½ cups brown sugar
2 eggs
2 cups flour
½ teaspoon salt
1 teaspoon baking soda
1 teaspoon baking powder
½ cup orange juice
1 teaspoon vanilla
2 cups rhubarb, finely cut

■ Preheat the oven to 350°F. Grease and flour a 13 x 9-inch pan and set aside.

■ Mix the granulated sugar, cinnamon, 1 tablespoon of the butter, 1 cup of the coconut, and nuts, if using, together to make the topping and set aside.

■ Beat the brown sugar, remaining ½ cup butter, and eggs in a large bowl until creamy.

■ Sift the flour, salt, baking soda, and baking powder. Add the flour mixture to the creamed sugar mixture alternately with the orange juice, stirring after each addition.

■ Add the vanilla, rhubarb, and remaining ⅓ cup coconut. Stir to mix and then pour the batter into the prepared pan. Sprinkle the topping over the batter and bake for 50 minutes, or when a toothpick inserted into the center comes out clean.

—Joan Fyock Norris
Lititz, Pennsylvania

SOUR CREAM POUND CAKE

When pastoring, oftentimes I would be short on time when preparing worship. This cake was simple and quick to prepare, and always a hit. When I was a child my Aunt Mary, who lived in a Virginia holler, would bake a lemon pound cake for my cousins and me to eat warm. Sometimes I substitute lemon extract for the vanilla, and it brings back that great memory. Yum.

Serves 12

> 1½ (3 sticks) cups butter, at room temperature
> 3 cups sugar
> 6 eggs, at room temperature
> 1 cup sour cream
> 3 cups flour
> 1 teaspoon vanilla (or lemon)

■ Preheat the oven to 325°F. Grease an 8-inch tube pan and set aside.

■ Beat the butter and sugar until creamy. Add the eggs one at a time. Beat thoroughly after each addition.

■ Add the sour cream and stir. Add the flour a little at a time and beat after each addition. Stir in the vanilla. Pour into the prepared pan.

■ Bake for 1 hour 20 minutes, or when a toothpick inserted into the center comes out clean.

—Judy Mills Reimer
Roanoke, Virginia

LILLIAN FLORY'S 3-DAY COCONUT CAKE

The cake has no leavening other than the eggs. It is a very delicious, moist cake. The longer it sits, the better it gets.

Serves 10 to 12

CAKE	FROSTING
1 cup (2 sticks) butter	2 cups sugar
3 cups sugar	1 (16-ounce) package sour cream
6 eggs	1 (12-ounce) package shredded
3 cups cake flour	coconut (4 cups), divided
Pinch of salt	2 cups frozen whipped topping,
1 cup whipping cream	thawed
2 teaspoons vanilla	Dash of vanilla flavoring
½ teaspoon almond extract	

■ Preheat the oven to 350°F. Line three 9-inch round cake pans with wax paper cut to fit the bottom. Do not grease.

■ To make the cake, beat the butter and sugar until light and fluffy. Add the eggs one at a time, beating well after each addition. Sift the cake flour and salt together. Combine the whipping cream, vanilla, and almond extracts. Add a little flour mixture to the egg mixture and then a little whipped cream mixture, stirring after each addition. Continue alternating until all the ingredients are combined.

■ Pour the batter into the prepared pans. Bake for about 35 minutes. Let the cakes cook in the pans for 10 minutes and then transfer to wire racks to cool completely.

■ To make the frosting, combine the sugar, sour cream, and 3½ cups of the coconut. Stir to mix thoroughly. Set aside 1 cup of the frosting. Spread the remaining frosting on top of two of the cakes and stack them with the unfrosted cake on top. Combine the reserved 1 cup frosting with the whipped topping and blend with a wire whisk.

■ Frost the sides and top of the cake. Sprinkle the remaining ½ cup coconut on top. Put the cake in an airtight container and place in the refrigerator for 3 days before serving.

—Marty Barlow
Dayton, Virginia

Lazy Daisy Cake

This is a classic Inglenook recipe. A variation of this is found in the
Granddaughter's Inglenook Cookbook (*p. 46*).

Serves 8 to 10

CAKE
2 eggs
1 cup sugar
½ teaspoon vanilla
1 cup flour
¼ teaspoon salt
½ teaspoon baking powder
½ cup milk
1 tablespoon butter

TOPPING
⅓ cup butter, softened
⅔ cup packed brown sugar
¼ cup evaporated milk
1 cup coconut
½ cup chopped pecans

■ Preheat the oven to 350°F. Grease a 9-inch cake pan and set aside.

■ To make the cake, beat the eggs, sugar, and vanilla until creamy. Sift in the flour, salt, and baking powder and beat until smooth.

■ Heat the milk and butter in a saucepan over medium heat just until boiling and then add to the flour mixture. Beat well.

■ Pour into the prepared cake pan and bake for about 30 minutes.

■ To make the topping, combine the butter, brown sugar, evaporated milk, coconut, and pecans, mix well, and then spread on the warm cake. Brown under the broiler about 1 minute.

—Carolyn Dooley
Hutchinson, Kansas

Basic Cheesecake

This cheesecake recipe is a good base for whatever topping you like: fresh strawberries, cherry pie filling, or lemon sauce.

Serves 8 to 10

> 12 ounces cream cheese, at room temperature
> 2 eggs
> ½ cup sugar
> 2 teaspoons vanilla, divided
> 1 (9-inch) graham cracker crumb piecrust
> 1 cup sour cream
> 2 tablespoons sugar

■ Preheat the oven to 350°F.

■ Beat the cream cheese, eggs, sugar, and 1 teaspoon of the vanilla together until creamy. Pour into the graham cracker crumb piecrust.

■ Bake for 30 minutes. Let cool for about 5 minutes.

■ Mix together the sour cream, sugar, and the remaining 1 teaspoon vanilla. Spread over the cheesecake and chill for 6 hours before serving.

—Annette L. Shafer
Creston, Ohio

NEW YORK CHEESECAKE

Serves 12

CRUST
¼ cup butter, melted
1 cup graham cracker crumbs (about 16 squares)

FILLING
1 teaspoon cream of tartar
6 eggs, separated
1½ cups plus 3 tablespoons sugar, divided
18 ounces cream cheese, at room temperature
3 tablespoons flour
½ teaspoon salt
2 cups (1 pint) sour cream
1 teaspoon vanilla

■ Preheat the oven to 375°F. Grease a 9-inch springform pan and set aside.

■ To make the crust, combine the butter and graham cracker crumbs; mix well. Press into the bottom of the prepared pan and set aside.

■ To make the filling, combine the cream of tartar and egg whites and beat until foamy. Add 3 tablespoons of the sugar, a tablespoon at a time. Beat after each addition and then until firm. Set aside.

■ Beat the cream cheese until soft. Add the remaining $1\frac{1}{2}$ cups sugar, flour, and salt to the cream cheese. Blend well. Add the sour cream and vanilla. Fold in the eggs white mixture. Pour into the prepared springform pan. Bake for $1\frac{1}{2}$ hours or until firm.

■ Turn off the oven and open the door slightly. Let the cheesecake rest in the oven for 10 minutes. Remove and cool completely.

—Teresa Anzalone
Johnstown, Pennsylvania

BLUEBERRY CHEESECAKE

My family requested this dessert for every family gathering or reunion. I made it at Christmas for years. Later I found out my father didn't like blueberries, but he ate it all those years so he wouldn't hurt my feelings!

Serves 12 to 16

CRUST
1 cup crushed graham crackers
½ cup sugar
½ cup (1 stick) butter, melted

BLUEBERRY TOPPING
½ cup sugar
2 cups blueberries, divided
1½ tablespoons cornstarch

CHEESECAKE
2 (8-ounce) packages cream cheese
1 teaspoon vanilla
4 eggs
½ cup sugar

■ Preheat the oven to 350°F.

■ To make the crust, combine the graham crackers, sugar, and butter and stir with a fork. Press into the bottom and up the sides of a 13 x 9-inch cake pan.

■ For the cheesecake, combine the cream cheese, vanilla, eggs, and sugar in a blender. Process on medium speed until well mixed. Pour into the crust.

■ Bake for 20 minutes or until set. Remove from the oven and cool.

■ To make the blueberry topping, mix ⅓ cup water, sugar, and ½ cup of the blueberries in a saucepan over medium-high heat. Bring to a boil and simmer for 3 minutes.

■ Mix the cornstarch with ⅓ cup water and add to the saucepan. Stir until the mixture thickens and then remove from the stove.

■ Fold in the remaining 1½ cups of blueberries. Pour over the cooled cheesecake.

Note: To save time, you can use a can of blueberry pie filling and a premade graham cracker crust.

—Diane E. Eveland
Plymouth, Indiana

Razzle Dazzle Berry Trifle

Serves 12 to 16

2 (3-ounce) packages raspberry gelatin
2 large bananas, sliced (2 cups)
1 (21-ounce) can blueberry pie filling
4 cups cubed angel food cake (see page 319)
½ cup orange juice
1 (5.1-ounce) package instant vanilla pudding
2½ cups milk
1 cup frozen whipped topping, thawed
Fresh blueberries and raspberries (optional)

■ Put the gelatin in a large bowl and add 1½ cups boiling water; stir until the gelatin dissolves, about 2 minutes. Add 1 cup cold water and 24 ice cubes. Stir until slightly thickened. Remove any unmelted ice cubes.

■ Stir in the bananas and blueberry pie filling; set aside.

■ Place the angel food cake in a trifle bowl. Drizzle the orange juice over the cake and toss well. Spoon the gelatin mixture over the cake, cover, and chill for 30 minutes.

■ Combine the vanilla pudding mix with the milk. Fold the whipped topping into the pudding and spread over the gelatin mixture. Cover and chill.

■ Garnish with blueberries and raspberries, if desired, just before serving.

Note: For a low-fat version use a fat-free pudding as well as fat-free whipped topping.

—Cheryl A. Johnson
Perrysburg, Ohio

EASY STRAWBERRY VANILLA TRIFLE

My church family enjoys both variations of this light dessert. I've included both below, and I'm sure there are more out there.

Serves 12 to 16

2 (3½-ounce) packages instant vanilla pudding
2 cups milk
1 teaspoon vanilla
8 ounces sour cream
8 ounces frozen whipped topping, thawed
16 ounces fresh strawberries, washed and sliced
1 angel food cake, cubed (see page 319)
½ cup chopped nuts (optional)

■ Combine the vanilla pudding mix and milk and beat until blended. Stir in the vanilla extract.

■ Fold in the sour cream and whipped topping. Use immediately or refrigerate overnight and use the next day.

■ When ready to assemble, in a trifle bowl, layer the angel food cake, pudding, and strawberries and repeat until all the ingredients are used, ending with fruit on top.

Variation: For a Raspberry Lemon Trifle use raspberries instead of strawberries. Use lemon pudding instead of vanilla pudding, and substitute lemon extract for the vanilla extract.

—Becky Meiers
Anderson, Indiana

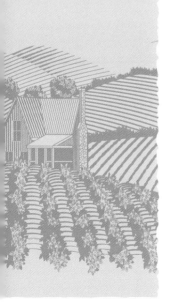

UPSIDE-DOWN DATE PUDDING CAKE

When pouring the brown sugar sauce over the cake mixture, pour
onto a spoon so it does not make a hole in the cake mixture.

Serves 12 to 14

CAKE
1 cup chopped pitted dates
1 cup boiling water
½ cup granulated sugar
½ cup packed brown sugar
1 egg
2 tablespoons butter, melted
1½ cups flour
1 teaspoon baking soda
½ teaspoon baking powder
½ teaspoon salt
1 cup chopped walnuts

SAUCE
1½ cups brown sugar
2 tablespoons butter
1½ cups boiling water

Whipped cream for topping (optional)

■ Soak the dates in 1 cup boiling water and let sit until cool.

■ Meanwhile, preheat the oven to 375°F. Grease a 13 x 9-inch baking dish and set aside.

■ To make the cake, blend the sugars, egg, and butter and stir until creamy.

■ Sift the flour, baking soda, baking powder, and salt. Add to the sugar mixture and blend. Stir in the nuts and cooled, undrained dates. Pour into the prepared baking dish.

■ To make the sauce, combine the brown sugar, butter, and 1½ cups boiling water. Stir until the sugar is dissolved and then pour over the cake batter.

■ Bake for about 40 minutes or until a toothpick inserted in the center comes out clean.

■ Cut into squares, invert on plates, and serve warm with whipped cream, if desired.

—Gladys E. Crawford
Greenville, Ohio

RHUBARB PUDDING

My grandmother and namesake, Essie Hood of the Oakley Brick Church of the Brethren in Cerro Gordo, Illinois, made this delicious dessert for me when I was a girl.

Serves 14 to 16

4 cups chopped rhubarb
1½ cups sugar
1 cup mini marshmallows
1½ cups flour
¾ cup sugar
1 egg
1¼ teaspoons baking powder
½ cup milk
⅓ teaspoon salt
1 teaspoon vanilla
1 tablespoon plus 1 teaspoon butter

■ Preheat the oven to 375°F. Grease a 12 x 8-inch cake pan and set aside.

■ Mix together the rhubarb, sugar, and marshmallows. Transfer to the prepared cake pan.

■ Combine the flour, sugar, egg, baking powder, milk, salt, vanilla, and butter. Stir to mix and pour on top of the rhubarb.

■ Bake for 30 to 45 minutes, or until set and the rhubarb is tender.

—Essie F. Pritts
Mount Pleasant, Pennsylvania

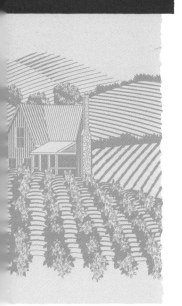

SUGARING UP

Grandma Mary Ann Rupel said the only way to make rhubarb pie tasty was to put in all the sugar you could stand, and then close your eyes and put in some more.

—Alice Rohrer
North Manchester, Indiana

CRANBERRY-PUMPKIN BREAD PUDDING

My family loves bread pudding and finds this to be a tasty variation, perfect for autumn.

Serves 9

PUDDING
3 eggs
1½ cups 2% milk
2 cups puréed pumpkin, canned or cooked fresh, divided
½ cup packed light brown sugar
1 teaspoon vanilla extract
¾ teaspoon pumpkin pie spice
5 cups cubed day-old bread
½ cup dried cranberries

TOPPING
¼ cup (½ stick) butter
¼ cup packed brown sugar
1 tablespoon corn syrup
¼ cup chopped walnuts

■ Preheat the oven to 350°F. Grease an 8 x 8-inch baking dish with cooking spray and set aside.

■ To make the pudding, combine the eggs, milk, 1 cup of the pumpkin purée, brown sugar, vanilla, and pumpkin pie spice in a large bowl. Stir in the bread cubes and cranberries.

■ Pour the mixture in the prepared baking dish, cover, and bake for 25 minutes. Uncover and bake for 10 to 15 minutes more, or until a knife inserted near the center comes out clean.

■ To make the topping, in a small saucepan over medium heat, combine the butter, brown sugar, and corn syrup and stir until the mixture is completely combined, about 5 minutes. Add the remaining 1 cup pumpkin and walnuts and stir to mix. Serve as a warm sauce for the pudding.

Notes: You can substitute 1 cup chopped fresh or frozen cranberries for the dried cranberries. If using canned pumpkin it will take one 15-ounce can.

—JoAnne Doody Leatherman
Damascus, Maryland

PRETTY GOOD PIE

It was Thanksgiving Day, about fifty-five years ago. I had experimented with my recipe for at least two years in an effort to get the spices just right, and I was anxious for the family to like my pumpkin pie. No one was saying anything, and I prepared myself to accept that it was just ordinary. Then Grandpa Leo, who never in his entire life had commented on the food he ate, in barely audible tones said, "Pretty good pie." Everyone gasped, the room exploded in laughter, and my day was made.

—Florence M. Crago
McPherson, Kansas

GRAHAM CRACKER PUDDING

Members of the Mohler Church of the Brethren, my grandmother Nora Bollinger and her sisters always vied with one another to make the best dishes. This is a vintage recipe from my grandmother. She concocted this recipe for a family dinner. Our children love it!

Serves 6

PUDDING
2 tablespoons butter
3 tablespoons brown sugar
3 tablespoons granulated sugar
2 tablespoons cornstarch
2 cups milk, divided
2 egg yolks, beaten
1 teaspoon vanilla
¼ teaspoon salt

TOPPING
⅓ cup graham cracker crumbs
¼ teaspoon cinnamon
2 tablespoons butter, melted

■ To make the pudding, melt the butter in a medium saucepan over medium heat. Add the sugars and cook until caramelized, stirring constantly. If it gets too thick, add a tablespoon of water.

■ Meanwhile, place the cornstarch in a medium bowl. Stir in ¼ cup of the milk and mix until smooth. Add the remaining milk, egg yolks, vanilla, and salt. Mix well.

■ Pour the milk mixture into the saucepan with the caramelized sugar and continue cooking over medium heat, stirring constantly, until the pudding thickens. Remove from the heat and pour into a 1½-quart dish or 6 ramekins.

■ To make the topping, combine the graham cracker crumbs, cinnamon, and melted butter. Toast in a 350°F oven for 3 minutes. Sprinkle over the pudding and let cool.

Note: To reduce the fat, you may use skim milk and egg substitute. The dish gets just as creamy.

—Susan B. Hertzog
Lebanon, Pennsylvania

FROZEN PUMPKIN PARFAIT SQUARES

Serves 9 to 12

1½ cups graham cracker crumbs
¼ cup granulated sugar
¼ cup (½ stick) butter, melted
1½ cups puréed pumpkin, canned or cooked fresh
½ cup packed brown sugar
½ teaspoon salt
1 teaspoon ground cinnamon
¼ teaspoon ground ginger
⅛ teaspoon ground cloves
1 quart vanilla ice cream, softened
8 ounces frozen whipped topping, thawed
⅔ cup chopped nuts (optional)

■ Mix the graham cracker crumbs, granulated sugar, and melted butter. Reserve ⅓ cup of the crumb mixture and press the remaining mixture into a 10-inch square pan.

■ Combine the pumpkin, brown sugar, salt, cinnamon, ginger, and cloves. Fold in the softened vanilla ice cream. Pour into the crumb crust. Sprinkle the reserved crumb mixture on top, cover, and freeze for at least 2 hours.

■ Cut into squares and serve with whipped topping and chopped nuts, if desired.

Note: To double this recipe, use a 13 x 9-inch pan.

—Deloris Corle
Williamsburg, Pennsylvania

PECAN DELIGHT

This dessert has been a favorite at many church gatherings and family dinners for years.

Serves 14 to 16

> 60 butter crackers
> ½ cup (1 stick) butter, softened
> 2 (3-ounce) packages instant coconut cream pudding
> 1½ cups milk
> 1 quart butter pecan ice cream, softened
> 8 ounces frozen whipped topping, thawed

■ Crush the crackers to fine crumbs and mix with the softened butter. Reserve ½ cup of the cracker crumbs for the topping.

■ Press the remaining cracker crumbs into a 13 x 9-inch pan.

■ Mix together the instant pudding mix, milk, ice cream, and whipped topping. Pour over the cracker crumbs. Top with reserved ½ cup crumbs and refrigerate for at least 1 hour, or until set.

Note: Don't substitute margarine for this recipe. It has too much water added and will make the crust very soggy.

—Joice B. Bernhard
Arcanum, Ohio

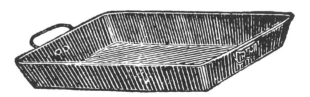

STIR AND ROLL PASTRY

Makes 2 (8-inch) piecrusts

2 cups flour
½ cup vegetable oil
Pinch of salt
¼ cup cold milk

■ Combine the flour, oil, salt, and milk in a bowl. Stir with a fork until a ball forms. Divide the dough in half and roll each half out to about 9 inches to fill an 8-inch pie pan.

■ An easy way to roll pastry dough is between two sheets of wax paper. Sprinkle a little water on your work surface first to keep the wax paper from sliding around. Drape one crust over an 8-inch pie dish and press into the bottom and up the sides. Freeze the other piecrust for later use or use to top the pie after filling it.

—Louise Smallwood
Fulks Run, Virginia

PIE BAKING DAY

As a young girl, I found it refreshing to rise early on a Saturday morning to help Mother work on various baking projects. My mother loved her kitchen, and I was thrilled as I became old enough to help with the mixing and the rolling for a whole gamut of special goodies. Times have changed, though, and with a family of my own I rarely have time to dedicate a day to baking. It's become a special occasion thing.

Though it had been many moons since I'd fashioned my own piecrust, one morning I pulled a recipe from the *Granddaughter's Inglenook Cookbook* that looked most promising—"Hot Water Pie Crust" (p. 225). Four months earlier, I'd purchased a pint of home-canned mincemeat at a local bazaar. A friend recommended it; I'd never experienced mincemeat (a mixture of chopped meat, fruits, and spices), so I treasured the possibility that my own family would enjoy such a classic.

Carefully I measured the shortening and salt; gingerly I poured in boiling water. And then I stirred as directed, but found more mashing and smashing were needed. Perhaps the shortening had indeed dissolved? How was I to know? As my chemist husband strolled through the kitchen, I launched these questions. He indicated the items in my bowl weren't likely to dissolve. As he sauntered away without further guidance, I stirred even more briskly before proceeding. I then poured the flour into the mixture and continued stirring as the dough began to take shape for the two crusts.

A brilliant idea struck as I chewed over my options for the second pie: A can of apple pie filling pulled from the back of the pantry would be a sure winner to contrast the little-known mince. I spread both into my homemade crusts. My mother would have been proud. She often improvised on the spot.

My pie dishes were all rather deep, so I needed to stretch both fillings. I added two portions of applesauce to both and was pleased with my concoctions. Each looked equally delicious. With the hasty addition of a bit more cinnamon, I was fully convinced my apple filling would be sure to taste homemade—at least I could hope so anyway. By this point, I had spent more time working on these desserts than any I'd prepared in a long while.

Fashioning the delicate edging is my favorite memory of baking pies with Mother, and my freshly crimped crusts looked gorgeous. I smiled, remembering the creative adaptations I'd tucked into these masterpieces, and settled them into the oven to bake. The delightful whiff of freshly baking pies brought back more memories as I cleaned the kitchen. Though I missed baking side by side with Mother, I had sensed her guidance. I used her helpful hints and improvisational techniques, along with my own creative genius, to turn my pie-baking venture into a morning to treasure.

The pies turned out great; however, next time I'd surely pause before making another one filled with mincemeat. My husband shivered after his first bite. My son refused to taste it until his girlfriend slipped her leftover portion onto his plate. Even then, he fussed for fear it might "contaminate" the apple pie he dearly loved. Personally, I rather enjoyed the unique taste, and so did my father-in-law.

Try making a piecrust yourself sometime. Linda Steele's "A Good Piecrust" is more user-friendly than the one I tried. Its instructions are modernized, even telling you what temperature to set your oven. Fill it with something your family will enjoy. Just be careful with using mincemeat; it's definitely an acquired taste.

—Yvonne R. Riege
Wakarusa, Indiana

HOT WATER PIE CRUST

½ c. shortening
½ tsp. salt
⅓ c. boiling water

2 c. flour
½ tsp. baking powder

Put shortening and salt in bowl; pour boiling water on it and stir with fork until shortening is dissolved. Then sift flour with baking powder into first mixture. Continue stirring with fork. This will make 2 large crusts.

—Miss Tryphena Mack, Dayton, Ohio

A Good Piecrust

Makes 2 (9-inch) piecrusts

3 cups flour
1⅓ cups shortening or butter, chilled
1½ teaspoons salt
½ cup cold milk
2 teaspoons vinegar

- Mix the flour, shortening or butter, and salt until coarse crumbs form.

- Add the milk and vinegar. Mix with a fork, then blend with your hands to form a soft dough. Don't overwork the dough.

- Divide the dough in half. Roll each half out onto a floured flat surface to about 10 inches in diameter. Drape one crust over a 9-inch pie dish and press into the bottom and up the sides. Freeze the other piecrust for later use or use to top the pie after filling it.

Note: To prebake your piecrust, line the pan with the crust and then freeze it for 30 minutes. When chilled, preheat the oven to 350°F, line the empty pie with parchment paper, and fill two-thirds full with dry beans or rice. Bake for 10 to 12 minutes. Remove the beans or rice, poke holes in the bottom with a fork, and bake for 7 to 8 more minutes. Cool completely before filling.

—Linda Steele
Decatur, Indiana

TENDER AND FLAKY

So, what makes piecrusts so tender and flaky? How do you prevent them from becoming leathery and tasteless? On paper they seem incredibly simple to make, containing humble ingredients, so where's the rub? Not to oversimplify, but it really boils down to the way flour (gluten) and fat interact in a bit of culinary chemistry. But the big question many ask is which fat makes the best crust—butter, lard, shortening, or some combination? Each camp has their reasoning, usually paired with strong emotions, whether it's the ease of use and availability or the final texture and taste. Ask your favorite baker and see what they say.

—Yvonne R. Riege
Wakarusa, Indiana

VELVETY CUSTARD PIE

Serves 8

   4 eggs
   ½ cup sugar
   ⅛ teaspoon salt
   1 teaspoon vanilla
   2½ cups hot milk
   1 (9-inch) unbaked piecrust (see page 347)

- Preheat the oven to 475°F.

- Mix the eggs, sugar, salt, and vanilla together. Slowly stir in the hot milk. Mix well and pour the mixture into an unbaked piecrust.

- Bake for 5 minutes. Reduce the oven temperature to 425°F and bake for 20 minutes longer, or until a knife inserted into the center of the pie comes out clean.

—Lois Ann Glessner
Mercersburg, Pennsylvania

KEY LIME PIE

8 servings

   1 (3-ounce) package lime gelatin
   1 (12-ounce) package key lime yogurt
   8 ounces frozen whipped topping, thawed
   1 (9-inch) graham cracker piecrust
   1½ cups sliced seasonal fruit (strawberry, blueberry, peach)

- In a large bowl, dissolve the gelatin in ¼ cup of boiling water. Whisk in the yogurt. Fold in the whipped topping. Spread the mixture into the piecrust. Refrigerate for at least 2 hours or overnight. Garnish with sliced seasonal fruit, as desired. Refrigerate leftovers.

Note: Match the flavor of the gelatin and yogurt with whatever seasonal fruit you add as a garnish.

—Bernice E. Petticoffer
Ephrata, Pennsylvania

Peanut Butter Pie

Serves 8

1 (6-ounce) package vanilla pudding
3 cups milk
1 cup peanut butter chips
¼ cup peanut butter
⅓ cup powdered sugar
1 (10-inch) graham cracker piecrust or baked piecrust
8 ounces frozen whipped topping, thawed

■ Cook the vanilla pudding and milk in a saucepan over medium-high heat until it comes to a boil. Stir in the peanut butter chips and stir until melted. Then remove from the heat.

■ In a bowl, combine the peanut butter and powdered sugar. Mix until it forms into small pieces. Spread the peanut butter mixture into the graham cracker crust or piecrust. Pour the pudding mixture on top and chill in the refrigerator for 2 hours. Top with whipped topping before serving.

—Faye Ervin Diehl
Waynesboro, Virginia

Zucchini Custard Pie

Serves 8

2 medium zucchini
1 cup evaporated milk
1 cup sugar
1 egg
¼ cup flour
1 teaspoon vanilla
1 (9-inch) unbaked piecrust (see page 347)
¼ teaspoon ground nutmeg or cinnamon

- Peel and deseed the zucchini by slicing in half lengthwise and gently scooping out the seeds. Steam the zucchini for about 5 minutes or until soft.

- Preheat the oven to 425°F.

- Place the zucchini, milk, sugar, egg, flour, and vanilla in a blender and process until puréed. Pour into the piecrust. Sprinkle with nutmeg or cinnamon.

- Bake for 10 minutes. Reduce the oven temperature to 325°F and bake for 20 to 25 minutes longer, or until a knife inserted into the center comes out clean.

—Joann C. Sanbloom
West Lafayette, Indiana

STRAWBERRY PIE

My mother-in-law used to live in Florida. She made this pie often when strawberries were in season.

Serves 8

> 1 cup sugar
> ¼ cup cornstarch
> ¼ cup strawberry gelatin (not sugar free)
> 1 tablespoon butter
> 1 quart fresh strawberries, coarsely chopped
> 1 (9-inch) baked piecrust (see page 347)
> Frozen whipped topping, thawed (optional)

■ Mix the sugar, cornstarch, and gelatin with 1 cup water in a saucepan over medium-high heat. Bring to a boil and boil for 1 minute, stirring continuously, until it forms a clear gel. Remove from the heat; stir in the butter until completely melted. Cool to room temperature.

■ Stir in the strawberries. Pour into the piecrust and refrigerate until set, about 2 hours.

■ To serve, top with the whipped topping, if desired.

Variations: For a strawberry glazed pie, boil the strawberries with ⅔ cup water for 3 minutes. Combine the cornstarch and sugar with ⅓ cup water, add to the strawberries, and boil for 1 minute. Pour into the piecrust and chill for 2 hours. Thanks to Grace Harrison of West Manchester, Ohio,

—Joann C. Sanbloom
West Lafayette, Indiana

PECAN PIE

Ron McAdams has made hundreds of these pies. He has special ovens that help him bake eighteen pies at a time. The pies are sold to help support church activities, service projects, and mission trips. He is famous in the Southern Ohio District for his delicious pecan pies.

Serves 8

PIECRUST	FILLING
1 cup flour	1 cup chopped pecans
½ teaspoon salt	3 eggs
⅓ cup canola oil	½ cup cane sugar
	1 cup white corn syrup
	¼ cup (½ stick) butter, melted
	Dash of salt
	¼ teaspoon vanilla

- Preheat the oven to 350°F.

- To make the piecrust, combine the flour, salt, oil, and 1 tablespoon ice water and mix until the dough gathers together and pulls away from the bowl, about 2 minutes. With your hands form the dough into a ball.

- Roll the dough into a 10-inch circle. An easy way to roll pastry dough is between two sheets of wax paper. Sprinkle a little water on your work surface first to keep the wax paper from sliding around.

- Place the dough in a 9-inch pie pan and press into the bottom and up the sides. Trim and crimp the edges.

- To make the filling, fill the piecrust with the pecans.

- With an electric mixer beat the eggs, sugar, syrup, butter, salt, and vanilla on medium speed. Pour over the pecans in the piecrust.

- Bake for 50 minutes or until the pie is firm.

—Ron McAdams
Union, Ohio

BLUEBERRIES AND CREAM PIE

This is a great crustless blueberry pie, but raspberries work well too.

Serves 8

FILLING
½ cup plus 1 tablespoon milk, divided
3 tablespoons butter, melted
1 egg
¾ cup flour
½ plus ⅓ cup sugar, divided
¼ cup cornstarch
¼ teaspoon salt
1 teaspoon baking powder
2 cups blueberries
1 (8-ounce) package cream cheese, softened

TOPPING
2 teaspoons sugar
⅛ teaspoon ground cinnamon

■ Preheat the oven to 350°F.

■ For the filling, beat ½ cup of the milk, butter, and egg in a bowl. Combine the flour, ⅓ cup of the sugar, cornstarch, salt, and baking powder. Stir into the egg mixture until just moistened.

■ Pour into a 9-inch pie plate coated with nonstick cooking spray.

■ Arrange blueberries over the batter to within ½ inch of the edge of the pie plate.

■ In a bowl, beat the cream cheese, the remaining ½ cup sugar, and 1 tablespoon of milk until smooth. Spread over the blueberries to within 1 inch of the edge of the berries.

■ For the topping, combine the sugar and cinnamon. Sprinkle over the cream cheese mixture.

■ Bake for 30 to 35 minutes or until set.

—Jim and Clareen Dunn
Mulberry Grove, Illinois

CAN'T MAKE JUST ONE

My father was a cook at the Brethren Service Center during his alternative service time in Brethren Volunteer Service. As a child, I remember watching him work in our kitchen to make a piecrust. After throwing away his first and second attempts, he was exasperated and said, "I can't make just *one* pie." He was so accustomed to making a large number of pies to feed everyone at the center that he truly couldn't make just one. So Dad then went on to make us two pies!

—Mark Liller
Hollidaysburg, Pennsylvania

Peach Crumb Pie

Serves 8

FILLING
5½ cups sliced peaches
1½ teaspoons lemon juice
1 cup sugar
4 tablespoons cornstarch
½ teaspoon ground cinnamon
¼ teaspoon ground nutmeg
¼ teaspoon almond extract
1 (9-inch) unbaked piecrust (see page 347)

TOPPING
1 cup flour
¼ cup sugar
¼ cup (½ stick) butter

- Preheat the oven to 425°F.

- To make the filling, mix the peaches and lemon juice together in a bowl.

- Stir together the sugar, cornstarch, cinnamon, nutmeg, and almond extract. Add to the peaches and stir to mix. Pour into the unbaked piecrust.

- To make the topping, combine the flour and sugar. Cut in the butter with a pastry blender or mix with fork until very fine crumbs form. Sprinkle over the top of the pie.

- Cover the edges of the crust with aluminum foil to prevent excess browning. Bake for 10 minutes. Reduce the heat to 400°F and continue baking for 35 minutes, or until bubbly.

—Marcia S. Myer
Manheim, Pennsylvania

FRUIT BODEN

This is my variation to my mom's authentic German boden recipe. "Boden" means floor or meadow. It looks like a pie with a decorative arrangement of sliced fruit on top to make a nice pattern. Perhaps someone thought it looked like a colorful meadow. I added the cream cheese and marshmallow filling.

Serves 10 to 12

½ cup (1 stick) butter, softened
1 cup sugar
2 eggs
1 teaspoon vanilla
2 cups flour
2 teaspoons baking powder
Pinch of salt
1 (8-ounce) package cream cheese, softened
1 (7-ounce) jar marshmallow crème
½ cup mint jelly
2½ cups fresh fruit (strawberries, kiwi, blueberries, raspberries)

■ Preheat the oven to 350°F. Grease and flour a 9-inch fluted tart pan.

■ Beat the butter and sugar until fluffy and creamy. Add the eggs and mix well. Add the vanilla and stir.

■ Combine the flour, baking powder, and salt and add to the butter mixture, stirring until thoroughly mixed. Press the dough into the prepared pan.

■ Bake for 15 to 17 minutes, or until it turns a light golden brown. Run a knife around the edge of the pan and turn out onto a plate to cool.

■ Combine the cream cheese and marshmallow crème thoroughly. Spread over the top of the cooled cake.

■ Stir the mint jelly and 1 tablespoon water to make a glaze. Slice and arrange the fresh fruit on top and drizzle the glaze over the fruit.

Note: If you don't have fresh fruit, use your favorite pie filling.

—Caroline E. Kaestner
Port Republic, Virginia

CHOCOLATE PIE

Serves 8

PIE
1 cup sugar
6 tablespoons flour
3 egg yolks
½ teaspoon salt
4 tablespoons cocoa
2½ cups milk
2 tablespoons butter
1 teaspoon vanilla
1 (9-inch) baked piecrust (see page 347)

MERINGUE
3 egg whites
6 tablespoons sugar
¼ teaspoon cream of tartar
½ teaspoon vanilla

- Preheat the oven to 400°F.

- To make the pie, combine the sugar, flour, and egg yolks together in a saucepan and stir until well blended. Add the salt, cocoa, and milk and cook over medium-high heat, stirring constantly until smooth and thick, about 7 minutes. Remove from the heat and add the butter and vanilla. Stir until well blended.

- Pour into the piecrust.

- For the meringue, beat the egg whites, sugar, cream of tartar, and vanilla until stiff peaks form. Spread over the pie and bake for 8 to 10 minutes, or until lightly brown on top.

—Brenda Foster Wine
Dayton, Virginia

Sweet Potato Pie

6 servings

2 cups cooked, mashed sweet potatoes
2 tablespoons butter, softened
2 eggs
1¼ cups sugar
1 tablespoon flour
½ teaspoon salt
½ cup buttermilk
¼ teaspoon baking soda
1 teaspoon vanilla
1 (10-inch) deep-dish unbaked piecrust

- Preheat the oven to 350°F.

- Combine the sweet potatoes, butter, and eggs. Mix well.

- In a separate bowl, combine the sugar, flour, and salt and add to the potato mixture and mix well.

- Combine the buttermilk and baking soda. Add to the potato mixture and mix well. Stir in the vanilla and mix well. Pour the batter into the piecrust. Bake for 1 hour 10 minutes.

—Shirley Pennington
Ironton, Missouri

A DUNKARD TREAT

Like scrapple and pickled beet eggs, I think you had to grow up with it. I did, and of course my mother makes the best shoofly pie! The name of this pie puzzles people, and many theories and legends try to explain both its roots and its name. Perhaps it was brought to America on ships crossing the Atlantic as the ingredients traveled easily? Did the French word for cauliflower—*chou-fleur*—produce the name due to the pie's bumpy surface? Others recall a brand of molasses called Shoofly. What I have always heard is that while cooling this sweet pie on a windowsill, you have to shoo away the flies!

It's interesting to note that there was no shoofly pie recipe in the 1911 edition of the *Inglenook Cook Book*. Maybe it was just too common to be included? But in the 1942 sequel, the *Granddaughter's Inglenook Cookbook*, it is found in two versions: "Shoo Fly Pie" and "Quakertown Pie" (p. 227). That's Quakertown, Pennsylvania, where I was born and baptized, in the heart of shoofly country.

Cake is the new pie these days. Years ago pie was the everyday dessert, while cake was served on special occasions. Sister Lesta Long Smith, member of the Mill Creek congregation in Port Republic, Virginia, told me years ago that in the late 1800s when Mill Creek had love feast, people would come from miles around for the weekend. Sometimes there would be twenty buggies parked around her grandfather preacher Isaac Long's house, as folks spent the night. The oven in the backyard was put to good use baking either ten loaves of bread or ten pies at a time. Nowadays you have to look hard between the sheet cakes at most potlucks to find a pie, especially a *shoofly* pie.

Some might say that shoofly pie is not very good for you. Although it has a lot of sugar, it packs a lot of energy if you plan to do active work all day. Pennsylvania Dutch farmers often ate it for breakfast. If your workday consists of sitting and typing at a computer, then yes, shoofly is best as an occasional treat. Actually molasses—the darker the better, and don't even think of making it with another sticky sweet syrup—has a number of nutrients, cinnamon is touted by many as something good for what ails you, and whole wheat flour ups the good-for-you quotient by providing added fiber. This eggless recipe makes it a welcome addition, whether you pull your chair up to the vegan table or the traditional Pennsylvania Dutch buffet. I can hear some of you shoofly connoisseurs *rutsching* over the spices in this recipe, saying it's too much like Thanksgiving, but this version of shoofly pie is a favorite of many, so give it a try.

Finally, Peggy Reiff Miller's classic recipe might be appropriately renamed "Shoofly Peace Pie." The battle over which bottom is better—a wet bottom or a dry bottom—has had folks *grexing* for years. The dry bottom dunks better in a good cup of coffee, so as a Dunkard I rest my case. But disagreements aside, here you can have your cake (in a piecrust) and eat it too. This recipe can go either way by a simple adjustment of baking time, bringing both sides of the debate to the table through common ingredients. What a nice pie for a historic peace church. Surely shoofly pie is on the menu in heaven!

—Marilyn E. Lerch
Bedford, Pennsylvania

SHOO FLY PIE

¾ c. flour	½ c. molasses
½ c. brown sugar	1 egg yolk beaten well
2 tb. shortening	½ tb. soda
¼ tsp. salt	¾ c. boiling water

Make crumbs of first 4 ingredients. Dissolve soda in boiling water. Put some liquid, then some crumbs in 2 pastry lined pans until all are used. Then bake in 300° oven.

—Ida Saul, Richland, Pennsylvania

MOM MILLER'S SHOOFLY PIE

Serves 6 to 8

CRUMBS
1½ cups whole wheat flour
½ cup packed brown sugar
¼ cup shortening

FILLING
¾ cup molasses
¾ teaspoon baking soda
¼ teaspoon salt
¼ teaspoon ground ginger
1 teaspoon ground cinnamon
½ teaspoon ground cloves
1 (9-inch) unbaked piecrust (see page 347)

■ Preheat the oven to 425°F.

■ For the crumbs, combine the whole wheat flour and brown sugar in a bowl. With a pastry blender, cut the shortening into the flour mixture to make fine crumbs. Set aside.

■ For the filling, combine the molasses, baking soda, salt, ginger, cinnamon, and cloves in a large bowl. Slowly stir in ³⁄₄ cup hot water. The mixture will foam up and expand.

■ Sprinkle ¹⁄₂ cup of the crumbs into the bottom of the piecrust. Drizzle ²⁄₃ cup of the filling into the piecrust over the crumbs.

■ Sprinkle ¹⁄₂ cup of the crumb mixture over the filling. Continue alternating layers with ¹⁄₃ cup filling and ¹⁄₂ cup crumbs, ending with the crumbs.

■ Bake for 15 minutes at 425°F and then reduce the temperature to 325°F and bake another 15 to 20 minutes, or until the pie cracks on top and is firm to the touch.

■ Remove the pie and let it cool before eating.

—Peggy Reiff Miller
Milford, Indiana

DRY BOTTOM OR WET BOTTOM?

This pie is a family tradition in the Miller family. We continue to serve it for breakfast on holidays and birthdays. This pie can be a wet bottom or dry bottom pie, depending on how long it is baked. For a dry bottom pie, there should be no jiggle left when touched and the cracks should be dry. It may take a trial or two until you master the consistency you like. The success of this pie depends on the interaction of the molasses with the baking soda. Do not substitute corn syrup for the molasses! This is not the butterscotch-type shoofly pie served at many Amish restaurants.

—Peggy Reiff Miller
Milford, Indiana

FRIED APPLE PIES

This recipe comes from my grandmother, Ada Alderman Weddle, a deaconess of Topeco Church of the Brethren. She dried her apples on a screen door balanced on two sawhorses in the yard. She made sure to rinse them because yellow jackets loved them. Substituting cooking oil for the shortening will result in greasier pies.

Serves 4

DOUGH	FILLING
4 cups flour	4 to 5 large dried apples, sliced
1⅓ cups shortening	(see note)
2 teaspoons salt	1⅓ cups sugar
	2 teaspoons ground cinnamon
	½ teaspoon salt
	1 cup shortening

■ To make the dough, combine the flour, shortening, and salt. Add ²/₃ cup cold water and stir. Add more water, a tablespoon at a time, until a smooth dough forms. Divide into fourths and set aside.

■ For the filling, stew the apples in simmering water until they are very tender and the water is almost evaporated, about 20 minutes.

■ Combine the stewed apples, sugar, cinnamon and salt. Beat with an electric mixer until nearly smooth, about 2 minutes. Cool to room temperature.

■ Roll out each piece of dough to about 8 inches. It should be pretty thin. Cut into about 6-inch circles; an upside-down cereal bowl works well as a guide.

■ Spread about ¼ cup of the apple mixture over half of a dough circle, staying ¾ inch away from the edge. Brush water around the dough's edge and fold the other side over, sealing the edges by pressing down with the tines of a fork.

■ Heat the shortening in a skillet over medium-high heat. When hot fry the pies, turning once to brown both sides. Drain on wire cooling racks over baking sheets.

Note: To dry your own apples, peel, core, and slice them ¼ inch thick. Spread on a baking sheet. They may touch but not overlap. Put in a 170°F oven for several hours, turning them once or twice to keep from sticking.

—Cheryl Ninmann Waldron
Bent Mountain, Virginia

FARM APPLE PIE

This pie is delicious both warm and cooled. It's a wonderful dessert to take to church gatherings.

Serves 15 to 20

5 pounds apples, peeled, cored, and sliced thin

4 teaspoons lemon juice

5 cups flour

½ teaspoon salt

½ teaspoon baking powder

¾ cup plus 4 teaspoons granulated sugar, divided

1½ cups shortening

2 egg yolks

¾ cup packed brown sugar

½ teaspoon ground nutmeg

1 teaspoon ground cinnamon

¼ teaspoon salt

½ cup powdered sugar

2 teaspoons milk

■ Preheat the oven to 375°F.

■ Mix the sliced apples with the lemon juice. Set aside.

■ Combine the flour, salt, baking powder, and 4 teaspoons of the granulated sugar. Cut in the shortening with a pastry knife or two forks until a crumb mixture forms.

■ Beat the eggs yolks with 1 cup water and add to the flour mixture. Stir until it forms a dough. Divide the dough in half and roll out one piece to 15 x 10 inches and lay in a jelly-roll pan.

■ Combine the remaining ³/₄ cup granulated sugar, brown sugar, nutmeg, cinnamon, and salt. Arrange ¹/₂ of the apple slices onto the dough. Sprinkle ¹/₂ of the sugar mixture over the layer of apples. Add the remaining apples and sugar.

■ Roll the remaining piece of dough to 15 x 10 inches and use as the top crust. Crimp the edges as with any pie. Vent the top by poking it with a fork. Bake for 20 minutes, or until brown.

■ Combine the powdered sugar and milk and mix until a frosting consistency. Frost the top of the pie with the powdered sugar glaze while still hot.

■ Cut into squares and enjoy!

—Karen Stover Shiflet
Dayton, Virginia

PERFECT CHERRY PIE

My grandmother, Wilma A. Snyder of the Holmesville Church of the Brethren, always made this for us when we were growing up. It is a perfect family favorite.

Serves 8

Pastry for 2 (10-inch) piecrusts
3 cups pitted frozen cherries
1 cup cherry juice
¾ cup sugar plus some for sprinkling
2 tablespoons quick-cooking tapioca
5 teaspoons cornstarch
⅛ teaspoon almond extract

■ Preheat the oven to 425°F.

■ Roll out the pastry dough to about 11 inches in diameter. Press one into a 10-inch pie plate. Cover with plastic wrap and chill. Cut the other rolled out dough into strips and set aside.

■ Thaw the cherries and reserve about 1 cup of the juice. Mix the cherry juice with the sugar, tapioca, and cornstarch in a saucepan over medium-high heat. Cook until the sugar is dissolved and the sauce begins to thicken, about 10 minutes. Remove from the heat, and set aside to cool.

■ Add the cherries and almond extract to the cherry filling. Pour into the prepared crust. For a lattice top, weave the reserved strips of dough in a crisscross pattern across the top. Pinch the edges of the pie to seal. Sprinkle with sugar.

■ Bake for 30 to 35 minutes until golden brown.

—Laura Dell-Haro
Holmesville, Nebraska

LEMON SPONGE PIE

My grandmother, Mattie Shellhaas of the Southern Ohio District, got this recipe from the radio station WLWD Cincinnati, Ohio.

Serves 8

> 2 tablespoons butter
> ¼ cup flour
> 1 cup sugar
> 1 cup milk
> 2 eggs, separated
> ¼ cup freshly squeezed lemon juice
> 1½ teaspoons grated lemon zest
> 1 (8-inch) unbaked piecrust

- Preheat the oven to 325°F.

- Combine the butter, flour, and sugar.

- In another bowl, mix together the milk, egg yolks (slightly beaten), lemon juice, and lemon zest. Add the milk mixture to the flour mixture and beat until the batter is smooth and well combined.

- Beat the 2 egg whites until stiff. Gently fold the egg whites into the batter. Pour the batter into the piecrust.

- Bake for 45 minutes or until set.

—Rebecca J. Rust Flickinger
Leo, Indiana

COCONUT CREAM PIE

Serves 8

PIE
2¾ cups milk
1 cup sugar
⅓ cup cornstarch
¼ teaspoon salt
4 egg yolks, lightly beaten
3 tablespoons butter
1 teaspoon vanilla
½ teaspoon coconut flavoring
1 cup flaked sweetened coconut
1 (9-inch) baked piecrust (see page 347)

MERINGUE
4 egg whites
½ teaspoon cream of tartar
8 tablespoons sugar
½ teaspoon vanilla

■ To make the pie filling, heat the milk in a saucepan over medium heat. Add the sugar, cornstarch, and salt and cook, whisking vigorously, until well incorporated, about 4 minutes. Pour 1 tablespoon of the milk mixture into the beaten egg yolks while stirring constantly to temper. Then add the tempered egg yolks to the milk mixture, stir continually, and cook until thick, about 4 minutes.

■ Add the butter, vanilla, and coconut flavoring. Fold in the coconut. Cook for 15 minutes; then pour into the piecrust. Preheat the oven to 350°F.

■ To make the meringue, beat the egg whites and cream of tartar. While beating, gradually add the sugar, 1 tablespoon at a time, and the vanilla. Beat until stiff and it forms soft peaks.

■ Spread the meringue over the pie, sealing to the edge of pastry, and bake for 12 to 15 minutes, or until set.

—Katy Stump
Leeton, Missouri

Peach Bee Hives

In the summer my family made a lot of these "bee hives" during peach season before the peaches spoiled. We would freeze them to enjoy during the winter when fresh peaches were not available.

Serves 4

HIVES	NUTMEG HARD SAUCE
Pastry for 2 piecrusts (see page 347)	¼ cup (½ stick) butter, softened
4 perfect large peaches	1 teaspoon vanilla
	¼ teaspoon ground nutmeg
	2 cups powdered sugar
	2 tablespoons milk

- Preheat the oven to 375°F.

- To make the hives, wash and dry the peaches but do not peel.

- Roll the pastry dough into a long rectangle about 6 x 12 inches. Cut into 1-inch strips lengthwise.

- Place a peach, stem end down, on the counter and starting at the top, wrap the pastry strips spiraling around the peach, overlapping each row until the peach is completely covered (looking a little like an apple dumpling). Press the pastry as you go so that there are no gaps or holes.

- Place the wrapped peaches in a shallow baking pan stem side down.

- Bake for 30 or 40 minutes, or until lightly browned.

- To make the sauce, beat the softened butter until creamy. Add the vanilla, nutmeg, powdered sugar, and milk and beat until well mixed. Add a little more milk to make a softer sauce.

- To serve, place bee hives in separate bowls. Each person should cut the bee hive in half from the top and down each side. After carefully opening it, remove the peach pit and fill the cavity with the nutmeg sauce. The sauce will melt and run over the peach and crust, making a sweet, flavorful dessert.

—Virginia Crim
Greenville, Ohio

Cherry Drop Dumplings with Fruit Juice

When my husband asked me to make this recipe for him, I had to go to his mother to find out what he was talking about. I had never heard of drop dumplings. She gave me the recipe, I liked it, and I served it in our home all the fifty-nine years we were married.

Serves 4

SAUCE
2 cups frozen or canned sour cherries (with juice)
½ cup sugar

DUMPLINGS
1½ cups flour
½ cup sugar
2 teaspoons baking powder
2 tablespoons butter
½ cup milk
½ teaspoon vanilla

■ For the sauce, bring to boil the cherries, sugar, and 2 cups water in a large saucepan over medium-high heat.

■ For the dumplings, combine the flour, sugar, baking powder, butter, milk, and vanilla in a bowl and stir until well mixed. Then drop the batter by spoonsful into the boiling cherries and fruit juices. Reduce the heat under the juice to medium and let boil for 20 minutes or until the dumplings are done. Serve with milk.

—Donna Marilyn Rehm
Smithville, Ohio

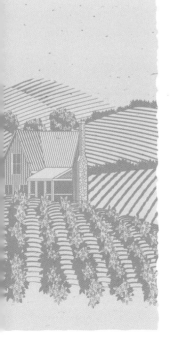

Mom's Southern Apple Dumplings

Serves 6 to 8

DUMPLINGS
2 cups peeled, chopped apples (3 medium apples)
3 teaspoons lemon juice
2 teaspoons sugar
2 cups flour
½ teaspoon salt
2 teaspoons baking powder
2 tablespoons cold shortening
　or butter
¾ cup cold milk

SAUCE
1 cup granulated sugar
½ cup brown sugar
2 tablespoons flour
½ teaspoon salt
⅛ teaspoon ground nutmeg
½ cup (1 stick) butter

■ Lightly grease a 13 x 9-inch baking pan and set aside.

■ Toss the apples with the lemon juice and sugar and set aside.

■ Sift together the flour, salt, and baking powder. Cut in the shortening with a pastry knife or two forks to form fine crumbs. Add the milk and stir until a soft dough forms. Roll out the dough on a floured surface to ¼-inch thickness and cut into 6 to 8 squares.

■ Place 2 to 3 tablespoons of chopped apples on each square. Moisten the edges of the squares with a little water and pinch together to seal.

■ Preheat the oven to 425°F.

■ To make the sauce, mix the sugars, flour, salt, and nutmeg in a saucepan. Add the butter and 2 cups water. Bring mixture to a boil over medium-high heat and cook for 1 minute. Pour into the prepared pan. Place the dumplings into the sauce seam side down. Cover and bake for 30 minutes. Remove the cover, baste the dumplings with the sauce, and continue baking until brown.

—Mary Good
Harrisonburg, Virginia

DUMPLINGS FOR RELIEF

Apple dumplings are much-anticipated delicacies in Pennsylvania. Each year the locals get restless when apples come into season and harvest approaches.

I grew up in Adams County, the heart of apple country. Musselman's was a trademark in our area. Each spring our family drove through the narrows to admire the apple blossoms. In August we circumvented winding roads to enjoy late summer succulence —Rambo, Stayman, Winesap, Smokehouse, and other varieties of apples. Limbs laden with apples were braced with stakes to support their weight. We stopped by roadside stands to purchase apples for pies and saucing. Rolling hills emitted an ambiance, almost akin to heaven, that heralded the apple harvest.

I first discovered apple dumplings when my mother-in-law, Amy Smith, was rolling pie dough in her kitchen. I watched her plop an apple in its center, fill it with sugar, cinnamon, and butter, and then seal it at the top. Then she drizzled a sugary syrup around the dumpling to create a mouth-watering delicacy.

After my husband and I were married I found a recipe over in Lebanon County. My husband's brother, Henry, got this recipe from coworkers at Hershey Chocolate Factory. The recipe was simple, similar to the rustic "Baked Apple Dumplings" recipe included here from the 1911 *Inglenook Cook Book* (p. 70). Once we made it, the first bite of this delicious delicacy converted me. (The modernized version of this recipe is found on page 369.)

BAKED APPLE DUMPLINGS

Pare, halve, and core 8 medium-sized apples; make enough pie crust for 2 pies, divide into 8 parts, roll out thin, set 1 apple on each crust, fill center full of sugar with a small pinch of cinnamon, roll crust up over each apple, then set dumplings in a dripping pan; fill the pan with water to half cover dumplings, set in oven and bake slowly to avoid burning till apples are soft when pierced with a fork. Serve with a sweetened cream.

—Sister Sarah Hayes, Rural, Oregon

In 1977, when our family moved to the Lick Creek Church of the Brethren in Bryan, Ohio, the church members had never heard of apple dumplings. That fall the church held an Apple Festival for CROP, the hunger arm of Church World Service, with apple butter a featured item. The night before, they peeled twenty bushels of apples, readying them for the cauldron. Men awakened before dawn to light the fire to simmer apple butter outdoors in a big iron kettle.

I decided to make apple dumplings for the Apple Festival based on my established recipe. As friendly a greeting as our apple butter got, my apple dumplings did not—until the church caretaker bit into one! From that moment on, apple dumplings mesmerized our members. Every fall since then, Lick Creek Church of the Brethren has baked apple dumplings for CROP, providing thousands of dollars to feed the hungry. Today they are CROP's top fundraiser in Ohio.

Several years later we moved to McPherson, Kansas. Our church decided to sponsor a year-long Hope for the Hungry project. Members were given seed money to use with fundraising projects based on their God-given talents. I chose apple dumplings. At the next potluck, our Outreach Team circled the tables for orders. Everyone looked perplexed, until we reached Merrin Godfrey, a native of Pennsylvania.

"Apple dumplings!" he exclaimed. "I'll take two dozen!"

Heads swirled around, and orders took off soaring. If Merrin enjoyed them that much, they *chust hat to be special*!

Later, the McPherson church featured apple dumplings at our International Bread Festival. Since 2005, at our Alternative Christmas Gift Markets we have sold these succulent delicacies for CROP and Trees for Life. Founded by members in the Wichita Church of the Brethren, Trees for Life plants orchards for hungry villagers in India. Today we are baking apple dumplings to sponsor a medical clinic in Haiti. While somewhat labor intensive, these special Pennsylvania Dutch treats are an act of love and definitely a winner.

—Jeanne Jacoby Smith
McPherson, Kansas

Pennsylvania Dutch Apple Dumplings

Serves 4 to 6

DOUGH
2 cups flour
1 teaspoon salt
⅔ to ¾ cup cold shortening

SYRUP
1½ cups sugar
¼ teaspoon ground cinnamon
¼ cup (½ stick) butter

ASSEMBLY
4 to 6 apples, peeled and cored
½ to ⅔ cup sugar, divided
1 to 1½ teaspoons cinnamon, divided
2 tablespoons butter, divided

- To make the dough, combine the flour and salt and cut in the shortening with a pastry knife or two forks. Work the pastry with your hands until the mixture is fine and crumbly.

- Add tablespoons of cold water one at a time, up to ½ cup, and knead the dough until it forms a ball and is soft. Divide the dough in fourths or sixths, depending on how many apples you have.

- To make the syrup, add 1½ cups water to a saucepan over medium heat. Add the sugar, cinnamon, and butter and bring to a boil. Boil for 5 minutes, or until reduced to a syrup. Stir to keep from scorching.

- Preheat the oven to 425°F.

- To assemble, roll out each piece of dough on a floured surface. Place one apple in the center of each piece of dough. Fill each apple cavity with about 1½ tablespoons sugar, a pinch of cinnamon, and 1 teaspoon butter. Wrap the dough up over the apple, and pinch to seal at the top, using a little water to ensure a tight seal. Place dumplings in a greased 13 x 9-inch cake pan. Pour hot syrup around them.

- Bake for 40 to 45 minutes, or until the apples are tender when pierced with a knife. Drizzle syrup over the tops and serve with hot milk.

—Jeanne Jacoby Smith
McPherson, Kansas

More on Relief

Each year the Chiques Church of the Brethren in Manheim, Pennsylvania, provides apple dumplings for the Brethren Disaster Relief Auction, sponsored by the Atlantic Northeast and Southern Pennsylvania Districts. The night before the big event, church members peel apples and roll thousands of dough rounds for dumplings. At 3:00 a.m. they light massive ovens at a local fire hall, delivering dumplings in time for breakfast. In 2012, they made 2,100 for the auction, with proceeds benefiting disaster relief ministries. Over the years, Chiques has donated some 40,000 apple dumplings.

—Jeanne Jacoby Smith
McPherson, Kansas

Fresh Peach Cobbler

Serves 6 to 8

¼ cup plus 2 tablespoons butter, melted
2 cups sugar, divided
¾ cup flour
2 teaspoons baking powder
⅛ teaspoon salt
¾ cup milk
2½ cups sliced peaches (or other fruit options below)

- Preheat the oven to 350°F.

- Pour the butter into a 2-quart baking dish.

- Combine 1 cup sugar, flour, baking powder, and salt. Add the milk and stir until mixed. Pour the batter into the baking dish, but do not stir.

- Toss the peaches with the remaining 1 cup sugar; add the peaches to the batter. Do not stir. Bake for 1 hour.

Fruit Variations: You can use whatever fruit you like. Here are some common alternatives. Use 2½ cups fruit to 1 cup sugar, adjusting the amount of sugar to the fruit and your taste.

- Blueberries with 1 teaspoon lemon juice

- Tart red cherries tossed with 1 tablespoon cornstarch

- Peeled and sliced apples sprinkled with 1 teaspoon cinnamon

- Raspberries, blackberries, boysenberries, or other berries in any combination

- Chopped rhubarb

- 1¼ cups chopped rhubarb tossed with 1¼ cups sliced straw- berries

—Phyllis E. Sorensen
Milford, Indiana

PUMPKIN COBBLER

This is a different twist on a seasonal favorite. It's simple to make *in spite of the large number of ingredients.*

Serves 10 to 12

BATTER
½ cup (1 stick) butter, melted
1 cup flour
1 cup sugar
4 teaspoons baking powder
½ teaspoon salt
1 cup milk
1 teaspoon vanilla

FILLING

2 eggs, beaten
1 cup milk
3 cups puréed pumpkin
1 cup granulated sugar
½ cup brown sugar
1 tablespoon flour

1 teaspoon ground cinnamon
¼ teaspoon ground ginger
¼ teaspoon ground cloves
¼ teaspoon ground nutmeg
¼ teaspoon salt

■ Preheat the oven to 350°F.

■ To make the batter, pour the melted butter in a 13 x 9-inch pan. Mix together the flour, sugar, baking powder, salt, milk, and vanilla. Pour this over the melted butter.

■ To make the filling, mix together the eggs, milk, pumpkin, sugars, and stir until blended. In a separate bowl, stir together the flour, cinnamon, ginger, cloves, nutmeg, and salt. Add this to the pumpkin mixture and stir until smooth.

■ Pour over the batter in the pan. Bake for 1 hour or until set.

■ Serve warm or cooled with whipped cream. Refrigerate any leftovers.

—Anita K. Heatwole
Waynesboro, Virginia

HEAVENLY BLUEBERRY CRISP

Top servings of this warm crisp with vanilla ice cream.

Serves 8

4 cups blueberries
½ cup granulated sugar
2 tablespoons cornstarch
2 tablespoons lemon juice
½ cup rolled oats
½ cup flour
¼ cup packed brown sugar
2 tablespoons chopped toasted walnuts
6 tablespoons butter

■ Preheat the oven to 375°F. Coat a 1-quart casserole dish with non-stick spray.

■ In a large bowl, mix the blueberries, granulated sugar, cornstarch, and lemon juice. Spoon into the prepared casserole.

■ In the same bowl, mix the oats, flour, brown sugar, and walnuts.

■ With a fork or pastry blender, cut in the butter until the mixture resembles coarse meal. Sprinkle over the berry mixture.

■ Bake for 45 minutes, or until lightly browned and bubbling.

—Joyce R. Fike
Doylestown, Ohio

RHUBARB CRISP

Serves 8 to 10

TOPPING
¾ cup flour
¾ cup packed brown sugar
½ teaspoon ground cinnamon
Dash of salt
½ cup chopped nuts (walnuts or pecans)
½ cup (1 stick) cold butter

FILLING
2 tablespoons flour
½ cup granulated sugar
½ teaspoon ground nutmeg
Dash of salt
4 to 5 cups chopped rhubarb (½-inch pieces)

- Preheat the oven to 350°F. Coat the sides and bottom of an 8- or 9-inch square baking dish with butter and set aside.

- To make the topping, combine the flour, brown sugar, cinnamon, salt, and nuts. Cut in the butter with a pastry knife or two forks until the mixture is crumbly. Set aside.

- To make the filling, combine the flour, granulated sugar, nutmeg, and salt. Add the rhubarb and toss to coat. Pour the rhubarb filling into the prepared baking dish. Spread the topping evenly over the fruit.

- Bake uncovered for about 45 minutes until lightly browned and bubbly. Serve warm topped with vanilla ice cream, whipped cream, or milk.

—Charlotte M. Wine
Imperial, Nebraska

APPLE CRISP

We live in apple country. My father and both grandfathers grew apples. When apples are ripe each fall, we enjoy kuchens, apple dumplings, and apple crisp. Of course, you can make these things any time of the year, but they are best enjoyed when the apples are fresh off the trees. This recipe has been passed down for generations.

Serves 8 to 10

> 4 to 6 tart cooking apples, peeled and sliced
> ¾ cup flour
> ¾ to 1 cup sugar (depending on tartness of apples)
> 1 teaspoon ground cinnamon
> 1 teaspoon salt
> ⅓ cup cold butter

- Preheat the oven to 350°F.

- Grease a 13 x 9-inch baking dish with butter. Arrange the apples in the bottom of the baking dish. Pour ¼ cup water over the sliced apples.

- Combine the flour, sugar, cinnamon, salt. Cut in the butter with a pastry knife or two forks until it forms crumbles. Top the apples with the flour mixture.

- Bake for 40 minutes or until the apples are tender.

—Leanne M. Ford
Wenatchee, Washington

FROZEN STRAWBERRY SALAD

Serves 12 to 15

1 (8-ounce) package cream cheese
½ cup sugar
8 ounces frozen whipped topping, thawed
1 (10-ounce) package frozen sliced strawberries, thawed
1 cup crushed pineapple, drained
1 cup chopped walnuts (optional)

■ Beat together the cream cheese and sugar. Fold in the whipped topping. Add the strawberries, pineapple, and walnuts, if using, and fold together.

■ Pour into a 13 x 9-inch glass baking dish and freeze.

■ Remove from the freezer 15 minutes before serving to soften it a little.

—Mary Lou Van Dyke
Lincoln, Nebraska

PRETZEL-STRAWBERRY SALAD

My mother, Susie Myers, described this recipe as super-duper!
It can be used as a dessert or a salad.

Serves 12

2 cups crushed pretzels
¾ cup butter, melted
3 tablespoons sugar
1 (8-ounce) package cream cheese, softened
1 cup sugar
8 ounces frozen whipped topping, thawed
1 (6-ounce) package strawberry gelatin
2 (10-ounce) packages frozen strawberries, thawed

■ Preheat the oven to 350°F.

■ Mix the pretzels, butter, and sugar together. Press into a 13 x 9-inch pan. Bake for 10 minutes and then let cool.

■ Mix the softened cream cheese and sugar together and then fold in the whipped topping. Spread over the cooled crust and chill.

■ Bring 3 cups water to a boil in a saucepan over medium-high heat. Add the gelatin powder and stir until dissolved. Remove from the heat and let the mixture cool to room temperature, about 15 minutes. Add the strawberries to the liquid gelatin.

■ When the mixture begins to set, pour over the cream cheese layer. Refrigerate until firm, about 1 hour.

—Bickey Myers Garber
North Manchester, Indiana

RASPBERRIES AND CREAM

Serves 8

1 (8-ounce) package cream cheese, softened
¼ cup sugar
2 cups heavy whipping cream
2 (10-ounce) packages frozen sweetened raspberries, thawed
2 tablespoons sugar
2 tablespoons cornstarch
Juice of ½ lemon
Fresh raspberries for garnish
Mint leaves for garnish

■ In a small bowl, beat the cream cheese and sugar until smooth. Set aside.

■ Beat the whipping cream until stiff. Gradually fold the whipped cream into the cream cheese mixture and chill in the refrigerator for 20 minutes.

■ Drain the raspberries, reserving the juice, and set aside. Add enough water to the raspberry juice to measure 1 cup; add sugar to taste, starting with $\frac{1}{8}$ cup.

■ Combine the cornstarch, lemon juice, and sweetened raspberry juice over medium heat. Stir until the cornstarch is completely dissolved and boil for 1 to 2 minutes or until thickened. Remove from the heat and let cool for about 5 minutes. Add the raspberries and stir. Cover and refrigerate until completely cool.

■ Divide the cream cheese mixture in half and pipe or spoon half of it into eight dessert dishes. Spoon the raspberry mixture on top of the cream cheese mixture and smooth the top. Pipe or spoon the remaining cream cheese mixture over the raspberry sauce. Decorate with fresh raspberries and a mint leaf. Cover and refrigerate.

Notes: This will keep for 2 to 3 days in the refrigerator. One large glass bowl can be substituted for the smaller dishes.

—Steve Dodge
Harrisburg, Pennsylvania

Peanut Butter Fudge

Makes 48 pieces

3 cups sugar
1 tablespoon butter
¾ cup milk
1 cup peanut butter
1 (7-ounce) jar marshmallow crème
1 teaspoon vanilla

■ Grease a 13 x 9-inch pan and set aside.

■ Combine the sugar and butter in a medium saucepan over medium heat. Add the milk and stir occasionally. When it starts boiling, cook for 5 minutes. Remove from the heat.

■ Add the peanut butter, marshmallow crème, and vanilla. Beat until smooth.

■ Pour into the prepared pan and let cool completely before cutting and serving.

Variation: To make chocolate peanut butter fudge, simply add 1 to 2 heaping tablespoons of cocoa with the sugar and butter.

—Treva Markey
York, Pennsylvania

Mamie's Million Dollar Fudge

Mamie Eisenhower was a gracious hostess and a real penny pincher. Her Million Dollar Fudge recipe has been enjoyed by housewives all over the country after it was reprinted in newspapers nationwide.

Makes 36 (1-inch) pieces

> 4½ cups sugar
> Pinch of salt
> 2 tablespoons butter
> 1 (12-ounce) can evaporated milk
> 2 cups marshmallow crème
> 1 (12-ounce) package semisweet chocolate chips
> 1 (12-ounce) package German-sweet chocolate
> 2 cups nutmeats (walnuts, pecans, etc.)

- Grease a 13 x 9-inch pan with butter and set aside.

- Heat the sugar, salt, butter, and evaporated milk in a heavy saucepan over medium heat. Bring to a boil and cook for 6 minutes.

- Combine the marshmallow crème, chocolate chips, chocolate, and nuts in a large bowl, pour the boiling syrup over the marshmallow-chocolate mixture, and stir until the chocolate is melted.

- Pour into the prepared pan. Let stand for 2 to 3 hours before cutting. Will keep in an airtight container for up to 1 month. Mamie Eisenhower said to store it in a tin box.

—Jeanette Reiste
Minburn, Iowa

PECAN PRALINES

Pralines originated in France, and then came to the United States in the 1700s with the French casket girls who were brought over to marry the colonists in Louisiana. They were originally made with almonds, but in the 1700s almonds were hard to come by in Louisiana, so the native and prevalent pecan was used. These delicious treats spread throughout the South and then to the rest of the country.

Makes 36 pralines

2 cups sugar
1 cup buttermilk
1 teaspoon baking soda
2 tablespoons corn syrup
3 tablespoons butter
1 tablespoon vanilla
3 cups pecan halves and pieces

■ Spread about 2 feet square of parchment paper onto a cutting board or heatproof surface. Brown paper or newspaper under the parchment paper will keep it from sticking to the work surface. Grease the parchment paper with butter or nonstick cooking spray.

■ Add the sugar, buttermilk, baking soda, and corn syrup to a large saucepan over medium heat. Cook, stirring constantly, until it reaches the softball stage (235°F). Remove from the heat.

■ Add the butter, vanilla, and pecan pieces. Beat until creamy. This is difficult to do with the pecans; you'll need to work fast. Quickly spoon the pecan mixture out onto the prepared parchment paper. If it hardens in the pan, heat it up again. Keep spreading the pecan mixture until it's all out of the pan. Let cool for 10 minutes and then break into pieces before serving or storing. It will keep for up to three weeks in an airtight container.

—Gail C. McGlothin
Tyler, Texas

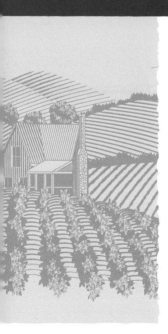

PEANUT BUTTER CANDY

Makes 48 candies

- 2 pounds powdered sugar
- 2 cups peanut butter, softened
- ½ cup (1 stick) butter
- 1 (8-ounce) package cream cheese, softened
- 2 teaspoons vanilla
- 24 ounces dipping chocolate
- 1 tablespoon evaporated milk or butter

- Combine the sugar, peanut butter, butter, cream cheese, and vanilla in a large bowl and mix well.

- Chill for at least 30 minutes and then roll into ½-inch balls. Place the balls in a plastic bag and freeze for at least 1 hour.

- Melt the chocolate with the evaporated milk or butter in a double boiler over medium heat or in the microwave, 30 seconds at a time, until completely melted. Dip the frozen balls into the chocolate and chill in the refrigerator for 30 minutes before serving.

—Gloria Baugher Miller
York, Pennsylvania

POTLUCKS AS CHURCH RENEWAL

Potlucks play an integral part of our church renewal work with congregations. Carry-in meals are often held prior to churchwide gatherings, providing space for renewal to begin. The spirit of such gatherings is always joyous. After the meal, persons join in table conversation and discuss the strengths of their church and how its work has touched their lives. They thank God for their gifts and thank others for what they mean to them. Together they build a composite picture of their church, which strengthens their vitality and gives them tools to discern God's vision for their continued ministry.

—David and Joan Young
Ephrata, Pennsylvania

FUDGE SAUCE FOR ICE CREAM

I never buy fudge topping for ice cream. This is so easy and inexpensive.

Makes 2 cups

1 cup sugar
¼ cup cocoa
2 tablespoons cornstarch
1 tablespoon butter
1 teaspoon vanilla

■ Combine the sugar, cocoa, and cornstarch in a saucepan. Add ³/₄ cup boiling water and bring to boil over medium heat, stirring constantly. Boil and keep stirring for about 1 minute to thicken.

■ When thickened, remove from the heat and add the butter and vanilla. Pour into a small serving pitcher or store in an airtight container in the refrigerator.

Variation: For a peanut butter sauce, add 2 tablespoons peanut butter instead of the butter.

—Janet C. Batdorf
Harrisburg, Pennsylvania

LEMON SAUCE FOR GINGERBREAD

I made this recipe when my daughters were growing up. They loved homemade gingerbread topped with this lemon sauce. After they married and each had a child, they called me for the recipe. Well, lo and behold, I had misplaced it. So when I found the recipe recently, everyone was so excited, including me.

Makes 2½ cups

½ cup sugar
2 tablespoons cornstarch
Dash of salt
2 tablespoons butter
2 tablespoons lemon juice
2 teaspoons grated lemon peel

■ Combine the sugar, cornstarch, and salt in a saucepan over medium heat. Stir in 1 cup water and cook, stirring constantly, until the mixture comes to a boil. Cook until slightly thickened and clear, about 7 minutes.

■ Remove from the heat. Stir in the butter, lemon juice, and lemon peel.

Variation: This recipe was also submitted by Thelma F. Michael of Mount Solon, Virginia, but without the salt, a little less cornstarch, and a tablespoon each of lemon juice and grated lemon peel.

—Joan G. Barker
Martinsville, Virginia

NEVER FAIL MERINGUE

This was given to me by a friend and it truly has never failed me.
Other recipes I have used always ended up getting watery, but not this one.

Serves 6 to 8

> 1 tablespoon cornstarch
> ½ cup sugar
> 3 egg whites

- Preheat the oven to 375°F. Combine ½ cup water, cornstarch, and sugar in a saucepan over medium heat. Cook until thick and clear. Cool completely.

- Beat the egg whites until frothy. Continue to beat the egg whites while pouring the cornstarch mixture into the whites, and then beat for about 5 minutes.

- Spread over your pie, sealing the edges well. Brown the meringue in the oven until lightly browned.

—Beverly J. Sheets
Akron, Ohio

CARAMEL ICING

This is an excellent icing for a chocolate cake.

Makes about 3 cups or enough for a 13 x 9-inch cake

> ½ cup (1 stick) butter
> 2 cups packed brown sugar
> ½ cup cream

- Combine the butter, brown sugar, and cream in a saucepan and bring to a boil over medium heat. Boil for 1½ minutes. Beat with an electric mixer on medium for 10 to 15 minutes. Pour on the cake while thin. It will harden.

Variation: For a little different icing from Brenda S. Hylton of Floyd, Virginia, use 1 cup brown sugar and ¼ cup evaporated milk instead of the cream.

—Linda Steele
Decatur, Indiana

Fluffy White Icing

This recipe belongs to my mother-in-law, Irene, who taught me much about the "fine art of cooking" country style. She was a farmer and kept things simple and easy to make. This is a semisweet icing that is nice and fluffy and does not get hard or dried out. I make a double batch of icing for a layer cake and will have about a cup left over. I freeze it for the grandkids' cupcakes. All you do is put it in the mixer for a few minutes after it is thawed out.

Makes about 3½ cups or enough for a 13 x 9-inch cake

- 1 egg at room temperature
- 1 tablespoon flour
- 2 tablespoons milk
- 1 tablespoon vanilla
- 2 cups powdered sugar, divided
- ¾ cup shortening or butter

■ Beat together the egg white, flour, milk, vanilla, and 1 cup of the powdered sugar. Beat until well mixed. Then add the remaining cup of powdered sugar and shortening or butter. Beat for 2 to 3 minutes. The icing will become nice and fluffy.

Variations: For a peanut butter icing, use ⅓ cup peanut butter instead of the vanilla. For an orange-flavored icing, use orange juice instead of milk and use ½ teaspoon of orange extract instead of the vanilla. Be creative with this recipe; I have done lots of variations with it.

—Donna Jean Shive
Seven Valleys, Pennsylvania

CREAM CHEESE ICING

This icing is especially good on a carrot cake.

Makes about 5½ cups or enough for a 10-inch layer cake

   1 (8-ounce) package cream cheese, softened
   4 cups powdered sugar
   ½ cup (1 stick) butter, softened
   2 teaspoons vanilla

■ Beat together the cream cheese, powdered sugar, butter, and vanilla. Spread over your cooled cake.

—Jennifer Hausfeld
Troy, Ohio

BUTTER CREAM FROSTING

Makes about 5 cups or enough for a 10-inch layer cake

   ½ cup shortening
   ½ cup (1 stick) butter, at room temperature
   1 teaspoon vanilla
   4 cups (1 pound) sifted powdered sugar
   2 tablespoons milk

■ Beat the shortening and butter together until creamy. Add the vanilla and powdered sugar 1 cup at a time, mixing after each addition. Gradually pour in the milk and keep beating until the frosting is light and fluffy, about 3 minutes.

Variation: To make chocolate frosting, add ¾ cup cocoa powder or 1 ounce melted chocolate. Increase the milk to 3 to 4 tablespoons.

—Karen Crim Dillon
Vandalia, Ohio

Peanut Butter Icing

Makes about 6 cups or enough for three 9-inch cakes

1 cup (2 sticks) butter, at room temperature
1 cup peanut butter
4 cups (1 pound) sifted powdered sugar
¼ cup milk
1 teaspoon vanilla

■ Beat together the butter, peanut butter, powdered sugar, milk, and vanilla until smooth. Spread on cake, cookies, cupcakes, or your finger.

—Jennifer Hausfeld
Troy, Ohio

God of Abundance

God of abundance, you see our full table; fill our hearts as well. You see our full lives; transform them to allow space for your presence. You see our full homes; may they be storehouses of riches for sharing. In our plenty may we bless and share with those in need. In our need may we find plenty in you, today and every day. Amen.

—Linda L. Alley
Harrisonburg, Virginia

ACKNOWLEDGMENTS

A major feast is usually the work of many people, and that is true for *The New Inglenook Cookbook.* Heartfelt thanks are extended to the staff, volunteers, and contributors whose collaboration makes this community cookbook a success.

A project of this scope would not have been possible without the creative vision and hard work of a core publishing team. James Deaton, managing editor, oversaw the project as a whole and—toward the end—labored day and night to get it to the table. Jeff Lennard, director of marketing and sales, brought creativity and energy as he helped shape the cookbook and then made sure it reached its intended audience.

A special thank you goes to Karen Crim Dillon, who has been an enthusiastic, full-time volunteer with the project since its beginning. She spent countless hours poring over recipes, sending them to testers, and processing evaluations as they came back. During the editorial phase, she made necessary adjustments to recipes based on tester feedback, reviewed each edited recipe, and tracked down unresolved issues. She even retested many recipes herself. Karen's passion for good food, lifelong experience with cooking, and organizational skills were an ideal combination for her work as coordinator of recipe testing.

Thanks also to Susan Fitze, who years ago made sure that the idea of a new Inglenook cookbook didn't get lost.

We're grateful to Jan Fischer Bachman, Perry Hudkins, and Mark Hartwig for website and database assistance. We don't know how we could have processed those thousands of recipes without their wizardry. Thanks also for strong support from Brethren Press team members Karen Stocking, finance and production assistant, and customer service representatives Steve Bickler, Margaret Drafall, and Diane Stroyeck.

Designer Paul Stocksdale did tremendous work creating the visual Inglenook world. He achieved a look that is contemporary but unquestionably Inglenook. Thanks to professional cookbook editor Geoff Stone, whose expert editing was just what we needed; to typesetter Debbie Anderson, who raced against the clock to meet the printing deadline; and to friends and colleagues who proofread pages.

Appreciation goes to each person who submitted favorite recipes, whether or not those recipes made the final selection. Around twenty-five hundred recipes were received from over nine hundred people all across this country and even outside the United States. The cookbook is also enriched by essays, poems, memories, and bits of wit and wisdom, and we thank the writers whose words give us food for thought.

Lastly, we're grateful to all the recipe testers, who volunteered many hours—and grocery money—toward the making of this cookbook. They provided honest assessment of the recipes, caught mistakes, and in some cases suggested improvements or variations to give the recipes broader appeal. More than one hundred testers served in an official capacity, but there were others who volunteered to test and taste recipes in more informal ways. Such gatherings included four couples in the Dayton, Ohio, area who met monthly to make and share Inglenook recipes. For them and for others, testing became a tangible way to build closer bonds with loved ones.

Each official Inglenook tester's name is listed below. A single asterisk identifies persons who tested an impressive twenty to thirty-nine recipes. And then there are four individuals, recognized with two asterisks, who provided exceptional help by testing forty or more recipes. We are deeply grateful to these and all other contributors.

—Wendy McFadden
Publisher

Inglenook Recipe Testers

Anna Marie Achilles*	Quinter, Kansas
Cheryl Snavely Allen	Woodland, Michigan
Christine Appl-Walsh*	Staunton, Virginia
Edith M. Arnold	Berne, Indiana
Emma E. F. Bachman	Chantilly, Virginia
Bettina Balmer	Big Creek, Kentucky
Janet C. Batdorf*	Harrisburg, Pennsylvania
Emily A. Bell*	Ravenna, Ohio
James L. Benedict	New Windsor, Maryland
Margaret Elaine Black*	Waters, Michigan
Nancy Shifflett Bowman*	Fishersville, Virginia
Susan Dianne Bratcher	Kansas City, Missouri
Carrie Lynn Bush	Kokomo, Indiana
Beverly Butterfield*	New Market, Virginia
Jeannie Campbell	Beavercreek, Ohio
Sandra T. Carroll	Salem, Virginia
Ruth A. Clark	Froid, Montana
Elizabeth Flora Cooper	Boones Mill, Virginia
Jane Snyder Cox	Kokomo, Indiana
Karen Orpurt Crim	Dayton, Ohio
Joan L. Daggett	Bridgewater, Virginia
Drew L. Deffenbaugh	Johnstown, Pennsylvania
Emilie M. Deffenbaugh	Johnstown, Pennsylvania
Dayna DiMarco*	Polo, Illinois
Melissa C. Dove	Delaware, Ohio
Laura K. Duane	Mason, Michigan
Jim and Clareen Dunn**	Mulberry Grove, Illinois
Kim E. Ebersole*	Elgin, Illinois
Phyllis Kulp Eller	La Verne, California
Anna Emrick	Milwaukee, Wisconsin
Dawn Emrick-Artwick	Holland, Michigan
Nancy E. Farringer	Martinsburg, Pennsylvania
Vicki Yoder Ferguson	Dayton, Ohio
Jill D. Fike	Willow Springs, Missouri
Joyce R. Fike*	Doylestown, Ohio
Charlene Foster	Brookville, Ohio
Ted Foster	Brookville, Ohio
Erma M. Foust*	Union, Ohio
Beth Gahm	Raytown, Missouri
Valda Ann Garber-Weider	Harrisonburg, Virginia
Carol June Glover	Daleville, Virginia
Rebecca A. Goldstein	Boise, Idaho
Oceana M. Goodwin*	Carlisle, Pennsylvania
Gail L. Harris	Spring Valley, Ohio
Beverly J. Hatten	Orrville, Ohio
Anita K. Heatwole**	Waynesboro, Virginia
Joyce E. Heisey	Troy, Ohio
Susan B. Hertzog	Lebanon, Pennsylvania
Lori J. Hill	Hatboro, Pennsylvania
Sandra M. Hughes	Palmyra, Pennsylvania
Cheryl A. Johnson*	Perrysburg, Ohio
Jessie Elizabeth Johnson	Hector, Minnesota
Becky Jones	Newton, Iowa
Linda L. Joseph	Onekama, Michigan
Caroline E. Kaestner*	Port Republic, Virginia
Ruth Karasek**	Lombard, Illinois
Rita R. Lane	New Carlisle, Ohio
Janice L. Largent	Muncie, Indiana
Jeff Lennard	Elgin, Illinois
Dorothy Liller*	Hollidaysburg, Pennsylvania
Diane E. Mason	Moulton, Iowa
Janette B. Matthews	Rocky Mount, Virginia
John McAvoy	Live Oak, California
Gail C. McGlothin	Tyler, Texas
April K. McGlothin-Eller	Chicago, Illinois
Kathryn L. Mellinger	Rossville, Indiana
Julia K. Miller*	Charleston, Illinois
Melanie A. Miller	Carrboro, North Carolina

Pearl Fruth Miller*	Warrensburg, Missouri	Raechel L. Sittig-Esser	Waterloo, Iowa
Sandra Bean Miller*	Lansdale, Pennsylvania	Brian Solem	Chicago, Illinois
Karen E. Millikin	Brookville, Ohio	Karen S. Staten	Troy, Ohio
Kirsten M. Mills	Arcanum, Ohio	Carly N. Staub	Federal Way, Washington
Nancy Miner	Elgin, Illinois	Karen Stocking*	South Elgin, Illinois
Sarah R. Minnich	Lisbon Falls, Maine	Anna L. Swindell	Everett, Pennsylvania
Marcia S. Myer*	Manheim, Pennsylvania	Beverly J. Swindell*	Everett, Pennsylvania
Sandra W. Myers*	Rocky Mount, Virginia	Mary Kay Snider Turner*	Gettysburg, Pennsylvania
Donna J. Nesselrodt*	Penn Laird, Virginia	Emily LaPrade Van Pelt	Dayton, Virginia
David A. Nickerson	Hutchinson, Kansas	Cheryl L. Voorhees*	Denton, Maryland
Janalyce K. Nicodemus	Osceola, Indiana	Sue Wampler	Union, Ohio
Catherine A. Patrick	Lindsborg, Kansas	Ellen S. Weaver*	Lancaster, Pennsylvania
Pauline E. Petry*	Beavercreek, Ohio	Rahila A. Weed*	Warrensburg, Missouri
Leslie Pettit	North Manchester, Indiana	Helen Wagoner Wenger	Anderson, Indiana
Jennie E. Ramirez	Everett, Pennsylvania	Rebecca Simmons Weybright	Manheim, Pennsylvania
Terri L. Raynor	Boise, Idaho	Carol M. Whybrew*	Peru, Indiana
Donna McKee Rhodes	Huntingdon, Pennsylvania	Carolyn S. Willoughby	Johnstown, Pennsylvania
Delora Mishler Roop*	Anderson, Indiana	Prudy M. Wilt	Everett, Pennsylvania
Merry Christina Roy	East Wenatchee, Washington	Margaret R. Witmer	Oxford, Ohio
Kathi L. Saffer	Fort Wayne, Indiana	Burt Wolf	Union, Ohio
Joann C. Sanbloom	West Lafayette, Indiana	Helen Wolf	Union, Ohio
Randall L. Schaurer	Phillipsburg, Ohio	Betty S. Yoder*	Fort Wayne, Indiana
Dorothy McWilliams Sheller*	Eldora, Iowa	Sarah Leatherman Young	Denver, Colorado
Michelle Shetler	Johnstown, Pennsylvania	Jolene L. Zeigler	York, Pennsylvania
Karen Stover Shiflet	Dayton, Virginia	Alissa Zience	Seattle, Washington
Sondra Eisenbise Simmons	Hershey, Pennsylvania	Kirsten Zoerhoff	Gilberts, Illinois

INDEX OF RECIPES

Emergency Ingredient Substitutions

Here are a few common ingredient substitutions that can be used in an emergency.

Baking Powder . . . Instead of 1 teaspoon baking powder, combine $\frac{1}{2}$ teaspoon cream of tartar plus $\frac{1}{4}$ teaspoon baking soda.

Brown Sugar . . . To make 1 cup light brown sugar, mix 1 cup granulated sugar with 1 tablespoon molasses.

Buttermilk . . . To make 1 cup buttermilk, combine 1 tablespoon vinegar or lemon juice plus enough milk to equal 1 cup. Stir to mix and let stand 1 minute. Or combine $\frac{3}{4}$ cup sour cream or plain yogurt with $\frac{1}{4}$ cup milk.

Cake Flour . . . To make 1 cup cake flour, remove 2 tablespoons from 1 cup all-purpose flour and replace it with 2 tablespoons cornstarch. Mix well.

Chocolate . . . To make 1 ounce (1 square) chocolate, mix 3 tablespoons cocoa powder with 1 tablespoon oil or butter.

Corn Starch . . . Instead of 1 tablespoon cornstarch, use 2 tablespoons flour.

Dry Mustard . . . Instead of 1 teaspoon dry mustard, use 1 tablespoon prepared mustard.

Fresh Herbs . . . Instead of 1 tablespoon fresh herbs, use 1 teaspoon dried herbs.

Garlic . . . Instead of 1 garlic clove, use $\frac{1}{8}$ teaspoon garlic powder.

Granulated Sugar . . . Instead of 1 cup white, granulated sugar, use 1 cup packed brown sugar or 2 cups sifted powdered sugar.

Honey . . . Instead of 1 cup honey, mix $1\frac{1}{4}$ cups sugar with $\frac{1}{4}$ cup liquid.

Ketchup or Chili Sauce . . . Instead of 1 cup ketchup or chili sauce, mix 1 cup tomato sauce with $\frac{1}{2}$ cup sugar and 2 tablespoons vinegar.

Marshmallows . . . Instead of 1 large marshmallow, use 10 mini marshmallows.

Thickening a Soup or Stew . . . To thicken a soup or stew, mix 1 tablespoon cornstarch, 2 tablespoons all-purpose flour, 2 tablespoons quick-cooking tapioca flour, or 2 tablespoons ground arrowroot with $\frac{1}{2}$ cup water and add to the soup or stew.